Economic and Environmental Regulation of International Aviation

The core structure of the regulatory regime for international civil aviation (the 'Chicago System') is *inter-national*. The features of the Chicago System were designed in an era when the world's airlines were State-owned, and the most pressing international concerns were for navigation and safety regulation. Economic liberalization and intense globalization since the Second World War have impacted on the industry; today, it is global.

This book observes the developing governance of global aviation, taking into account the concepts of sovereignty, jurisdiction and territoriality, and the proliferation of actors and participants as partners in a global public policy network, to posit that an upgraded system of *global governance* for civil aviation helps to explain the emerging complex landscape for global governance of civil aviation.

As evidence of the emerging, complex matrix of governance of global aviation, this book identifies and reviews a selection of contemporary, trans-national economic and environmental challenges facing the globalized aviation sector, e.g. fair competition safeguards, consumer protection, noise pollution and greenhouse gas emissions, and the respective 'legal' and policy actions taken at national level (United Arab Emirates, Qatar and People's Republic of China), regional level (the European Union) and international level (UN Framework Convention on Climate Change and International Civil Aviation Organization).

The book concludes that economic and environmental regulation of international aviation, designed for an *inter-national* world of yesterday, evolves into global governance of aviation, which is more suited for today's global world.

This book will be of particular interest to scholars and practitioners of aviation law, competition law and environmental law, as well as in the areas of transnational law, global governance and international relations.

Steven Truxal is senior lecturer in law at City, University of London.

Routledge Research in International Commercial Law

Available titles in this series include:

International Commercial and Marine Arbitration
Georgios l. Zekos

International Commercial Arbitration and the Arbitrator's Contract
Emilia Onyema

Jurisdiction and Arbitration Agreements in International Commercial Law
Zheng Sophia Tang

Progressive Commercialization of Airline Governance Culture
Jan Walulik

Economic and Environmental Regulation of International Aviation

From Inter-national to Global Governance

Steven Truxal

Routledge
Taylor & Francis Group
LONDON AND NEW YORK

First published 2017 by Routledge

2 Park Square, Milton Park, Abingdon, Oxfordshire OX14 4RN
52 Vanderbilt Avenue, New York, NY 10017

Routledge is an imprint of the Taylor & Francis Group, an informa business

First issued in paperback 2018

British Library Cataloguing in Publication Data
A catalogue record for this book is available from the British Library

Library of Congress Cataloging in Publication Data
Names: Truxal, Steven, author.
Title: Economic and environmental regulation of international aviation : from inter-national to global governance / Steven Truxal.
Description: Abingdon, Oxon [UK] ; New York : Routledge, 2017. |
Series: Routledge research in international commercial law | Includes bibliographical references and index.
Identifiers: LCCN 2016029644 | ISBN 978-1-138-84345-5 (hbk) |
ISBN 978-1-315-73100-1 (ebk)
Subjects: LCSH: Aeronautics—Law and legislation | Aeronautics—Economic aspects. | Aeronautics—Environmental aspects.
Classification: LCC K4095 .T78 2017 | DDC 343.09/7—dc23
LC record available at https://lccn.loc.gov/2016029644

ISBN: 978-1-138-84345-5 (hbk)
ISBN: 978-0-367-07545-3 (pbk)

Typeset in Galliard
by Fish Books Ltd.

Contents

Table of cases, decisions and legislation

Cases

U.S.

F Hoffmann-La Roche Ltd v. *Empagran SA*, 315 F 3d (2004)
Heller v. *United States*, 776 F 2d 92 (3d Cir 1985)
Hinman v. *Pacific Air Transport and United Airlines Transport Corp*, 84 F 2d 755 (9th Cir 1936)
Kiobel v. *Royal Dutch Petroleum Co*, 621 F 3d 111 (2nd Cir 2010), 133 S Ct 1659 (2013)
Restatement (3d) of Foreign Relations Law of the United States (1987)
United States v. *Causby*, 328 U.S. 256 (1946)
Virgin Atlantic Airways v. *British Airways plc*, 257 F.3d 256 (2nd Cir 2001)
Vitamins Antitrust Litigation (Re), 120 F 2d 58 (DDC 2000)

EU

Ahmed Saeed Flugreisen and Silver Line Reisebüro GmbH v. *Zentrale zur Bekämpfung unlauteren Wettbewerbs E.V.* (Case 66/86) [1989] ECR 803, [1990] 4 CMLR 102
Alitalia (C-26/08) [2009] OJ L52
Air Transport Association of America and Others v. *Secretary of State for Energy and Climate Change* (C-366/10) [2011] ECR I-0000
Andrejs Eglītis and Edvards Ratnieks v. *Latvijas Republikas Ekonomikas ministrija*, (C-294/10) [2011] ECR I-03983
Charleroi [2003] OJ C18/03
Christopher Sturgeon and Others v. *Condor Flugdienst GmbH* (C-402/07) and *Stefan Böck and Cornelia Lepuschitz* v. *Air France SA* (C-432/07) [2009] ECR I-10923
Commission v. *Federal Republic of Germany* (C-476/98) [2002] ECR I-9855

Commission v. *France (Re French Merchant Seamen)* (C-167/73) [1974] ECR 359, [1974] CMLR 216.
Commission v. *Grand Duchy of Luxembourg* (C-472/98) [2002] ECR I-9741
Commission v. *Kingdom of Belgium* (C-471/98) [2002] ECR I-9681
Commission v. *Kingdom of Denmark* (C-467/98) [2002] ECR I-9519
Commission v. *Kingdom of Sweden* (C-468/98) [2002] ECR I-9575
Commission v. *Republic of Austria* (C-475/98) [2002] ECR I-9797
Commission v. *Republic of Finland* (C-469/98) [2002] ECR I-9627
Commission v. *United Kingdom* (C-466/98) [2002] ECR I-9427
Emeka Nelson, Bill Chinazo Nelson, Brian Cheimezie Nelson v. *Deutsche Lufthansa AG* (C-581/10) and *The Queen, on the application of TUI Travel plc, British Airways plc, easyJet Airline Co. Ltd, International Air Transport Association* v. *Civil Aviation Authority* (C-629/10), 15 May 2012
Emirates Airlines – Direktion für Deutschland v. *Diether Shenkel* (C-173/07) [2008] ECR I-5237
Friederike Wallentin-Hermann v. *Alitalia* (C-549/07) [2008] ECR I–11061
Intertanko (C-308/06) [2008] ECR I-04057
Pan Am Airways v. *The Queen* [1981] 2 SCR 565 (UK)
Sabena [1991] OJ L300/48, 31 October 2001
Sandy Siewert and Others v. *Condor Flugdienst GmbH* (C-394/14) 14 November 2014 (a preliminary ruling)
The Queen on the Application of International Air Transport Association, European Low Fares Airline Association v. *Department for Transport* (C-344/04) [2006] ECR I-403
Vodafone and Others (C-58/08) [2010] ECR I-4999

Other jurisdictions

Chile v. *European Community* ITLOS (2000) 40 ILM 475
Island of Palmas Case (or Miangas), United States v. *Netherlands*, Award (1928) II RIAA 829 ICGJ 392
Lighthouses in Crete and Samos, France v. *Greece* (1937) PCIJ Ser. A/B No 62 ICGJ 322
Pan American World Airways Inc. v. *The Queen* [1981] 2 SCR 565 (Canada)
Shrimp/Turtle WTO Case No 58 (1998)
Tuna/Dolphin GATT Case (1991, 1994)

List of decisions and legislation

Air Transport Agreement between the United States of America and the Member States of the European Union, [2007] OJ L134/4, 25 May 2007

Charter of Fundamental Rights of the European Union [2000] C364/01, 18 December 2000

Commission Decision 94/118/EC of 21 December 1993 concerning aid to be provided by the Irish government to the Aer Lingus group [1994] OJ L54/30

Commission Decision 94/653/EC of 27 July 1994 concerning the notified capital increase of Air France [1994] OJ L254

Commission Decision 94/696/EC of 7 October 1994 on the aid granted by Greece to Olympic Airways [1994] OJ L273

Commission Decision 94/698/EC of 6 July 1994 concerning increase in capital, credit guarantees and an exemption in favour of TAP [1994] OJ L279

Commission Decision 2000/74 of 14 April 1999 relating to a proceeding under Article 82 of the EC Treaty (IV/D-2/34.780 – Virgin/British Airways) [2004] OJ L30/1, 4 February 2004

Commission Decision 2001/539/EC on the conclusion by the European Community of the Convention for the unification of certain rules for international carriage by air ('the Montreal Convention') [2001] OJ L194/38, 28 June 2004

Commission Decision of 9 November 2010 relating to a proceeding under Article 101 of the Treaty on the Functioning of the European Union, Article 53 of the EEA Agreement and Article 8 of the Agreement between the European Community and the Swiss Confederation on air transport [2010] OJ C371/11

Commission Decision C (2010) 7694 final relating to a proceeding under Article 101 TFEU, Article 53 of the EEA Agreement and Article 8 of the Agreement between the European Community and the Swiss Confederation on Air Transport

Commission Implementing Regulation (EU) 295/2012 of 3 April 2012 amending Council Regulation (EC) 474/2006 establishing the Community list of air carriers which are subject to an operating ban within the Community [2012] OJ L98/13, 4 April 2012

Commission Regulation (EC) 2150/2005 of 23 December 2005 laying down common rules for the flexible use of airspace [2005] OJ L342/20

Conférence internationale de navigation aérienne, Paris 18 mai-28 juin 1910, Exposé des vues des puissances d'après les mémorandums adressas au gouvernement français (1909) Paris Imp. Nationale (France)

Convention on International Civil Aviation ('the Chicago Convention'), signed at Chicago on 7 December 1944.

Convention for the Unification of Certain Rules Relating to International Carriage by Air, as amended and supplemented by the Hague Protocol of 28 September 1955, the Guadalajara Convention of 18 September 1961, the Guatemala Protocol of 8 March 1971, and the four additional Montreal Protocols of 25 September 1975 ('the Warsaw Convention'), originally signed at Warsaw on 12 October 1929

Council Decision 2001/539/EC of 5 April 2001 on the conclusion by the European Community of the Convention for the unification of certain rules for international carriage by air ('the Montreal Convention') [2001] OJ L194/38
Council Directive 90/314/EEC of 13 June 1990 on travel, package holidays and package tours [1990] OJ L158/59
Council Directive 2002/30/EC of the European Parliament and of the Council of 26 March 2002 on the establishment of rules and procedures with regard to the introduction of noise-related operating restrictions at Community airports [2002] OJ L85/40
Council Directive 2008/101/EC of the European Parliament and of the Council of 19 November 2008 amending Directive 2003/87/EC so as to include aviation activities in the scheme for greenhouse gas emission allowance trading within the Community [2008] OJ L8/3
Council Directive 2009/29/EC of the European Parliament and of the Council of 23 Apr. 2009 amending Directive 2003/87/EC so as to improve and extend the greenhouse gas emission allowance trading scheme of the Community [2009] OJ L140/63
Council Regulation (EC) 193/2004 of 20 January 2004 on the control of concentrations between undertakings (the EC Merger Regulation) [2004] OJ L24/2
Council Regulation (EC) 261/2004 of the European Parliament and of the Council of 11 February 2004 establishing common rules on compensation and assistance to passengers in the event of denied boarding and of cancellation or long delay of flights, and repealing Regulation (EEC) No 295/91 [2004] OJ L46/1
Council Regulation (EEC) 295/91 of 4 February 1991 establishing common rules for a denied-boarding compensation system in scheduled air transport [1991] OJ L36/5
Council Regulation (EC) 411/2004 of 26 February 2004 repealing Regulation (EEC) No 3975/87 and amending Regulations (EEC) No 3976/87 and (EC) No 1/2003, in connection with air transport between the Community and third countries [2004] OJ L68/1
Council Regulation (EC) 785/2004 of the European Parliament and of the Council of 21 April 2004 on insurance requirements for air carriers and aircraft operators [2004] OJ L138/1, 30 April 2004
Council Regulation (EC) 889/2002 of the European Parliament and of the Council of 13 May 2002 amending Council Regulation (EC) No 2027/97 on air carrier liability in the event of accidents [2002] OJ L140/2, 30 May 2002
Council Regulation (EC) 1008/2008 of the European Parliament and of the Council of 24 September 2008 on common rules for the operation of air services in the Community, OJ [2008] L293/3
Council Regulation (EC) 1107/2006 of the European Parliament and of the Council of 5 July 2006 concerning the rights of disabled persons

and persons with reduced mobility when travelling by air [2006] OJ L204/1, 26 July 2006

Council Regulation (EC) 2027/97 of 9 October 1997 on air carrier liability in the event of accidents [1997] OJ L285/1, 17 October 1997

Council Regulation (EC) 2111/2005 of the European Parliament and of the Council of 14 December 2005 on the establishment of a Community list of air carriers subject to an operating ban within the Community and on informing air transport passengers of the identity of the operating air carrier, and repealing Article 9 of Directive 2004/36/EC, [2005] OJ L344/15, 27 December 2005

European Parliament, Resolution on Climate Change [2007] OJ C287 E/344

Exposé des vues des puissances d'après les mémorandums adressas au gouvernement français (1909) Paris, Imp. Nationale (France)

Federal Law No. 4 of 2012 on the Regulation of Competition (United Arab Emirates)

Ordonnance de police qui defend de lancer des Ballons ou Machines aérostatiques dans la Ville & Fauxbourgs de Lyon du 21 Novembre 1783. Extrait des Minutes du Greffe de Police de la Ville, Fauxbourgs & Banlieue de Lyon (France)

Tokyo Convention on Offences and Certain Other Acts Committed on Board Aircraft (1963)

Treaty on the Functioning of the European Union (consolidated version) [2012] OJ C326/1, 26 October 2012

United Nations Framework Convention on Climate Change (UNFCCC), 'Kyoto Protocol and the UN Climate Change Secretariat: A Global Framework to Tackle Climate Change' (2007) 37 ILM 32

UK Alien Tort Claims Act 1789

U.S. European Union Emissions Trading Scheme Act of 2011 (enacted 27 November 2012) insert: U.S. Federal Aviation Act of 1958

Abbreviations

ADIZ	air defence identification zone
AEA	Association of European Airlines
ASA	air services agreement
ASEAN	Association of Southeast Asian Nations
ATConf	Air Transport Conference
ATM	air traffic management
BRICS	Brazil, Russian Federation, India, People's Republic of China and South Africa
CAAC	Civil Aviation Administration of the People's Republic of China
CAEP	Committee on Aviation Environmental Protection
CAPA	Centre for Aviation
CBDR	common but differentiated responsibilities
CJEU	Court of Justice of the European Union
CNG	carbon neutral growth
CO_2	carbon dioxide
CORSIA	Carbon Offsetting and Reduction Scheme for International Aviation
DCAA	Dubai Civil Aviation Authority
DWC	Dubai World Central
DXB	Dubai International Airport
EAG	Environment Advisory Group
EC	European Community
ECAC	European Civil Aviation Conference
ECN	European Competition Network
EEA	European Economic Area
EEC	European Economic Community
EEZ	exclusive economic zone
ELFAA	European Low Fares Airline Association
EPA	Environmental Protection Agency
ETS	Emissions Trading System
EU	European Union
EUC	emissions unit criteria

EUR	euros
FOCJ	functional, overlapping and competing jurisdictions
FTK	freight tonne-kilometre
GATS	General Agreement on Trade in Services
GATT	General Agreement on Tariffs and Trade
GHG	greenhouse gas
GIACC	Group on International Aviation and Climate Change
GLADs	Global Aviation Dialogues
GMBM	global market-based mechanism
GNI	gross national income
HLG-GMBM	High-Level Group on a Global MBM Scheme
IAG	International Airlines Group
IATA	International Air Transport Association
ICAN	International Commission for Air Navigation
ICAO	International Civil Aviation Organization
ICJ	International Court of Justice
ICN	International Competition Network
ILO	International Labour Organization
IMF	International Monetary Fund
INDC	intended nationally-determined contribution
IPCC	Intergovernmental Panel on Climate Change
LCC	low-cost carrier
LDC	Least Developed Country
LLDS	Landlocked Developing Country
MBM	market-based measure
MENA	Middle East and Northern Africa
MRV	monitoring, reporting and verification
NAP	National Allocation Plan
NCLB	No Country Left Behind
NO_x	nitrogen oxide
nvPM	non-volatile particulate matter
OECD	Organisation for Economic Co-operation and Development
PICAO	Provisional International Civil Aviation Organization
POFS	Partnership for Open and Fair Skies
RPK	revenue passenger-kilometres
RTK	revenue tonne-kilometre
SARP	standard and recommended practice
SDR	special drawing right
SIDS	Small Island Developing States
SSC	significant safety concern
TFEU	Treaty on the Functioning of the European Union
UAE	United Arab Emirates
UK	United Kingdom
UN	United Nations
UNCLOS	United Nations Convention on the Law of the Sea

UNCTAD	United Nations Conference on Trade and Development
UNEP	United Nations Environment Programme
UNFCCC	United Nations Framework Convention on Climate Change
U.S.	United States
USD	United States Dollars
USSR	Union of Soviet Socialist Republics
WMO	World Meteorological Organization
WTO	World Trade Organization
WOQOD	Qatar Fuel

To Christian

Acknowledgements

First of all, I wish to thank The City Law School at City, University London for providing me with the sabbatical that allowed me the time to finish this book. I am also grateful to the Centre for Enterprise Liability at the Faculty of Law, University of Copenhagen, for including me in its productive research environment. In addition, I am thankful to the Faculty of Law, McGill University, for the extended stay I enjoyed at the Institute of Air and Space Law.

The advice and feedback I received from friends in government circles and within industry have been invaluable to me; thank you for the many insights!

Many thanks also go to Gabrielle Carrouset for paying close attention to detail, to Nicole Asprou for helping with preliminary research and to Dr Elaine Fahey for supporting me in my global thinking.

Preface

The core structure of the regulatory regime for international civil aviation, the so-called 'Chicago System', is *inter-national*. The Chicago System takes its name from the primary source of international law relating to civil aviation, the Convention on International Civil Aviation, signed at Chicago on 7 December 1944 ('Chicago Convention'). The Chicago Convention has a dual function; it serves as a source of international air law and as the constitution of the International Civil Aviation Organization (ICAO), headquartered in Montréal, the specialized agency of the United Nations (UN) mandated to administer the Convention.[1] In this function, ICAO serves as the special forum for inter-State relations on civil aviation. The Chicago Convention came into force on 4 April 1947; today it has practically universal membership.[2] Wherever the Chicago System is mentioned in this book, I refer broadly to the Chicago Convention and its Annexes, ICAO Council, Assembly and Secretariat, ICAO-instituted committees and working groups, and the 191 UN Member States of ICAO. Through inter-State dialogue facilitated by ICAO, States agree at the international level relevant standards, recommended practices and policies for civil aviation, which are subsequently implemented nationally. ICAO is the forum for developments in international air law and therefore also domestic air law.[3] Responsibility for implementation and enforcement, therefore, lay with individual States. States are the key subjects of the Chicago System.

The Chicago Convention provides that aircraft take the nationality[4] and must bear[5] the respective mark of the State of registration. An aircraft's

1 See Paul Stephen Dempsey, *Public International Air Law* (McGill University 2008).

2 As at May 2016: see www.icao.int/about-icao/Pages/member-states.aspx for a complete list of ICAO Member States. There are 193 Member States of the United Nations: see www.un.org/en/sections/about-un/overview/index.html.

3 See Ruwantissa Abeyratne, *Convention on International Civil Aviation: A Commentary* (Springer 2014). Standards and recommended practices are agreed internationally and implemented nationally. See Annex 2, Chicago Convention 'Rules of the Air'.

4 ICAO, Doc. 7300, *Convention on International Civil Aviation 1944* ('Chicago Convention 1944') Art 17.

5 Ibid., Art 20.

registration may be changed from one State to another, with the caveat that aircraft cannot be validly registered in more than one State.[6] Without a doubt, this nationality or flag concept, most immediately apparent from visual markings on aircraft livery, promulgates national identity and perceived connotations of State power. One cannot help but notice that just as States acquire aircraft for military purposes – at whatever the cost – they also tend to procure aircraft to establish national airlines for civil aviation. State ownership of civilian aircraft and airlines is commonplace. The moment a civilian aircraft flying the national flag travels beyond its home airspace, if not before, it may serve as an important symbol of State power on the world stage. It is understandable that States would therefore seek to promote and protect national flag carriers in the State, national or public interest. But to what extent? The experience in Europe shows that some bankrupt national flag carriers have exited the market, while others in financial difficulties have been acquired by foreign companies.[7] Swiss and Austrian registered aircraft flying Swiss and Austrian flags, respectively, retain their individual identities but are now owned by Lufthansa, a German company. Air France and KLM Royal Dutch Airlines formed a single group in 2004, Air France–KLM. Also, British Airways, Iberia and Vueling (Spain), and Aer Lingus (Ireland) are a single group, International Airlines Group (IAG).

As seen from an *economic* standpoint, international civil aviation is shedding its flag obsession to become more global. It can be said that in some parts of the world prestige and political power associated with national flag carriers now are less prevalent. There are fewer national airlines owned and controlled by States, and protected at all costs from the risks and opportunities associated with the free market. Instead, one can witness an increase in the number of new and diverse multinational airlines operating on the global market as major global businesses.

Growth is strong in the sector.[8] In many respects, the global market for aviation is booming.[9] But competition is also fierce, particularly in liberalized and deregulated markets in which market entry is unrestricted, and innovative low-cost and low-fare business strategies flourish. Yet, on the global market, fair competition is often more theory than praxis. In an inherently cooperative airline industry, there has been a prevalence of regional and global price-fixing cartels. The highly competitive market also gives way to

6 Ibid., Art 18; see also Chicago Convention Art 77 and the possibility of 'common mark' registration.

7 National flag carrier bankruptcies in Europe include SABENA (Societé Anonyme Belge d'Exploitation de la Navigation Aérienne) of Belgium (2001), Malév Hungarian Airlines (2012) and Cyprus Airways (2015). The Lufthansa Group, which includes Lufthansa Passenger Airlines, Germanwings and Eurowings, acquired Swiss International Air Lines (2005) and Austrian Airlines (2009).

8 See further discussion on this point in Chapters 3 and 4.

9 The low price of oil is a major contributing factor, noting also the 'boom to bust' cyclical nature of the airline industry and today's capitalist economies in general.

instances of price discrimination, and increasingly, allegations of State guarantees and subsidies.

In spite of these challenges, airlines devise innovative and cooperative strategies as well as try out new business structures in an attempt to survive the competitive global market. But for historical, protectionist ownership and control rules in place in most jurisdictions, economic theory suggests major global airlines would benefit from consolidation across national (territorial) borders. Over the past decade, there have been numerous successful airline consolidations in the United States and Europe. Consolidation often makes good business sense in network industries. More often than not, American and European competition authorities have approved resulting market concentrations.

The Chicago System, however, continues to operate on the basis of traditional Westphalian State sovereignty. This continues to restrict the international aviation community, whose 'attempt since 1944 to establish on a multilateral basis rights of aircraft of contracting states to fly into each others' territories, whether engaged in scheduled air services or in non-scheduled flights, has largely failed'.[10] Indeed, in some respects, attempts to liberalize civil aviation further seem to have slowed or even ground to a halt; some suggest liberalization is actually rolling back.[11] These areas of economic regulation are traditionally handled by national regulators on the argumentation that they are a matter of *national* policy. Such an exclusively State-based system has many shortcomings; one could possibly argue it is no longer fit for purpose.

It is not difficult to cite instances in which one State's antitrust and securities laws have been (successfully[12]) applied to foreign firms with extra-territorial effect. On the one hand, this gives way to polycentric, fragmented, multi-layered and overlapping governance[13] and competition between authorities, and also produces confusing and at times conflicting regulation of a single actor at multiple levels. On the other hand, it provides an opportunity for collaboration and convergence in competition policy to ensure consistent practice on global markets[14] whereby States 'reorient their

10 Peter Malanczuk, *Akehurst's Modern Introduction to International Law* (7th edn, Routledge 1997) 200.

11 *See* Barry Humphreys, 'The Gulf Carrier Row: Real Risk of Pantomime?' (May 2015) *Aviation Strategy* (online).

12 In a judicial sense, noting that finding of 'right' jurisdiction and enforcement are other challenges.

13 Parallels with international human rights regime: 'substantial majority of states [post-Second World War] either supported or acquiesced in the development of a comprehensive international human rights regime. The contemporary human rights regime consists of overlapping global, regional and national institutions and conventions', David Held *et al.*, *Global Transformations: Politics, Economics, and Culture* (Polity Press 1999) 67.

14 The European Commission and U.S. Department of Transportation 'cooperate' on competition issues affecting European Union and United States airline markets, e.g. mergers and acquisitions, joint ventures and airline alliances.

particular policy work or broader state agendas toward the requirements of the global economy even as they continue to be coded as national'.[15] If, in the context of economic (market) globalization, it can be said that 'denationalization'[16] manifests itself in both public and private realms – i.e. States' policy reorientation alongside airlines as private actors taking on a global character as they engage in 'borderless', *transnational* activities – then, a more *transnational* regime for economic regulation of global airlines is perhaps most appropriate.

The aviation sector also contributes to global climate change; it must also take an active role in finding solutions to this complex problem. Unlike with economic regulation, some environmental aspects of international civil aviation are being addressed by international law. Whilst the international community has identified climate change as a serious problem that deserves a global response, which is under development, some States and groups of States have already delivered solutions for limiting and reducing the impact of aviation emissions on the environment. These environmental policies in action have not necessarily been met with universal appreciation. In response to the perceived unilateral nature of the European Union's inclusion of aviation activities in its Emissions Trading System (ETS), some States have issued joint declarations opposing it while other States have enacted blocking legislation or threatened 'trade war'. All the same, there is a genuine opportunity for global civil aviation vis-à-vis transnational environmental governance to contribute to innovation in global climate change policy. If we accept the transnational nature of the problem and the limits of the international system generally, we may be able to reorientate the Chicago System, authority and governance of international civil aviation away from the exclusive, monopolistic State. Whilst this book does not propose the traditional conception of 'supranationality' as the solution, it does recognize that by accepting such an unbounded spectrum for types of decision making, one can create the space required to observe and advocate the emergence of a global governance regime for civil aviation that is not confined to States. To elevate from international to global governance, one must not dwell on the 'great divide' of internal/external, international/national.[17] Rather, the approach of this book allows for a new, globalist perspective on law and governance as an 'alteration in mood' or altogether 'new mood' for global aviation law and governance in a globalized era, to create a means by which we can describe what is currently taking place.[18]

15 Saskia Sassen, *Territory, Authority, Rights: From Medieval to Global Assemblages* (Princeton University Press 2008) 223.

16 Ibid.

17 Ian Clark, *Globalization and International Relations Theory* (Oxford University Press 1999).

18 Neil Walker, *Intimations of Global Law* (Cambridge University Press 2015) 24.

In short, I attempt in this book to stand above the wider debate on transnational challenges in international law as observer of the global aspects of international civil aviation. By 'going global', I seek to extend the scope of the territorial sovereignty-based Chicago System by including not only States but also non-State actors and private actors. In this book, I accept that globalization diminishes the authority of the State, however highly contested that theory may be.

The first part of this book's title – Economic and Environmental Regulation – implies *multilevel* regulation, that is, not only vertical regulation but the complex matrix of governance occurring often simultaneously at local, national, regional, international, supranational, transnational and global levels.[19] International aviation refers in the main to international *civil* aviation but also bears in mind the broader characteristics of its historical development as presented in Chapter 1. The subtitle – From Inter-national to Global Governance – represents the book's central thesis and conclusion.

This book observes the developing governance of civil aviation, taking into account the proliferation of actors and participants as partners in a global public policy network, to posit that a *global* governance system for civil aviation – citing in Chapter 2 the relevant scholarship on sovereignty, jurisdiction and territoriality – helps to explain the emerging complex landscape for global governance of civil aviation. The relevant theories applied to international civil aviation suggest that the transnational law approach, moving beyond the contractual model of international law towards greater use of norms and processes that reflect community values rather than only State interests, would lead to better outcomes vis-à-vis non-consensual law-making mechanisms.[20] I question the use of subsidiarity in the law of jurisdiction for the global interest, for instance, as a possible means of fostering more productive interaction at multiple levels of civil aviation regulation, stronger decision-making and more innovative design of norms and processes.

Chapter 3 identifies a selection of economic and environmental challenges facing the globalized aviation sector as matters that also affect the wider global neighbourhood, namely fair competition safeguards, consumer protection, noise pollution and greenhouse gas emissions. This chapter reviews the 'legal' and policy actions taken at national level (United Arab Emirates, Qatar and People's Republic of China), regional level (the European Union) and international level (UN Framework Convention on Climate Change and ICAO), so as to provide evidence for the complex matrix of governance of aspects of civil aviation.

19 See Andreas Føllesdal *et al.* (eds), *Multilevel Regulation and the EU: The Interplay between Global, European and National Normative Processes* (Martinus Nijhoff Publishers 2008).

20 Nico Krisch, 'The Decay of Consent: International Law in an Age of Global Public Goods' (2015) *AJIL* 108.

To end with, Chapter 4 questions whether 'classical' international law that is mediated by States vis-à-vis the Chicago System can or should continue in light of the very much changed global nature of the aviation business. I present the ongoing work of ICAO in the economic and environmental domains set out in the previous chapter. The global market-based mechanism (GMBM) for international aviation emissions provides special impetus for this book insofar as support from States, non-state actors and private actors has led to resounding agreement that a GMBM scheme for global aviation must be implemeted. This reveals an unprecedented shift from the traditional 'standard-setting' authority of ICAO, including *environmental* regulation, towards an upgraded system of global *economic* regulation that brings with it more inclusive norm-setting and decision-making processes as well as responsibility for non-State and private actors. Whilst the stated objective is to overcome the hurdles of the Westphalian order of States under the Chicago System and associated political roadblocks, ultimately I recognize that a major risk to this will be the reality of territorial enforcement.

1 'Airspace' as linked to State territorial sovereignty

Introduction

Leonardo da Vinci is famous for producing countless imaginative sketches during his lifetime. With that said, few may be acquainted with his drawings of the construction of a flying machine, or 'ornithopter' (ca. 1485). Da Vinci's 'ornithopter' – the title taken from the Greek *ornithos* ('bird') and *pteron* ('wing') – evidences his genius as inventor of a possible solution to the dream of flight, modelled on the winged anatomy of birds and bats. Whether da Vinci himself ever managed to construct wings and fly is unknown; however, as da Vinci's drawings illustrate, the artist, inventor and scientist lived well ahead his time.[1]

In Paris, some three centuries later, Professor Jacques Charles and the Robert brothers[2] built and launched the world's first hydrogen balloon on 23 August 1783. The balloon was unmanned and is said to have flown for 45 minutes to land 21 kilometres away in the small village of Gonesse, where terrified locals reportedly attacked and destroyed it as it touched down.

At around the same time, the Montgolfier brothers[3] launched an unmanned balloon called the *Aerostat Réveillon*. This led to a subsequent launch at the Royal Demonstration at the Palace of Versailles on 19 September 1783, but this time with an (unlikely) crew of three animals on board: a sheep, a duck and a rooster! King Louis XVI of France and Queen Marie Antoinette were in attendance.[4] The craft flew for eight minutes covering over three kilometres, and landed safely. On 21 November 1783, the balloon was launched again, this time over Paris and with a crew of two men.[5]

1 Bill Gunston (ed.), *Chronicle of Aviation* (JL Publishing 1992) 43.

2 Anne-Jean Robert (1758–1820) and Nicolas-Louis Robert (1760–1820).

3 Joseph-Michel Montgolfier (1740–1810) and Jacques-Étienne Montgolfier (1745–1799).

4 Charles Coulston Gillispie, *The Montgolfier Brothers and the Invention of Aviation 1783–1784* (Princeton University 1983).

5 The craft was piloted by Nicolas-Louis Robert and Jacques Charles. See Archives Municipalesde Nantes, 'L'aérostat nantais des années 1783 à nos jours'. Online at: www.archives.nantes.fr/PAGES/DOSSIERS_DOCS/aerostats_nantais/pages/accueil.html

Remarkably, these major events took place more than a century before the Wright brothers took to flight in *Kitty Hawk* in 1903. Nonetheless, the consensus view is that the *Aerostat Réveillon* was the first functioning flying machine.[6]

It seems that public enthusiasm for balloons and other *machines aérostatiques* was developing quickly in France, where in 1783, according to the Lieutenant Général de Police of Lyon,

> plusieurs Citoyens lancent journellement, dans la Ville [de Lyon] & Fauxbourgs, des Ballons, ou Machines aérostatiques, dans lesquels ils mettent des artifices et ou des rechaux chargés de feux; que ces Ballons, souvent mal construits, s'enflamment dans l'air, & peuvent, en tombant, causer les plus grands malheurs.[7]

The public welfare concern expressed in the statement above is that flying objects may be dangerous. On one reported occasion a group of inexperienced young men launched a balloon having imprudently attached a bale of straw to it. The balloon and straw caught fire and fell on a house, causing a terrible fire. This incident took place on the evening of Sunday 16 November 1783:

> Dimanche, 16 de ce mois [novembre], sur les 11 heures du soir, des jeunes gens, sans expérience, en lancerent un [Ballon] de la Place des Terreaux, auquel ils avoient eu l'imprudence d'attacher une botte de paille, à laquelle ils avoient mis le feu; que ce Ballon tomba tout en feu sur une maison; ce qui auroit pu occasioner l'incendie le plus affreux, si l'on ne s'en étoit apperçu; qu'il est de notre prudence d'empêcher que l'on n'abuse si cruellement d'une découverte qui peut un jour devenir très-utile.[8]

In response, an *ordonnance de police* (police order) was issued, under which any 'pilots' of unauthorized balloons and other flying machines to which anything was attached, including fire, were to be subject to a hefty fine and liable for consequential losses:

> Très-expresses défenses sont faites à toutes personnes, de quelque qualité & condition qu'elles soient, de lancer, sans y être autorisées, dans la Ville

6 R. G. Grant, *Flight: The Complete History* (DK Publishing 2007).

7 *Ordonnance de police qui défend de lancer des Ballons ou Machines aérostatiques dans la Ville & Fauxbourgs de Lyon du 21 Novembre 1783. Extrait des Minutes du Greffe de Police de la Ville, Fauxbourgs & Banlieue de Lyon.* 11173. ('Every day, some citizens throw balloons in the air and, because they are poorly constructed, they often catch fire in the sky'.)

8 Ibid. ('A group of young men launched a balloon in the air and attached to it a bale of straw. The balloon and straw caught fire and fell on a house, causing a terrible fire. We shall prevent people from abusing this major discovery'.)

> ou Fauxbourgs, des Ballons, ou Machines aérostatiques, auxquels elles auront adapté des artifices, ou du feu, de quelque manière que ce puisse être; le tout sous peine de 300 livres d'amende, & d'être responsables des dommages qu'ils pourroient occasioner.[9]

This *ordonnance* is noteworthy because it appears to be the first ever air law on record. Whilst it is obviously limited in its jurisdictional scope, it is nevertheless quite important beyond Lyon insofar as it acknowledges the safety risks associated with improper use of flying objects. It also makes special reference to (pre-)flight authorization. But who should authorize balloon launches? Presumably the relevant authority at the time was the police, but what of private landowners' rights to enjoy their land and things adjacent to it, such as 'airspace'? This book's starting point is to delve into the concept and status of 'airspace'.

In the eighteenth century, the maxim in Roman law and common law, 'cuius est solum eius est usque ad coelum et ad inferos', prevailed. This maxim provides that property rights in land are extended to the heavens and down to hell.[10] However, the phrase 'usque ad coelum' began to fall out of favour following increasing frequency of manned hot air balloon flights.[11] This will be discussed in further detail below.

Development of the 'airspace sovereignty' concept

As balloon flights became a more regular occurrence, and began to cover ever longer distances, crossing between the territorial limits of States without authorization, it is no surprise that this phenomenon should contribute to

9 *Ordonnance de police 21 Novembre 1783* (n 7) ('It is forbidden to launch, without authorization, balloons with fire. This would be punished with a 300£ fine and to be liable for the damages that they might be causing'.) This fine is a considerable sum of money: 'donne à son épouse sa vie durant la légitime jouissance du revenu de sa terre et de sa baronnie de Fluviat d'une valeur de onze cent livres par année', tells us the real value – 1100 livres per annum for a Baron's lands. For the amount in gold, see Jean Monange, 'De la valeur des choses dans le temps' (Histoire-Généalogie). Available online at: www.histoire-genealogie.com/spip.php?article398&lang=fr

10 'The property story and the sovereignty story began identically, with the invention of the airplane, but they ended differently. The owner of land ended up without the right to exclude aircraft from flying overhead, except at very low altitudes. Nations, by contrast, ended up with the right to exclude foreign aircraft from flying overhead, except at extremely high altitudes. In the airspace used most frequently, from a few hundred feet up to several miles, nations have a power that individuals lack'. Stuart Banner, *Who Owns the Sky?* (Harvard University Press 2008) 290.

11 Against this, one might consider the power of a State to take private property that is to be put to public use or for public safety reasons, e.g. for constructing interstate road or railway infrastructure. A few notable examples include United States 'eminent domain'; UK, Ireland, Australia and New Zealand 'compulsory purchase'; Hong Kong 'resumption'; and Brazil, Canada and South Africa 'expropriation'.

concerns over protection of national security. Indeed, military interests in aviation – interpreted widely as defensive and offensive – appeared as early as 1899 in discussions that took place at the First International Peace Conference, held at The Hague.[12]

Whilst the *Aerostat Réveillon* was the first functioning flying machine, the *Kitty Hawk* is widely considered to have marked the birth of civil aviation.[13] The invention of the aeroplane brought a new dimension to transport; transport of persons by air beyond national territorial borders was now a reality.

A general rise in recreational flying over France and along the edges of her territorial borders led to the establishment in 1905 of a non-governmental, non-profit organization, the Féderation aéronautique internationale (International Aeronautical Federation), to promote astronautical and aeronautical activities in France, and later to establish rules for the control and certification of world records.[14] Famously, Louis Blériot flew an aeroplane across the English Channel in 1909 – from Calais, France to Dover, England – without prior authorization, aircraft markings or pilot identification.

As well as regarding recreational flights, concerns over military flights began to arise, too. To be precise, '[b]etween April and November of 1908 at least ten German balloons crossed the frontier and landed in France carrying over twenty-five aviators at least half of whom were German officers'.[15] Debates in the French *Sénat* concluded that the situation 'should be considered both for its effect on national defense and on international commercial relations, and that regulation of the aerial frontiers must therefore be studied'.[16]

It followed that the French government invited delegates from the major European powers to Paris in 1910 to attend a diplomatic conference, the

12 ICAO, 'The Postal History of ICAO'. Available online at: www.icao.int/secretariat/PostalHistory/1910_the_paris_convention.htm

13 17 December 1903. It should be noted that the first commercial (passenger-carrying) civil aviation operation began on 1 January 1914, the St Petersburg–Tampa, Florida Line in the U.S. (Smithsonian National Air and Space Museum, 'America by Air'. Available online at: https://airandspace.si.edu/exhibitions/america-by-air/online/early_years/early_years01.cfm). The fierce rivalry between France and the United States as 'first to fly' is discussed in more detail in Laurence E. Geseel and Paul Stephen Dempsey, 'Aircraft and Aviation Technology' in *Air Transportation: Foundations for the 21st Century* (3rd edn, Coast Air Publications 2010) Ch. 2.

14 Today, this survives as The World Air Sports Federation. See www.fai.org

15 John Cobb Cooper, 'The International Air Navigation Conference Paris 1910' (1952) 19 *J. Air L. & Com.* 127, 128 citing Gaston Bonnefoy, *Le Code de l'air* (M. Rivière 1909) 186–190; See also Giulio Castelli, 'Il dominio dell'aria' (1908) 47 *Rivista internazionale di scienze sociali e discipline ausiliarie* 315–323.

16 Cooper, 'The International Air Navigation Conference Paris 1910'; see Speech by General Mercier in the French Sénat in *Journal official 1908* (Paris, 5 November 1908) quoted by Georges Montenot, 'La Circulation Adrienne envisagée au point de vue juridique' (Thesis Dijon, 1911) 5.

Conférence internationale de navigation aérienne (International Air Navigation Conference).[17] The goal of the conference was to formulate principles of international law relating to air navigation. Unfortunately, the parties to the conference could not agree on equal treatment of all civil aircraft, national or foreign, within usable airspace. There were two main camps: the first advocated a general principle of 'freedom of the air', in parallel to that of the sea; the second argued that national (State) sovereignty extended into 'international airspace'. Ultimately, the conference ended in political failure without any State signatories. A subsequent attempt to resume talks in Brussels in 1913 also failed.

Whereas commentators tend to agree that the Paris Conference 1910 was a failure for lack of explicit agreement, most would also acknowledge the importance of the debates it produced as well.[18] Indeed, Cooper explains that although the Conference was 'technically a diplomatic failure … [its] subsequent developments mark it as second in historical importance only to the 1919 conference after World War I when the celebrated Paris Convention [1919] was drafted and signed'.[19]

It is useful to consider that when the parties convened in Paris in 1910, they were initially faced with the dilemma of how, if at all, they should treat 'airspace'. It was possible for the conference to proceed in any one of four ways with regard to the recognition of airspace as: (1) free airspace; (2) territorial airspace; (3) sovereign airspace; or (4) modified sovereign airspace. Each of these 'treatments' will be elaborated below.

The first, free airspace, denotes a complete freedom of aerial navigation. Under this variety, analogous with freedom of navigation in maritime law that is based on the *pleno jure gentium* rule of law, there would be no restriction on the use of airspace. Whilst Nys stated in 1902, 'Let us beware lest we destroy "the *liberty* of the air" or reduce it to a very slight significance',[20] his theory received criticism 'for the simplistic way in which it equated air law with maritime law, and it has never received wide support

17 The attendees were Austria-Hungary, Belgium, Bulgaria, Denmark, France, Germany, Great Britain, Italy, Luxembourg, Monaco, Netherlands, Portugal, Romania, Russia, Spain, Sweden, Switzerland and Turkey. The Conference excluded the U.S. as it was deemed out of reach of incidents such as those that transpired in France, and was thus limited to Europe. Source: Cooper, 'The International Air Navigation Conference', 128.

18 There was, however, as Cooper argues, implicit agreement on the fundamental principles. See Cooper, 'The International Air Navigation Conference', 140, and discussion below.

19 Cooper, 'The International Air Navigation Conference', 127.

20 In the report by Professor M. Nys of Brussels to the Institute of International Law 1902, as cited in Harold D. Hazeltine, *The Law of the Air* (University of London Press 1911), referred to in Jae Woon Lee, 'Revisiting Freedom of Overflight in International Air Law: Minimum Multilateralism in International Air Transport' (2013) 38(4/5) *Air & Space Law* 356 (emphasis added).

since its inception'.[21] Against Nys's position, it could be argued, 'Il y a une différence fondamentale entre la mer et l'air: le fond de la mer n'appartient à personne; aucun Etat n'y peut prétendre exercer de souveraineté'.[22]

The second possible line to take would be to treat territorial airspace in a similar fashion to how the territorial sea was already treated in customary international maritime law. The foremost proponent of this view was Frenchman Paul Fauchille, who proposed the following: 'The air is free. States have in the air in time of peace and in time of war only those rights which are necessary for their preservation. These rights relate to the prevention of espionage, to customs and sanitary regulations, and to the necessities of defence'.[23]

It is possible that Fauchille's position would have received more widespread support had it not been for the rising tensions in Europe leading up to outbreak of the First World War (1914–1918).

The third variant would be to treat airspace as being entirely within State sovereignty. This actually led to the so-called 'sovereignty of the air' school of theorists that advocated for a *sovereign right* in the air. The sovereignty of the air also 'accords the State the rights of legal and political supremacy'.[24] In the words of Lee, 'In general, writers of this school give the State full sovereign rights in the entire atmosphere above its territory because it is necessary for the State to guard itself against the dangers incident to aerial navigation'.[25] Thus, the sovereignty of the air variant takes a defensive position on aerial navigation, extending upwards to include the entire atmosphere above a State's territory.

Finally, it was possible to recognize State sovereignty over airspace and also to grant the right of innocent passage for foreign aircraft in that sovereign airspace. This would give rise to questions around qualification of a limited or unlimited height, and if unlimited, then the possible need to grant permission of innocent passage above a certain pre-determined height. In his pioneering treatise, *The Law of the Air* (1911), Hazeltine concluded 'that the proper view was the doctrine of *full* sovereignty – without any restriction on height, and without the concession of a right of passage'.[26]

21 Lee, 'Revisiting Freedom of Overflight in International Air Law' 356, referring to Nicholas Mateesco Matte, *Treatise on Air-Aeronautical Law* (McGill University 1981) 74, 75.

22 'The sea and the air are fundamentally different as no State can exercise its sovereignty over the seabed'. Conférence internationale de navigation aérienne, Paris 18 mai–28 juin 1910, *Exposé des vues des puissances d'après les mémorandums adressas au gouvernement français* (Paris, Imp. Nationale, 1909) 268. Available online at: https://archive.org/stream/procsverbauxde00conf/procsverbauxde00conf_djvu.txt

23 Taken from Paul Fauchille's draft code submitted to the Institute of International Law in 1902, as translated by Hazeltine, *The Law of the Air*, 16–17, Lee, 'Revisiting Freedom of Overflight in International Air Law, 356.

24 Lee, 'Revisiting Freedom of Overflight in International Air Law, 357.

25 Ibid. referring to Hazeltine, *The Law of the Air*, 28.

26 Lee, 'Revisiting Freedom of Overflight in International Air Law', 359 referring to Hazeltine, *The Law of the Air*, 51 (emphasis added).

In the early twentieth century, 'jurists were still divided between those who contended that the air, like the high seas, should be free to all, and those who believed that States possessed sovereignty over their superincumbent airspace'.[27] This was also reflected in the positions of the State participants at the Paris Conference 1910. Whilst the French advocated for freedom of the air, the British argued for State sovereignty. The German position is also set out below.[28]

EXPOSÉ DE LA DÉLÉGATION FRANÇAISE

Sur la question de la libre circulation aérienne.

Il ne parait pas à la Délégation française que la Conférence doive examiner la question de savoir si les Etats ont sur l'espace un droit de souveraineté parce que l'espace constitue un accessoire inséparable du sol ou si, au contraire, l'atmosphère doit, comme la haute mer, être déclarée libre, insusceptible de souveraineté.

En réalité, – et c'est le second motif de l'écarter, – la question n'a pas, en fait, dans la pratique, toute l'importance qu'elle semble avoir. En effet, les partisans du principe de la souveraineté comme ceux du principe de la liberté de l'atmosphère sont d'accord pour admettre que le principe ne doit pas être absolu mais souffre un tempérament nécessaire: le droit de souveraineté de l'État territorial sur l'espace est mitigé par le droit de passage innocent reconnu aux aéronefs; le principe de la liberté de l'atmosphère est tempéré par la reconnaissance à l'Etat territorial, sur l'atmosphère, des droits nécessaires à sa conservation. Or, avec ces tempéraments, chacune des deux opinions conduit, pour ainsi dire sur tous les points, tout au moins en temps de paix, aux mêmes conséquences pratiques.[29]

EXPOSÉ DE LA DÉLÉGATION BRITANNIQUE

Sur le principe de l'admission de la navigation aérienne dans les limites et au-dessus du territoire étranger.

... dans la mesure du possible, encourager et développer la navigation aérienne, il est évidemment nécessaire de sauvegarder les intérêts et la

27 Keith Hamilton, *Bertie of Thame: Edwardian Ambassador* (Royal Historical Society 1990) 200, 201.

28 See also Matte, *Treatise on Air-Aeronautical Law*.

29 Conférence internationale de navigation aérienne, 242. In summary, according to the French delegation, the question of the sovereignty of a State over the atmosphere did not seem to be a key issue; indeed, the right of state sovereignty is tempered by the right of way of aircraft.

> souveraineté des Etats … Nous essayerons maintenant d'expliquer pourquoi nous considérons comme inutile toute déclaration de principe sur la question de la liberté de navigation ou de la souveraineté des Etats dans les airs.[30]

According to Hamilton's comprehensive study on Edwardian diplomacy, which the British position expressed above notably reflects, 'The conference had not … been expected by the British government to deal with the legal status of the air … both the French and German delegations proposed in written *exposés* that the conference should consider the *usage* rather than the *status* of airspace'.[31]

In the end, as the major powers attending the Paris Conference 1910 appeared to be at loggerheads over fundamental concepts on the regulation of aerial navigation, it should come as no surprise that the conference ended without a written agreement. Nonetheless, 'the Paris 1910 conference did not break down because of a fundamental difference between Great Britain on one side and Germany on the other as to sovereignty or freedom of usable space',[32] contrary to popular belief.

Interestingly, the British position foreshadows Britain's national legislative action taken only a very short while after the conference concluded. Fearful of possible intrusion by air via the English Channel, the United Kingdom (UK) Parliament passed the Aerial Navigation Act 1911 (amended in 1913), which recognized UK power to close all British airspace, including parts of the English Channel as territorial waters, to foreign navy or military aircraft.[33]

The German position,[34] according to Cooper, 'provided that aircraft of a *contracting* State should be *authorised* to take off, land, and fly over the territory of other contracting States'.[35] In keeping with Cooper, 'By providing for authorization of foreign flight and limiting it to aircraft of contracting States, the convention thus in effect denied any general international law right of innocent passage or of entry of all foreign aircraft'.[36]

Nonetheless the conference also voiced unease at this.

> Le projet allemand n'avait pas moins souci de ces intérêts, mais obéissant à une pensée dominante, et entendant conserver dans toute son intégrité

30 Ibid., 210, 271 (Air navigation should be encouraged, while safeguarding the principle of sovereignty in the air).
31 Hamilton, *Bertie of Thame*, 201; Hazeltine, *The Law of the Air*; Conférence internationale de navigation aérienne, 239–244 (emphasis added).
32 Cooper, 'The International Air Navigation Conference', 140.
33 Lassa Oppenheim and Ronald Roxburgh, *International Law: A Treatise, Volume 1 – Peace* (3rd edn, New Jersey 2005) 353–354.
34 Translated from the original text as 'Admission of Air Navigation within the Limits of or above Foreign Territory'. Conférence internationale de navigation aérienne, 93–104.
35 Cooper, 'The International Air Navigation Conference', 132.
36 Ibid.

> le principe de la souveraineté territoriale en ce qui concerne les mesures de police, il préférait qu'il n'y eût pas de stipulations internationales de cette nature. Aussi, proposait-il de décider seulement que «tout Etat contractant pourra prescrire que, dans le cas où l'aéronef d'un autre Etat contractant atterrit sur son territoire, l'aéronaute en avise l'autorité de police».[37]

For reference, the key articles of the draft agreement from the Paris Conference 1910 are reproduced below.

> Article 2: An aircraft is only governed by the present Convention if it possesses the nationality of a contracting State. None of the contracting States shall permit a free balloon or airship to fly over its territory unless it complies with the above condition, though special and temporary authorization may be granted.

> Article 23: The restrictions and reservations contemplated in Articles 19, 20, 21, and 22 shall immediately be published and notified to the Governments concerned. The forbidden zones shall be defined with sufficient precision to enable them to be shown on aeronautical maps of a scale of at least 1/500000. The contracting States shall be obliged to communicate these maps to one another.

> Article 24: As soon as the pilot of any aircraft perceives that he has entered the airspace above a forbidden zone he must give the signal of distress specified in Article 16 of Annex (c) and land as soon as possible; he must also land if requested to do so by warning given from the ground. Each State shall give notice of the warning signals which it has adopted.

> Article 29: The authorities of the country will always have the right to visit the aircraft on its departure and landing, and to exercise in the atmosphere above their territory police jurisdiction and customs supervision. Each State can enact that if an aircraft of another contracting State lands on its territory the nearest police or customs authorities must immediately be notified ... The personnel on board the aircraft must conform strictly to the police regulations and provisions of the customs laws of the country.

> Article 80: Each State undertakes to enact that all aircraft within the limits of, or above, its territory, and all its own aircraft within the limits

37 Conférence internationale de navigation aérienne, 93–104. The German position wanted to preserve the principle of sovereignty in relation to police measures, namely notification to police before landing on the territory of another State.

of, or above, the territory of another contracting State shall comply with the 'Rules relating to Aerial Traffic' annexed to the present Convention (Annex (6)) and to punish those which fail to do so.

Article 84: The carriage of goods by air can only take place in virtue of special conventions between the States concerned or of the provisions of their own legislation.

Article 85: The carriage by aircraft of explosives, arms, and munitions of war, and of traveler and other carrier pigeons, is forbidden in international traffic.

Article 86: Each State can forbid or regulate the carriage or use of photographic apparatus above its territory. It can cause the negatives found on board a foreign aircraft landing on its territory to be developed, and can, if necessary, seize the apparatus and negatives.

Article 88: Each State has the right to authorize aircraft within the limits of and above its territory to carry on board a radio-telegraphic apparatus. Such apparatus cannot, without special permission, be used except when the safety of the aircraft is concerned.[38]

Ultimately it was political, not legal, disagreement that produced the stalemate. As Cooper analyses, an examination of these:

articles of the draft convention approved at the plenary session of the conference shows that the government delegations then understood and acted upon the legal assumption that flight-space over the national lands and waters was part of the territory of the subjacent State in which such State had complete and exclusive power to control all human activity including foreign flight.

Article 2 of the draft convention would alone determine the correctness of this assertion … This is an undertaking by each contracting State to prohibit the entry of all free balloons or airships except those possessing the nationality of contracting States or those specially authorized by such State. It is equivalent to the assertion of full and absolute sovereignty of the superjacent State with exclusive power to control all flight over its surface territories. Article 30 is equally conclusive. Taken almost directly from the German draft convention, it provided that each State

38 This list is provided as a summary in Cooper, 'The International Air Navigation Conference', 142; see Conférence internationale de navigation aérienne, 188–189. English translation from *Reports of the Civil Aerial Transport Committee*, London, H. M. Stationery Office, 1918, Cd. 9218 (Appendix A to Report of Special Committee No. 1).

undertakes to require the observance by all aircraft 'within the limits of or above its territory' of the rules relating to air traffic contained in an annex to the convention and 'to punish those which fail to do so'.[39]

Although at the outbreak of the First World War no international agreement was in place for the regulation of aerial navigation, one State's (military) trespass into the airspace over another State's territory would of course have amounted to wartime transgression. The general principles and draft provisions of the Paris Conference, albeit not agreed upon in writing, were accepted in principle by State participants, which, according to Cooper, evidences that 'States had concluded that they were entitled to regulate flight over their territories as fully as they had historically regulated other forms of human activity in national territory, and that no general freedom of international transit (innocent passage) for aircraft of all States existed as a matter of international law in the usable space over sovereign States'.[40]

One such Paris Convention provision, which would shortly prove significant, was the common understanding that military aircraft are the only 'national mark' of the sovereignty of a State, and markings representing that sovereign State should be notified to other States: 'Les aéronefs militaires porteront comme seule marque nationale le signe de souveraineté de leur Etat. Chaque Etat contractant notifiera aux autres Etats contractants les signes de souveraineté dont il fera usage'.[41]

Cooper concludes by stating that 'at the close of the conference no State denied its legal *right* to restrict foreign flight over its surface territories. Agreement, though tacit, existed as to the legal status of flight-space. The only open problem was the political extent to which States should exercise their existing powers of control without unnecessarily impeding future development of international flight'.[42]

First World War and return to Paris

The First World War began on 28 July 1914, and continued until Armistice Day, 11 November 1918. In Europe, all civil air travel was suspended from the moment the war started.[43] This war was the first time in history that aircraft were employed in large-scale military combat.

After the war had ended, an environment of reinforced sense of national - ism and common recognition that aircraft could be used for strategic military

39 Cooper, 'The International Air Navigation Conference', 141.

40 Ibid., 128.

41 'Military aircraft are the only "national mark" of the sovereignty of a State, and markings representing that sovereign State should be notified to other States'. Conférence internationale de navigation aérienne.

42 Cooper, 'The International Air Navigation Conference', 140.

43 Oppenheim and Roxburgh, *International Law*, 354.

purposes placed the regulation of aerial navigation high upon national political agendas, and crucially this time also upon the *international* agenda. On the one hand, 'States recognized the possible commercial advantages of technological advances in aircraft, [however] they tended to be more concerned about the military aspects of aircraft development'.[44]

On the other hand, interest amongst private citizens for conducting longer flights that would cross national borders was also intensifying. John Alcock and Arthur Whitten-Brown conducted the first non-stop transatlantic flight in June 1919, from St John's, Newfoundland to Clifden, Ireland. This feat demonstrated that the technology, along perhaps with requisite courage, had advanced sufficiently to support the ambition of transatlantic flight.[45] With that said, it took two more decades until *commercial* transatlantic operations would become practical.

At the same time, at the Congrès de la Paix (Paris Peace Conference) held between 1919 and 1920, negotiations were held on the theme of cooperation and collaboration on future development of international aviation, bearing in mind its two components: State and civil aviation. The outcome was the Convention portant réglementation de la navigation aérienne (Paris Convention Relating to the Regulation of Aerial Navigation), which was signed by 27 States on 13 October, 1919, and entered into force in 1922. By 1940, the Convention was in force for 33 States, comprising many members of the League of Nations, but excluding Brazil, China, the USSR and the United States.[46]

Recalling the failure of the 1910 Paris Conference to reach a binding agreement, the attendees in 1919 met under even greater impetus to agree a binding solution for regulation of airspace; most were also allies emerging from a very costly – in human casualties and financial loss – First World War. In fact, already in 1916, an Inter-Allied Aviation Committee was established, signalling a common objective of the Allies: France, Great Britain, Italy and the United States. The committee's mandate was to coordinate aircraft manufacturing and in particular standardization of aircraft motors.

At the Paris Peace Conference in 1919, returning to the unresolved deliberations from the 1910 conference, an Inter-Allied Aeronautical Commission was created. Its principal task was 'to consider the limits on commercial aviation to be allowed to the defeated Germany … [and] to prepare a Convention on international aerial navigation in the time of peace'.[47]

44 Lee, 'Revisiting Freedom of Overflight in International Air Law', 358–359.

45 14–15 June, 1919.

46 Although U.S. President Woodrow Wilson formulated the concept of the League of Nations and was awarded the Nobel Peace Prize in 1919, U.S. Congress did not ratify the Charter of the League of Nations owing to the contractual nature of Article X, which called on members of the League to provide assistance if another member experienced external aggressions.

47 Michael Milde, *International Air Law and ICAO* (Eleven Publishing 2008) 10.

To that end, Great Britain proposed a draft core principle: 'The High Contracting Parties recognise the full and absolute sovereignty of every State over the air above its territories and territorial waters'.[48] Thus, the British remained steadfast on their 1910 position.

A delegate from the United States, Rear Admiral Knapp, recommended the following for adoption:

> Recognition:
> (1) of the principle of the full and absolute sovereignty of each State over the airspace above its territories and territorial waters carrying with it the right of exclusion of foreign aircraft;
> (2) of the right of each State to impose its jurisdiction over the airspace above its territory and territorial waters.[49]

Thus, the American position advocated dually for recognition of State sovereignty *and* the right to impose national jurisdiction.

After deliberations, the Legal Subcommittee accepted the following extended articulation in its report to the Inter-Allied Aeronautical Commission:

> full and exclusive subjection of the airspace to the sovereignty of the territory underlying it … is only when the column of air rests upon a *res nullius* or *communis*, the sea, that freedom becomes the rule of air … It follows that in consequence of its sovereignty the underlying State within the limits of its frontiers may forbid flight over, and *a fortiori*, landing upon its territory.[50]

Reference to jurisdiction was dropped.

This version gave rise to the following, final agreed language in Article 1 of the 1919 Paris Convention:

> The High Contracting Parties recognise that every Power has complete and exclusive sovereignty over the airspace above its territory.

Interestingly, in the French version of the Convention, 'airspace' appears as 'l'espace atmosphérique'; in the Italian version it is 'spazio atmosferico'. Thus there are discrepancies in the languages of the convention, which could lead to alternative legal interpretations of 'airspace'. No clear definition of airspace is provided.

48 John Cobb Cooper, 'Sovereignty in Space' (1959) 64(1) *Flying* 31.
49 Ibid.
50 Ibid., 31–32.

Nevertheless, a partial definition is provided for 'territory' in the second part of Article 1 of the Paris Convention, which continues:

> For the purposes of this Convention the territory of a State shall be deemed to be the land areas or territorial waters adjacent thereto under the sovereignty, suzerainty, protection or mandate of such State.

Thus, the Paris Convention 1919 *recognized* full sovereignty of States over airspace above their lands and territorial seas. Milde sums up the effect of these provisions:

> The concept of complete and exclusive air sovereignty means in the first place the *exclusive jurisdiction* of the State concerned to adopt laws and regulations relating to the status and uses of its airspace and to implement such laws by administrative decisions and sanctions – all to the exclusion of any other State's jurisdiction.[51]

Against that, Goedhuis questions:

> [D]id the authors of [the first] article want to indicate that the power of the state over the air was an unrestricted power? Was that the reason why the words 'complete and exclusive' were added to the term 'sovereignty'? Or were they simply meant to convey that only the subjacent state is entitled, to the exclusion of all others, to exercise legal power?[52]

He answers himself by providing a *qualification* of sovereignty, namely that '[i]n the Report of the Legal Sub Commission it was stated that, whereas the right of sovereignty was to be vigorously maintained in regard of third (i.e. ex-enemy) states, this right was not to be exercised in regard of states that trusted each other'.[53]

Finally able to reach agreement on the language of Article 1 of the 1919 Paris Convention, the High Contracting Parties 'put an end to almost two decades of academic discussions' and intense diplomatic debate.[54] 'In the shadow of the war time experience states firmly and unequivocally confirmed the complete and exclusive sovereignty of states over their airspace'.[55] Milde argues that the Convention provides 'no "freedom to fly" – [but rather]

51 Milde, *International Air Law and ICAO*, 35 (emphasis added).

52 D. Goedhuis, 'The Air Sovereignty Concept and United States Influence on its Future Development' (1955) 22 *J. Air L. & Com.* 209, 211.

53 Ibid., 209, 212.

54 Milde, *International Air Law and ICAO*, 11.

55 Ibid.

every aspect of aviation is regulated in great detail and foreign aircraft have no right to enter the airspace of another State otherwise than in conformity with the applicable laws and regulations'.[56]

The 1919 Paris Convention also created the International Commission for Air Navigation (ICAN), a commission placed under the League of Nations, a precursor in part to the International Civil Aviation Organization (ICAO)[57] and International Air Transport Association (IATA).[58]

Returning to the text of the Convention, Article 2 grants the freedom of innocent passage in time of peace; it reads:

> Each contracting State undertakes in time of peace to accord freedom of innocent passage above its territory to the aircraft of the other contracting States, provided that the conditions laid down in the present Convention are observed.
>
> Regulations made by a contracting State as to the admission over its territory of the aircraft of the other contracting States shall be applied without distinction of nationality.

In addition, Article 3 limits the freedom of innocent passage in the light of military and other safety concerns; it reads:

> Each contracting State is entitled for military reasons or in the interest of public safety to prohibit the aircraft of the other contracting States, under the penalties provided by its legislation and subject to no distinction being made in this respect between its private aircraft and those of the other contracting States from flying over certain areas of its territory.
>
> In that case the locality and the extent of the prohibited areas shall be published and notified beforehand to the other contracting States.

Therefore it can be concluded that, following the 1919 Paris Convention, the sovereignty of a State over its airspace may be *limited*.

56 Ibid., 35.

57 Today, the Air Navigation Committee of ICAO continues to be a crucial component of ICAO governance. It has 19 members and has recommended for adoption 16 of the 19 Annexes to the Chicago Convention 1944 containing international standards and recommended practices (SARPs). See ICAO, 'Air Navigation Commission: Special 200th Session Commemorative Review' (Fall 2015). Available online at: www.icao.int/about-icao/AirNavigationCommission/Documents/ANC-200_final_web.pdf

58 See below; it should be acknowledged that today IATA is a very important forum for airline industry discussions. See IATA, 'About us', online at: www.iata.org/about/Pages/index.aspx

Second World War and onwards to Chicago

The UN environment

In the midst of the Second World War, the League of Nations was replaced by the United Nations (UN). The next steps in the regulation of international civil aviation took place within the UN environment. Some understanding of the driving principles of the organization would be helpful.

We may begin with the signing of the Atlantic Charter on 14 August 1941,[59] which itself embodies the 'common program of purposes and principles' later adopted by the signatories of the United Nations Declaration. Two of these stand out, namely that the State parties:

> (Third) respect the right of all peoples to choose the form of government under which they will live; and they wish to see *sovereign rights* and self-government restored to those who have been forcibly deprived of them.
>
> (Fifth) desire to bring about the *fullest collaboration between all nations* in the economic field with the object of securing, for all, improved labour standards, economic adjustment and social security.[60]

On 30 October 1943, the Foreign Ministers of the United States, the United Kingdom, the USSR and the Chinese Ambassador to Moscow issued the Declaration of Four Nations on General Security, which 'contemplated the establishment at the earliest practicable date of a *general international organization* ... [which was to be] based upon the principle of the sovereign equality of all peace–loving States and open to membership by such States, large and small, for the maintenance of international peace and security'.[61]

U.S. President Franklin D. Roosevelt, British Prime Minister Winston S. Churchill and USSR leader Joseph Stalin signed the Yalta Agreement in February 1945, the objective of which was 'to prevent aggression and to remove the political, economic and social causes of war through the *close and continuing collaboration* of all peace-loving peoples'.[62]

59 The Atlantic Charter was a joint declaration made by the President of the United States (Franklin D. Roosevelt) and the Prime Minister of the United Kingdom (Winston S. Churchill). www.unmultimedia.org/searchers/yearbook/page.jsp?volume=1946-47&bookpage=1

60 U.S. Department of State Bulletin (18 February 1945) vol XII, 213–216, https://archive.org/stream/departmentofstat1245unit#page/n253/mode/2up; Report of the Crimea (Yalta) Conference (London H. M. Stationery Office, 11 February 1946) [Miscellaneous No. 5 (1945) Cmd. 6598.] (emphasis added).

61 U.S. Department of State Bulletin (6 November 1943) 307–311 (emphasis added).

62 U.S. Department of State Bulletin (18 February 1945) 213–216; Report of the Crimea (Yalta) Conference (emphasis added).

At the San Francisco Conference held in June 1945, hosted by U.S. President Harry Truman, the UN Charter was unanimously approved by all 50 delegate nation-states. In fact, the language in the previous version of the Charter that read 'all peace-loving States' was changed to read 'all its Members', and reflected 'sovereign equality' of all Members. The term, 'sovereign equality', according to the report of the Rapporteur of Committee I/1, means:

(1) that States are juridically equal;
(2) that each State enjoys the right inherent in full sovereignty;
(3) that the personality of the State is respected as well as its territorial integrity and political independence; and
(4) that the State should, under international order, comply faithfully with its international duties and obligations.[63]

According to Article 2 of the UN Charter:

> The Organization and its Members, in pursuit of the Purposes stated in Article 1, shall act in accordance with the following Principles.
>
> 1. The Organization is based on the principle of the sovereign equality of all its Members.
> 2. All Members, in order to ensure to all of them the rights and benefits resulting from membership, shall fulfil in good faith the obligations assumed by them in accordance with the present Charter.
> 3. All Members shall settle their international disputes by peaceful means in such a manner that international peace and security, and justice, are not endangered.
> 4. All Members shall refrain in their international relations from the threat or use of force against the territorial integrity or political independence of any state, or in any other manner inconsistent with the Purposes of the United Nations.
> 5. All Members shall give the United Nations every assistance in any action it takes in accordance with the present Charter, and shall refrain from giving assistance to any state against which the United Nations is taking preventive or enforcement action.
> 6. The Organization shall ensure that states which are not Members of the United Nations act in accordance with these Principles so far as may be necessary for the maintenance of international peace and security.

63 UN, 'Yearbook of the United Nations: 1946–1947' 19. Available online at: www.unmultimedia.org/searchers/yearbook/page.jsp?volume=1946-47&bookpage=1

> 7. Nothing contained in the present Charter shall authorize the United Nations to intervene in matters which are essentially within the domestic jurisdiction of any state or shall require the Members to submit such matters to settlement under the present Charter; but this principle shall not prejudice the application of enforcement measures under Chapter VII.[64]

Thus, the UN Charter reflects the UN as a 'world community of sovereign states'.[65]

Post-war civil aviation

During the Second World War (1939–1945), major advancements were made with respect to technology such as radar, and aircraft were employed by the Allies and Axis powers as strategic tools for the air force and military, for carrying out reconnaissance missions, as fighters and bombers, and for providing important airlift services. Naval aerial warfare, particularly the use of aircraft carriers, also advanced significantly during this global war.

The air commands of the major powers had developed networks of airways in the course of the First and Second World Wars. As the end of the Second World War drew near, '[i]t became abundantly clear that rules for the conduct of civil aviation – mutually workable among the nations of the world – must be evolved and enforced by common consent'.[66] It was feared that the post-war world would otherwise be 'confronted by a state of disorder in the air, containing the seeds of much economic and political strife, and capable of poising international relations'.[67] These hopes and fears led to the organization of the International Civil Aviation Conference that met in Chicago on 1 November 1944. Fifty-two nation-states were represented in total.

As he opened the conference, Adolf A. Berle, Jr., President of the Conference and Chairman of the Executive Committee, delivered a memorable address:

> The use of the air has this in common with the use of the sea: it is a highway given by nature to all men. It differs in this from the sea: that it is subject to the sovereignty of the nations over which it moves. Nations ought therefore to arrange among themselves for its use in that manner which will be of the greatest benefit to all humanity, wherever situated.[68]

64 Charter of the United Nations, Ch. 1. Available online at: www.un.org/en/sections/un-charter/chapter-i/index.html

65 Held *et al.*, *Global Transformations*.

66 'The Postal History of ICAO' 9.

67 Ibid.

68 'Proceedings of the International Civil Aviation Conference' (Chicago, 1 November–7 December 1944) vol. I, 55, online at: www.icao.int/ChicagoConference/Pages/proceed.aspx

One observes thusly that at Chicago just as twice before in Paris, there were various courses of action that could be pursued, including possible adoption of certain 1919 Paris Convention provisions while seeing to the wider and more diverse membership of contracting States. These courses included, according to prevailing trends at the time:

(1) the American trend, advocating complete freedom of competition in air transport;
(2) the British trend, suggesting the creation of an International Organisation to coordinate air transport and to assume the duties of apportioning the world's air routes and making decisions on frequencies and tariffs;
(3) the Canadian trend, recommending support for the British proposals, but in a rather more elaborate version;
(4) an Australian and New Zealand plan for the internationalization of major airlines under the direction of a single authority in which all states would participate.[69]

Diederiks-Verschoor and Kopal go on to note that '[t]he Netherlands and the Scandinavian countries followed the American trend. However, none of the proposals exerted a significant influence in determining the ultimate scope and contents of the Convention'.[70] Instead, the 1919 Paris Convention principle found in Article 1, 'complete and exclusive sovereignty over airspace', remained the *legal standard* for the Chicago Convention.

The Chicago participants adopted a number of resolutions and recommendations alongside the Final Act of the Conference, which contained the following instruments adopted by the Conference in plenary:[71]

(1) the Convention on International Civil Aviation (Chicago Convention)
(2) the International Air Services Transit Agreement
(3) the International Air Transport Agreement

69 I. H. Diederiks-Verschoor and Vladimir Kopal, *An Introduction to Space Law* (3rd edn, Kluwer Law International 2008) 13.

70 Ibid.

71 See 'The Postal History of ICAO', Ch. 1, 9. It should be noted that U.S. law follows the Chicago Convention. For detail on this, see Legal Information Institute, 49 U.S. Code §40103 'Sovereignty and use of airspace' for a condensed version. See also U.S. Federal Aviation Act of 1958 §1108(a), for the full version, which reads: 'The United States of America is hereby declared to possess and exercise complete and exclusive national sovereignty in the airspace of the United States, including the airspace above all inland waters and the airspace about those portions of the adjacent marginal high seas, bays and lakes over which by international law or treaty or convention the United States exercises national jurisdiction'.

(4) the Interim Agreement on International Civil Aviation[72]
(5) 12 technical Annexes to the Chicago Convention
(6) a Standard Form of Bilateral Agreement

Convention on International Civil Aviation (Chicago Convention)

The Chicago Convention was opened for signature on 7 December 1944. It came into force once the 26th contracting State ratified the text on 4 April 1947.[73] Unlike the 1919 Paris Convention, the United States did sign the Chicago Convention, and subsequently ratified it in 1946.[74] Brazil and China also ratified the convention in 1946.[75] In 1970, the USSR notified ICAO of its adherence to the Convention.[76]

The Preamble to the Chicago Convention reads:

> WHEREAS the future development of international civil aviation can greatly help to create and preserve friendship and understanding among the nations and peoples of the world, yet its abuse can become a threat to the general security; and
>
> WHEREAS it is desirable to avoid friction and to promote that cooperation between nations and peoples upon which the peace of the world depends;
>
> THEREFORE, the undersigned governments having agreed on certain principles and arrangements in order that international civil aviation may be developed in a safe and orderly manner and that international air transport services may be established on the basis of equality of opportunity and operated soundly and economically;

Have accordingly concluded this Convention to that end.

There are four key themes which stand out in the Preamble. They are:

(1) there is an opportunity for international civil aviation to unite the world in cooperation and under peace;

72 This Agreement brought into being the Provisional International Civil Aviation Organization (PICAO).

73 Fifty-two States signed the Chicago Convention on 7 December 1944. The Convention came into force on 4 April 1947, on the thirtieth day after deposit with the government of the United States. See Abeyratne, *Convention on International Civil Aviation*, 3.

74 Legal Information Institute, U.S. Code, Title 49 para 40103, 'Sovereignty and use of airspace', online at: www.law.cornell.edu/uscode/text/49/40103

75 ICAO, Convention on International Civil Aviation (Chicago, 7 December 1944), online at: www.icao.int/secretariat/legal/List%20of%20Parties/Chicago_EN.pdf

76 Ibid.

(2) the world community must be mindful that international civil aviation, if misused, could pose a risk to security;
(3) agreed principles should guide the development of international civil aviation;
(4) safety and order are paramount; and
(5) there should be equal opportunity for all involved.

These themes also reflect the values of the later-established UN that are referred to above.

Retaining the legal standard on airspace sovereignty agreed in the 1919 Paris Convention, the parties to the Chicago Convention agreed to reproduce in Article 1:[77]

> The High Contracting Parties recognize that every State has complete and exclusive sovereignty over the airspace above its territory.

Again, whereas the Chicago Convention does not provide a definition of airspace,[78] it is commonly understood that airspace 'is essentially the region where aerodynamic *lift* provides the upward movement of aircraft, as opposed to the centrifugal force needed to escape the earth's gravity. While air can be found many miles above earth, the Von Karman line, at 52 to 56 miles above the earth, is where centrifugal force must be substituted for aerodynamic lift'.[79]

Article 2 of the Chicago Convention reads:

> For the purposes of this Convention the territory of a State shall be deemed to be the land areas and territorial waters adjacent thereto under the sovereignty, suzerainty, protection or mandate of such State.

Therefore, the sovereign State is ***recognized*** as having exclusive 'control' of the airspace over its territory (land) and the territorial sea (waters).[80] A 'freedom of innocent passage' is granted to seafarers in territorial seas, however, this freedom is not applied to law of international flight.[81]

77 Noting that the spelling changed from 'recognised' (British) to 'recognized' (American) standard.

78 Noting the earlier point made about French and Italian language discrepancies in the respective versions of the Paris Convention.

79 Paul B. Larsen, Joseph Sweeney and John Gillick, *Aviation Law: Cases Laws and Related Sources* (2nd edn, Martinus Nijhoff Publishers 2012) 40.

80 Article 3 of the 1982 UN Convention on the Law of the Sea (UNCLOS) extends the coastal state's exclusive control into the territorial waters to a total distance of 12 miles from the low-water mark. See below for additional discussion, and in Larsen, Sweeney and Gillick, *Aviation Law* Ch. 1.

81 UNCLOS Art 3, 'Innocent Passage in the Territorial Sea', online at: www.un.org/depts/los/convention_agreements/texts/unclos/UNCLOS-TOC.htm

Article 5 of the Chicago Convention reads:

> Each contracting State agrees that all aircraft of the other contracting States, being aircraft not engaged in scheduled international air services shall have the right, subject to the observance of the terms of this Convention, to make flights into or in transit non-stop across its territory and to make stops for non-traffic purposes without the necessity of obtaining prior permission, and subject to the right of the State flown over to require landing. Each contracting State nevertheless reserves the right, for reasons of safety of flight, to require aircraft desiring to proceed over regions which are inaccessible or without adequate air navigation facilities to follow prescribed routes, or to obtain special permission for such flights.
>
> Such aircraft, if engaged in the carriage of passengers, cargo, or mail for remuneration or hire on other than scheduled international air services, shall also, subject to the provisions of Article 7, have the privilege of taking on or discharging passengers, cargo, or mail, subject to the right of any State where such embarkation or discharge takes place to impose such regulations, conditions or limitations as it may consider desirable.

Generally speaking, Article 5 of the Chicago Convention applies to flights that are not labelled as scheduled. Aircraft carrying out non-scheduled services may fly over contracting States and stop for non-traffic purposes (refuel and repairs) without obtaining prior permission. Unfortunately, the Chicago Convention does not define scheduled and non-scheduled flights in its Article 96, where definitions of terminology used elsewhere in the Convention are otherwise contained. According to Larsen *et al.*, 'Charter services, unknown in 1944, would need some form of definition: no more than eight to 12 flights per month between the same points. The ICAO considered scheduled flight to be so frequent that they constitute a recognizable systematic series'.[82]

In 1952, ICAO Council adopted a definition of scheduled air services. It reads:

> A scheduled international air service is a series of flights that possess all the following characteristics:
>
> a. it passes through the airspace over the territory of more than one State;
> b. it is performed by aircraft for the transport of passengers, mail or cargo for remuneration, in such a manner that each flight is open to use by members of the public;

82 Larsen, Sweeney and Gillick, *Aviation Law* 45.

c. it is operated so as to serve traffic between the same two or more points; either
   1. according to a published timetable, or
   2. with flights so regular or frequent that they constitute a recognisable systematic series.[83]

ICAO also published a definition in 2004, according to which a non-scheduled air service is 'a commercial air transport service performed as other than a scheduled air service'.[84] It follows that a *scheduled* air service is 'an air service open to use by the general public and operated according to a published timetable or with such a regular frequency that it constitutes an easily recognizable systematic series of flights'.[85]

It should be noted that '[t]hough the terms non-scheduled and charter (i.e. a contractual arrangement between an air carrier and an entity hiring or leasing its aircraft) have come to be used interchangeably … not all commercial non-scheduled operations are charter flights'.[86]

Moving on to scheduled air services, Article 6 of the Chicago Convention provides:

> No scheduled international air service may be operated over or into the territory of a contracting State, except with the special permission or other authorization of that State, and in accordance with the terms of such permission or authorization.

It should be noted that the phrase 'over or into the territory' used in Article 6 makes clear that there is no freedom of overflight; in other words 'special permission' first must be obtained. Article 6 on scheduled international air services, which shows States' agreement on the requirement for special permission or other authorization to operate scheduled international air services over or into the territory of a contracting State before a flight may be operated, combined with Article 1, recognizing the principle of national sovereignty over territorial airspace, as well as failed efforts to establish a multilateral regulatory regime for commercial aviation, cumulatively evidence that bilateral air service agreements are required for cross-border flight operations (international air services).

There has been extensive use of bilateral agreements to regulate international air transport. According to ICAO's *Manual on the Regulation of*

83 ICAO, Doc. 7278-C/841, *Definition of Scheduled International Air Service* (1952) 3.

84 ICAO, Doc. 9626, *Manual on the Regulation of International Air Transport* (2nd edn, 2004). Available online at: www.icao.int/Meetings/atconf6/Documents/Doc%209626_en.pdf

85 Ibid.

86 EUROCONTROL, 'ATM Lexicon', online at: www.eurocontrol.int/lexicon/lexicon/en/index.php/Non-scheduled_air_service

International Air Transport, the

> [b]ilateral agreements now in force, which constitute the largest volume of international air transport regulatory documents, largely date from after the 1944 International Civil Aviation Conference held in Chicago ... bilateral negotiations and the agreements they produced emerged as the preferred method for States to exchange commercial rights for air services and to agree on ways of regulating capacity, tariffs and other matters.[87]

There have been attempts, however, to create a multilateral regulatory regime, beginning with the convention at Chicago itself.[88] The two multi - lateral agreements, the transit and transport agreements outlined below, were both proposed at Chicago and can be traced as the starting point for today's bilateral and multilateral system of the exchange of air traffic rights. These are typically negotiated through air services agreements or on an ad hoc basis, or they are provided for under the International Air Transit Agreement where States are parties to it.

Thus it can be said that the Chicago Convention, in particular Articles 1, 2, 5 and 6, provides the framework, or 'backbone',[89] to the Chicago system of exchange of traffic rights. Whilst the International Transit and Transport Agreements are meant to strengthen this system, they have not both received the widespread support that was anticipated.

International Air Services Transit and Transport Agreements

The International Air Services Transit Agreement,[90] which is also known as the Two Freedoms Agreement named after the first two 'Freedoms of the Air',[91] provides for the multilateral exchange of rights of overflight and non-

87 ICAO, Doc. 9626, 'Part 2 – Introduction of Bilateral Regulation' in *Manual on the Regulation of International Air Transport* (2nd edn, Secretary General 2004). Available online at: www.icao.int/Meetings/atconf6/Documents/Doc%209626_en.pdf. There are an estimated 3000 or more bilateral air service agreements currently in force.

88 It may be argued that the presentation by the German government at the 1910 Paris Conference was the first multilateral air navigation convention; it was only presented, not agreed. Cooper 'The International Air Navigation Conference'.

89 According to Lee, 'Revisiting Freedom of Overflight in International Air Law'.

90 ICAO, Doc. 7500, *Administrative package for acceptance of the international air services transit agreement* (Chicago 1944) online at: www.icao.int/secretariat/legal/Administrative%20Packages/transit_en.pdf; also reproduced in Doc. 9587, online at: www.icao.int/sustainability/pages/doc9587.aspx

91 ICAO, 'Freedoms of the Air', online at: www.icao.int/Pages/freedomsAir.aspx

traffic stop for scheduled air services among its contracting States.[92] The first two 'Freedoms of the Air' are:

> First Freedom of the Air – the right or privilege, in respect of scheduled international air services, granted by one State to another State or States to fly across its territory without landing (also known as a First Freedom Right).
>
> Second Freedom of the Air – the right or privilege, in respect of scheduled international air services, granted by one State to another State or States to land in its territory for non-traffic purposes (also known as a Second Freedom Right).[93]

The Transit Agreement has 130 Parties.[94] In contrast to the International Air Transport Agreement,[95] which has only 11 Parties,[96] it appears that States' preference for the Transit Agreement is likely a reflection of strong commercial interests. The Transit Agreement does not grant commercial rights, only rights of overflight and for technical landings. With that said, some of the largest States in terms of land area, i.e. Russian Federation, China, Canada, Brazil and Indonesia, are not parties to the Transit Agreement. Thus, we can conclude that this does not really evidence 'freedom of the air' in international aviation.

Whilst the Transport Agreement established the fundamental five 'Freedoms of the Air' for scheduled air services, which are of significant importance for States when negotiating bilateral and multilateral air service agreements, it is fair to say that this agreement is otherwise of relatively little importance today.[97]

Instead, in the absence of a universal agreement, and bearing in mind economic benefits associated with civil aviation, in effect a system of tradeable traffic rights for contracting States and their aircraft (operators) was created. Recalling the provisions in Articles 5 and 6 of the Chicago Convention, on non-scheduled and scheduled international air services respectively, it is needful to consider the possibility of gaining 'special

92 The Transit Agreement grants overflight rights for scheduled air services to an 'air transport enterprise' that is substantially owned and effectively controlled by nationals of a contracting State to the IASTA. ICAO, Doc. 9626, 'Part 4 – Air Carrier Ownership' in *Manual on the Regulation of International Air Transport.*

93 ICAO, 'Freedoms of the Air'.

94 ICAO, 'International Air Services Transit Agreement', online at: www.icao.int/secretariat/legal/List%20of%20Parties/Transit_EN.pdf

95 ICAO, Doc. 9587.

96 The International Air Transport Agreement was originally signed by 19 States, eight of which subsequently denounced it. See ICAO, 'International Air Transport Agreement', online at: www.icao.int/secretariat/legal/List%20of%20Parties/Transport_EN.pdf

97 ICAO, 'Freedoms of the Air'.

permission or other authorization' for most services, perhaps offering some reflection of liberalism on one hand and the position on so-called 'cabotage'[98] on the other hand, which continues to be characterized by protectionism.

Article 7 of the Chicago Convention reads:

> Each contracting State shall have the right to refuse permission to the aircraft of other contracting States to take on in its territory passengers, mail and cargo carried for remuneration or hire and destined for another point within its territory. Each contracting State undertakes not to enter into any arrangements which specifically grant any such privilege on an exclusive basis to any other State or an airline of any other State, and not to obtain any such exclusive privilege from any other State.

The two so-called 'Freedoms of the Air' that relate to cabotage are:[99]

> Eighth Freedom of the Air – the right or privilege, in respect of scheduled international air services, of transporting cabotage traffic between two points in the territory of the granting State on a service which originates or terminates in the home country of the foreign carrier or (in connection with the so-called Seventh Freedom of the Air) outside the territory of the granting State (also known as an Eighth Freedom Right or 'consecutive cabotage').
>
> Ninth Freedom of the Air – the right or privilege of transporting cabotage traffic of the granting State on a service performed entirely within the territory of the granting State (also known as a Ninth Freedom Right or 'stand alone' cabotage).[100]

Additional attention to exchange of economic (traffic) rights by way of air services agreements incorporating some, or in the case of a true open skies agreement all, 'Freedoms of the Air' is given below in Chapters 2 and 3.

Other relevant sources of air law

The primary source of international (and domestic) air law clearly is the Chicago Convention. But, tracing the legislative development back to the 1919 Paris Convention, which was 'the historically first multilateral

98 Cabotage taken from the French *caboter*, meaning to sail along the coast. Defined in English as 'trade or transport in coastal waters or airspace or between two points within a country'.

99 The first five 'Freedoms of Air' are recognized in the International Air Transport Agreement. The remaining four are referred to as 'so-called' Freedoms of the Air.

100 ICAO, 'Freedoms of the Air'.

instrument of international law relating to air navigation', it should be remembered that Paris 'helped to formulate also the principles of the domestic law of contracting states, many of whom did not have any law governing aviation'.[101] Found in the Annexes to the Convention are international standards and recommended practices (SARPs). The SARPs are in effect legislation on one hand and guidelines on the other, produced by the International Civil Aviation Organization (ICAO). Article 44 of the Chicago Convention sets out the technical and administrative powers of the ICAO Assembly and Council, including the mandate 'to develop the principles and techniques of international air navigation and to foster the planning and development of international air transport'.

Other sources of air law include multilateral conventions,[102] bilateral air service agreements, general principles of international law, national law, supranational law,[103] judicial decisions of national, supranational and international courts, contracts between states and airlines, contracts between airlines and groups of airlines, and contracts between airlines and firms in sectors complementary to air transport.[104]

Before considering another relevant multilateral convention (on the law of the sea) and the extent to which it pertains also to aspects of aviation, it is interesting firstly to note two established legal maxims: the first is *mare liberum*, which refers to the sea; the second is the land-based *cuius est solum eius est usque ad coelum et ad inferos*, also referred to earlier. Each of these will be discussed in greater detail below.

First let us consider Hugo Grotius's pioneering work, *Mare liberum* (*The Free Sea*), published in 1609.[105] In this great treatise, Grotius makes powerful statements on the right to freedom of trade and navigation, whereby sparking 'wider and more enduring controversy regarding the foundations of international relations, the limits of national sovereignty, and the relationship between sovereignty (*imperium*) and possession (*dominium*) that would guarantee its lasting fame and notoriety'.[106] Thus the concept 'freedom of the sea' gained its momentum in the early seventeenth century.

It goes without saying that maritime trade and transport cannot be practicably compared with transport and trade by air; the latter is a post-modern invention. Maritime law and governance have had significantly more time to mature and to adapt to trade practices. Generally speaking, it can be

101 Milde, *International Air Law and ICAO* 10.

102 Diederiks-Verschoor argues these are primary sources of air law (Diederiks-Verschoor and Kopal, *An Introduction to Space Law*). Take for instance UNCLOS as it relates to aspects of aviation.

103 E.g. European Union law.

104 Diederiks-Verschoor and Kopal, *An Introduction to Space Law* 4.

105 Hugo Grotius, *Mare liberum, 1609–2009* (Robert Feenstra Brill 2009).

106 David Armitage, 'Introduction' in Hugo Grotius (ed.), *The Free Sea* (Richard Hakluyt tr, Indianapolis: Liberty Fund, 2004) 15. Available online at: http://scholar.harvard.edu/files/armitage/files/free_sea_ebook.pdf

said that in maritime law, States have taken an open freedom approach to regulation of navigation, for example. This can be gleaned from the fact that major trading powers of the world have codified international maritime laws since the Second World War, for instance vis-à-vis the 1958 Geneva Conventions on the Law of the Sea, which led to the conclusion of the United Nations Convention on the Law of the Seas 1982 (UNCLOS).[107] The freedom is qualified on the 'high seas' and innocent passage in territorial waters.[108] Thus it prescribes a regime in which sovereignty and sovereign rights are limited, and vary, according to particular zones of the sea. The following are the relevant provisions in UNCLOS useful to our discussion on airspace:

> Article 53
>
> 1. An archipelagic State may designate sea lanes and air routes thereabove, suitable for the continuous and expeditious passage of foreign ships and aircraft through or over its archipelagic waters and the adjacent territorial sea.
> 2. All ships and aircraft enjoy the right of archipelagic sea lanes passage in such sea lanes and air routes.
>
> ...
>
> 4. Such sea lanes and air routes shall traverse the archipelagic waters and the adjacent territorial sea and shall include all normal passage routes used as routes for international navigation or overflight through or over archipelagic waters and, within such routes, so far as ships are concerned, all normal navigational channels, provided that duplication of routes of similar convenience between the same entry and exit points shall not be necessary.
> 5. Such sea lanes and air routes shall be defined by a series of continuous axis lines from the entry points of passage routes to the exit points. Ships and aircraft in archipelagic sea lanes passage shall not deviate more than 25 nautical miles to either side of such axis lines during passage, provided that such ships and aircraft shall not navigate closer to the coasts than 10 per cent of the distance between the nearest points on islands bordering the sea lane.
>
> ...
>
> 12. If an archipelagic State does not designate sea lanes or air routes, the right of archipelagic sea lanes passage may be exercised through the routes normally used for international navigation.
>
> ...

107 UN, 'The United Convention on the Law of the Sea, a historical perspective' (Office of Legal Affairs 2012), available online at: www.un.org/depts/los/convention_agreements/convention_historical_perspective.htm

108 On exercise of sovereignty over the high seas, see also *Pan Am Airways* v. *The Queen* (1981) 2 RCS 565–573.

Article 58

1. In the exclusive economic zone, all States, whether coastal or land-locked, enjoy, subject to the relevant provisions of this Convention, the freedoms referred to in article 87 of navigation and overflight and of the laying of submarine cables and pipelines, and other internationally lawful uses of the sea related to these freedoms, such as those associated with the operation of ships, aircraft and submarine cables and pipelines, and compatible with the other provisions of this Convention.

...

Article 87

1. The high seas are open to all States, whether coastal or land-locked. Freedom of the high seas is exercised under the conditions laid down by this Convention and by other rules of international law. It comprises, inter alia, both for coastal and land-locked States:
   (a) freedom of navigation;
   (b) freedom of overflight;
   (c) freedom to lay submarine cables and pipelines, subject to Part VI;
   (d) freedom to construct artificial islands and other installations permitted under international law, subject to Part VI;
   (e) freedom of fishing, subject to the conditions laid down in section 2;
   (f) freedom of scientific research, subject to Parts VI and XIII.

...

Article 89

No State may validly purport to subject any part of the high seas to its sovereignty.

To sum up, Article 38 of UNCLOS provides 'new' transit rights for aircraft, including overflight of foreign aircraft over certain straits used for international navigation. Article 53 of UNCLOS provides for overflight over archipelagic waters.

Article 58 of UNCLOS provides freedom of overflight over a State's exclusive economic zone (EEZ). Over the high seas, no State has sovereignty. There have been numerous incidents involving treatment by one State of airspace over an EEZ as its territorial airspace, rather than merely exercising sovereign (economic) rights in the EEZ, whereas another State recognizes the same waters as the high seas.[109] This continues to be a

109 Larsen, Sweeney and Gillick, *Aviation Law* 42–44; See also K. Hailbronner, 'Freedom of the Air and the Convention on Law of the Sea' (1983) 77 *Am. J. Int'l L.* 490.

troublesome area in the conflicted South China Sea, for maritime and airspace usage.[110]

It can be concluded that these parts of UNCLOS operate very much in tandem with the Chicago Convention as primary international air law. As any future conflict over territorial seas or EEZs will always involve the respective airspace above the seas, whereby giving rise to questions around 'complete and exclusive' sovereignty, or at a minimum on sovereign rights, UNCLOS will continue to be read together with the Chicago Convention to identify the underlying principles of international law of transport.

Moving from *mare liberum* to the land-based maxim, *cuius est solum eius est usque ad coelum et ad inferos*, we consider the landmark *United States* v. *Causby* case that came before the U.S. Supreme Court in 1946.[111] This case raised questions around individual (property) rights and their immediate reaches insofar as there are connections to land – who owns the airspace above *private* property? The *Hinman* case[112] in 1936 centred on the conflict between private land rights and airspace. In *Hinman*, the U.S. Court of Appeals held:

> We own so much of the space above the ground as we can occupy or make use of, in connection with the enjoyment of our land. This right is not fixed. It varies with our varying needs and is coextensive with them. The owner of land owns as much of the space above him as he uses, but only so long as he uses it. All that lies beyond belongs to the world.
>
> The case differs from the usual case of enjoining a trespass. Ordinarily, if a trespass is committed upon land, the plaintiff is entitled to at least nominal damages without proving or alleging any actual damage. In the instant case, traversing the airspace above the appellant's land is not, of itself, a trespass at all, but it is a lawful act unless it is done under circumstances which will cause injury to appellant's possession.[113]

In the 1986 *Nicaragua* case, the International Court of Justice (ICJ) ruled: 'The principle of respect for territorial sovereignty is also directly infringed

110 Robert Beckham, 'The UN Convention on the Law of the Sea and maritime disputes in the South China Sea' (2013) 107(1) *Am. J. Int'l L.* 142; Ian Storey, 'Japan's maritime security interests in Southeast Asia and the South China Sea dispute' (2013) 65(2) *Political Science* 135; Ronald O'Rourke, 'Maritime territorial and exclusive economic zone (EEZ) disputes involving China: Issues for Congress' (2014) 23(1/2) *Current Politics and Economics of Northern and Western Asia* 1–66.

111 *United States* v. *Causby*, 328 U.S. 256 (1946).

112 *Hinman* v. *Pacific Air Transport; same* v. *United Airlines Transport Corp*, U.S. Court of Appeals (9th Circuit), 20 July 1936, 1 Avi 640; [1936] USAvR, 1; [1936] JAL 624.

113 Ibid.

by the unauthorised overflight of a state's territory by aircraft belonging to or under the control of the government of another state'.[114]

This takes us full circle from the point at which we began at the 1910 Paris Conference, and the following statement, which began this line of reasoning, namely: 'Les aéronefs militaires porteront comme seule marque nationale le signe de souveraineté de leur Etat. Chaque Etat contractant notifiera aux autres Etats contractants les signes de souveraineté dont il fera usage'.[115]

Airspace and outer space

The existence of a myriad of bilateral and multilateral agreements between States seems sufficiently to qualify the *usque ad coelum* part of the land-based maxim – but so too does the upper limit of sovereignty. In the wake of the USSR's launch of the world's first atmospheric satellite, *Sputnik I*, in 1957, and subsequent events,[116] there was a call for the development of a 'new' law on 'outer space'.[117] Prior to this event, given that for technological reasons high-altitude flight was limited, State sovereignty was 'understood to extend for an unlimited distance into the airspace (*usque ad coelum*),[118] although this has been modified by the new law on outer space'.[119] Before 1957, discussions were mainly academic; they questioned if airspace was 'limitless' or if an upper limit existed at a fixed level, or was to be determined by usable airspace or by maximum exercise of control.

According to Cooper, 'With this background, various definitions of the term airspace have been suggested seeking to fix the upper limit of the right of a State to admit or refuse the entry of flight instrumentalities in space above its lands and waters'.[120] In addition, Shaw suggests,

> It soon became apparent that the *usque ad coelum* rule, providing for state sovereignty over territorial airspace to an unrestricted extent, was

114 ICJ Reports (1986) 14, 128; 76 ILR, 1.

115 'Military aircraft are the only "national mark" of the sovereignty of a State, and markings representing that sovereign State should be notified to other States'. Conférence internationale de navigation aérienne.

116 See also O. J. Lissitzyn, 'Some Legal Implications of the U-2 and RB-47 Incidents' (1962) 56 *Am. J. Int'l L.* 135.

117 See for instance C. Q. Christol, *The Modern International Law of Outer Space* (Pergamon Press 1982); Nicolas M. Matte, *Aerospace Law* (Sweet & Maxwell 1969); B. Cheng, *Studies in International Space Law* (Oxford University Press 1997); B. Cheng, 'The Legal Status of Outer Space' [1983] *Journal of Space Law* 89; K. H. Böckstiegel and M. Berkö, *Space Law: Basic Legal Documents* (Martinus Nijhoff 1991); C. Q. Christol, *Space Law* (Eleven publishing 2005); Diederiks-Verschoor and Kopal, *An Introduction to Space Law*; Wybo P. Heere, 'Problems of Jurisdiction in Air and Outer Space' (1999) 24 *Air & Space Law* 70.

118 Based on common law principles; See W. Blackstone, *Commentaries on the Laws of England* (Oxford University Press 1765–1769) vol. 2, Ch. 2, 18 (note in original).

119 Malcolm N. Shaw, *International Law* (5th edn, Cambridge University Press 2003) 464.

120 Cooper, 'Sovereignty in Space' 32, 58.

> not viable where space exploration was concerned. To obtain the individual consents of countries to the passage of satellites and other vehicles orbiting more than 100 miles above their surface would prove cumbersome in the extreme and in practice states have acquiesced in such traversing. This means that the sovereignty of states over their airspace is limited in height at most to the point where the airspace meets space itself.[121]

Turning our attention back to the Chicago Convention, it clearly treats 'only' airspace, not outer space. As Larsen *et al.* point out, 'Airspace involves territorial sovereignty, whereas there is no sovereignty in outer space. In the 1967 Treaty on Outer Space, the boundary between sovereign airspace and non-sovereign outer space is treated ambiguously'.[122]

It is now settled public international law that airspace sovereignty ends where non-sovereign outer space begins. Unfortunately, more discussion on the fascinating area of the law of outer space is beyond the scope of the current project.

The aim of this chapter was to provide a brief historical review on the development of the 'airspace' concept, and how it is regulated. Airspace is clearly defined. We understand from the Chicago Convention that it is also linked to the territory of the State. And States have complete and exclusive sovereignty over their airspace. Thus, airspace is regulated vis-à-vis the territorial sovereignty-based Chicago System.

Whilst we understand from this that airspace and its territorial link will be difficult to separate, in Chapter 2, this book will explore the ways in which it is suggested that State sovereignty and territory could be unbundled.

121 Shaw, *International Law* 480.

122 Larsen, Sweeney and Gillick, *Aviation Law*; see also Francis Lyall and Paul B. Larsen, *Space Law: A Treatise* (Ashgate Publishing Group 2009), Ch. 6.

2 Sovereignty, jurisdiction and territory

> The time of absolute sovereignty and exclusive sovereignty, however, has passed; its theory was never matched by reality.
>
> Former UN Secretary General Boutros Boutros-Ghali (1992)[1]

Introduction

In this book, international aviation is presented as a case study on the wider debate on international law, transnational law and global governance, as viewed through the lens of the emerging economic and environmental concerns of the global neighbourhood. This project first located international law on civil aviation within its historical and ideological contexts in the previous chapter. Now, we turn to examine the core concepts of sovereignty and jurisdiction, and related scholarship that suggests they are changing.

This chapter explores what we shall term 'the tri-dimensional web' of State territory – 'the territorial sphere of validity of the national legal order, [which] is not a plane, but a space of three dimensions'[2] – and its relationship with the territorial sovereignty-based Chicago System and more broadly-defined international law and governance. The aim is to consider the concepts of sovereignty, territory and jurisdiction in the context of international civil aviation, and the ways in which they are shifting.[3] We begin this journey by exploring how the traditional interpretations of these legal doctrines are under pressure in an increasingly globalized world, owing in

1 *An Agenda for Peace*, Report of the Secretary General, para 17, United Nations, NY, June 1992; UNDPI publication 1247.

2 Hans Kelsen, *General Theory of Law and State* (Anders Wedberg tr., Harvard University Press 1949), as cited in Cooper, 'Sovereignty in Space' 58.

3 The author attributes his inspiration for the phrase 'tri-dimensional web' to: (1) Kelsen, *General Theory of Law and State*; and (2) Gbenga Oduntan for his conceptualization of territory and its 'apportionment in a tridimensional manner' in the context of sovereignty and jurisdiction in airspace and outer space. See Gbenga Oduntan, *Sovereignty and Jurisdiction in the Airspace and Outer Space: Legal Criteria for Spatial Delimitation* (Routledge 2012).

particular to the borderless nature of transnational challenges facing contemporary society. To do this, we must first recognize the notion that the 'carved up' world of Westphalian sovereignty has been outmoded, and its pillars of State exclusiveness are thinning.

To say that the legal doctrines of sovereignty and jurisdiction are complex would be an understatement; each is subject to countless interpretations and analyses. It is not the objective of this project to dispute the critical discourse that interprets and analyses the doctrines. Instead, bearing in mind that '[p]ostmodern critical theory has spent a lot of time in the quicksand of sovereignty and, more recently, jurisdiction',[4] this project provides a narrative on sovereignty and jurisdiction – and territory – to the extent that the two doctrines impact on and implicate selected regulation of 'airspace' vis-à-vis the Chicago System in the light of the contemporary changes and challenges. Throughout, we are mindful of the changing 'role of State sovereignty against the complexities of current developments in international society and in international law'.[5] International civil aviation provides an ideal case study on sovereignty and jurisdiction; this study offers a contribution to the existing scholarship.

This chapter will consider, and attempt to synthesize a selection of theories that all suggest State sovereignty is in flux. Scholars maintain that this transpires in different ways and to varying degrees: it has been or will eventually be transformed, fragmented or eroded. Thus, we locate the common call to unbundle sovereignty's link with territory – something almost imaginable in the realm of State sovereignty over airspace as we understand from Chapter 1 – and additionally to separate sovereignty and jurisdiction, the political and legal. Extraterritoriality and territorial extension are common features in many areas of the international commercial world – civil aviation is no exception. This exposes the territorial bias of the law of jurisdiction and, at the same time, reveals that the foundations of jurisdiction are indeed shifting. As dialogue between jurisdictions matures in character and increases in mode, jurisdiction emerges as a possible, new dual form of governance that delivers substantive justice for the international community, yet is also a space for political power struggles.

The first section of this chapter will introduce the doctrines of sovereignty and jurisdiction from a generalist perspective before turning to consider the influence of 'Westphalian sovereignty' on the territorial foundations of the Chicago System. A look at the transfer of national authority (competence) to the international level in specific areas of civil aviation regulation reveals that there may be impetus for transfer, or surrender, of State sovereignty, pooled

4 Asha Kaushal, 'The Politics of Jurisdiction' (2015) 78(5) *The Modern Law Review* 780.

5 Marcel Brus, 'Bridging the Gap between State Sovereignty and International Governance: The Authority of Law' in Gerard Kreijen (ed.), *State, Sovereignty, and International Governance* (Oxford University Press 2002) 7.

or shared sovereignty, and non-territorial sovereignty – as technical and economic sovereignty – in a supranational or even post-sovereignty era.

In the context of civil aviation, one has in recent years increasingly borne witness to seemingly legitimate sovereignty being extended through the exercise of jurisdiction, territorial extensions[6] and subsidiarity in the law of jurisdiction. In the second part of this chapter, this book will explore the relevant jurisdiction scholarship: jurisdiction as territory, as community and as governance.[7]

In areas of civil aviation, absent of international or multinational regulation and supervision, doubts loom for global justice. Thus this author also considers *alternatives* to territorial jurisdiction (non-territorial jurisdiction) and to the jurisdictional rules of reason (subsidiarity in the law of jurisdiction). Subsidiarity in the law of jurisdiction may prove a useful tool against States, non-state actors and private actors whose actions or omissions harm the global interest. The basic premise in the law of subsidiarity is that one State acts, or appears to act, as a 'trustee of mankind',[8] or as regards global public goods through the exercise of unilateral jurisdiction.

In conclusion, this chapter will offer two possible theoretical platforms – the transnational law approach to international law, and international law as global governance – which advocate for a move away from traditional, seemingly restrictive forms of sovereignty in the light of transnational and therefore global neighbourhood problems that will be reviewed in Chapter 3 as a framework for theorizing the emerging complex global governance regime for international aviation in Chapter 4.

Sovereignty and jurisdiction in international law

To begin, it is needful to say a few words on sovereignty.

First and foremost, we acknowledge that sovereignty is not a static concept. Indeed, the meaning of sovereignty changes continuously; it has even been called a 'sponge concept'.[9] There are also competing conceptions of sovereignty.[10] The 'doctrines of sovereignty down the ages have differed

6 Joanne Scott and Lavanya Rajamani, 'Contingent Unilateralism: International Aviation in the European Emissions Trading Scheme' in Bart Van Vooren, Steven Blockmans and Jan Wouters (eds), *The EU's Role in Global Governance: The Legal Dimension* (Oxford University Press 2013) 209–223.

7 In some cases, jurisdiction may be viewed as an extension of (legitimate) sovereignty. It is accepted that arguments for nation-state territoriality, communities and legitimacy are supported by some, but for others they are unconvincing.

8 Cédric Ryngaert, 'The Concept of Jurisdiction in International Law' in Alexandre Orakhelashvili (ed.), *Research Handbook on Jurisdiction and Immunities in International Law* (Edward Elgar Publishing 2015) 67; also available online at: https://unijuris.sites.uu.nl/wp-content/uploads/sites/9/2014/12/The-Concept-of-Jurisdiction-in-International-Law.pdf

9 Jens Bartleson, *The Geneology of Sovereignty* (Cambridge University Press 1995) 237.

10 Walker, *Intimations of Global Law*.

from time to time for the very reason that they reflected the needs and problems of their own particular times and were designed to do so'.[11] At the same time, there is no clear definition of the *notion* of sovereignty. In the words of Hinsley, sovereignty is 'the *idea* that there is a final and absolute political authority in the political community ... and no final and absolute authority exists elsewhere'.[12] And, as Crawford succinctly puts it, '[s]overeignty comes in all shapes and sizes'[13] – take for example the many archipelagic and island states with little *terra firma* but rather great expanses of territorial waters. According to Caporaso:

> Sovereignty has to do with relations among authority structures. The sovereign authority – the state – is the final authority, the authority that claims the ultimate right to decide. As Hinsley[14] points out, sovereignty did not evolve in perfect synchrony with the state. It lagged the emergence of the Westphalian state by several centuries. Sovereignty, as a claim about ultimate rule within a territory, came after the state itself, even if we today confusingly define the state as sovereign ... The view of sovereignty as final and exclusive rule cuts through the subtle and more differentiated discussion of the concept by Krasner and others.[15]

Under the Westphalian order of sovereign States, named after the Peace of Westphalia (1658),[16] there are three key understandings:

(1) The ruler has sole authority over his territory;
(2) States are judicially equal; and
(3) States are subject only to laws to which they consent.[17]

11 Robert Jennings, 'Sovereignty and International Law' in Gerard Kreijen (ed.), *State, Sovereignty, and International Governance* (Oxford University Press 2002) 29.

12 F. H. Hinsley, *Sovereignty* (C. A. Watts & Co. 1966) 26 (emphasis added); Derek Croxton, 'The Peace of Westphalia of 1648 and the Origins of Sovereignty' (1999) 21(3) *The International History Review* 569, 570.

13 James Crawford, *The Creation of Studies in International Law* (2nd edn, Oxford Univer - sity Press 2007) 47.

14 F. H. Hinsley, *Sovereignty* (2nd edn, Cambridge University Press 1986) 21 (note in original).

15 James A. Caporaso, 'Changes in the Westphalian Order: Territory, Public Authority, and Sovereignty' (2000) 2(2) *International Studies Review* 10; Stephen D. Krasner, *Sovereignty: Organized Hypocrisy* (Princeton University Press 1999); Janice E. Thomson, 'State Sovereignty in International Relations: Bridging the Gap between Theory and Empirical Research' (1995) 39(2) *International Studies Quarterly* 213–233.

16 The Peace of Westphalia refers to the treaties of Münster and Osnabrück signed in 1648 to end the Thirty Years War. Westphalia is commonly referred to as marking the shift from canon law to secular law under a new, mutual recognition between sovereign States.

17 Daniel Philpott, *Revolutions in Sovereignty: How Ideas Shaped Modern International Relations* (Princeton Studies in International History and Politics, Princeton University Press 2008); Croxton 'The Peace of Westphalia' 569–591.

The State is 'depicted as a realm to which one belongs or from which one is banned, whose interests one serves or one injures, and whose sovereignty should be respected but is persistently at risk'.[18] What we attribute to the Westphalian order therefore is an 'emphasis on *territory* [which] may be evidence for a changing conception of the state from rule over people to rule over *territory*, but [also noting that this] is hardly a definitive indication of sovereign statehood'.[19]

Internal or domestic sovereignty must first be distinguished from external sovereignty, yet this is not a simple task. Jackson proposes that sovereignty has both positive and negative attributes; positive sovereignty stems from a freedom *to* act – a positive liberty, whereas negative sovereignty is a negative liberty – freedom *from* interference, reflecting the 'right' to self-determination.[20] Whilst Grotius, in a very different era, 'liked to identify sovereignty with freedom',[21] we can say that this 'freedom' is actually seriously limited for sovereign States of today and their governments. According to Sir Robert Jennings, governments

> nowadays have very seriously limited choices in the exercise of their supposedly sovereign competence, because their theoretically important areas for decisions are much restricted and hemmed in by treaties, by customary international law, and by the consequences, and especially the economic consequences, of the sheer interdependence of all sovereign States of today.[22]

It can be said that many States do not have 'strong governments that are able in fact to exercise sovereign powers';[23] thus, there is change to come for some parts of the world. Jennings argues that sovereignty is largely a myth for sovereign governments, at least on the international plane. The exception of course is when sovereignty 'is used as a word to describe a State's title to territory ... The State remains a sovereign State in international law and continues to be able to guide its future destiny within the limits that it has itself accepted'.[24] The most relevant aspect of sovereignty for the current study on the international system is precisely this external aspect.

18 Kaushal, 'The Politics of Jurisdiction' 770 citing Note, 'Constructing the State Extraterritorially: Jurisdictions Discourse, The National Interest, and Transnational Norms' (1990) 103 *Harvard Law Review* 1273.
19 Croxton, 'The Peace of Westphalia of 1648' 569–591 (emphasis added).
20 Robert H. Jackson, *Quasi-States: Sovereignty, International Relations and the Third World* (Cambridge University Press 1990).
21 Jennings, 'Sovereignty and International Law' 29.
22 Ibid., 31.
23 Ibid., 29.
24 Ibid., 32 citing Elihu Lauterpacht, 'Sovereignty: Myth or Reality' (1997) 73 *Int'l Aff.* 137.

Taking the orthodox view, territorial sovereignty is defined as supreme and exclusive authority within a State's territory, thereby defining the 'territorial State'. Coxton flags up the challenge presented by positive and negative notions of sovereignty and the link to territory. He says:

> A key problem with studying the origins of sovereignty is that any ruler is likely to claim the sole authority to make decisions in his *territory*, while unwilling to concede the same authority to his neighbours within theirs. The difficulty is not finding a ruler who considers himself to be sovereign, but a group of rulers who recognize each other's sovereignty.[25]

Relating this view to State sovereignty as the foundation of international law and the international legal order, Goldsmith and Posner make the case against the efficacy of international law, alongside the work of international relations (realists) such as Slaughter Burley on the 'disaggregated state',[26] and Berman who argues that 'international law is sometimes important, but only as a mechanism by which nation-states negotiate power, not as an independent limitation on the prerogatives of state governments'.[27] Berman continues that 'in this so-called realist vision each state single-mindedly pursues its rational state interest and therefore obeys alternative legal norms only to the extent that such norms serve those pre-existing interests ... international law is sometimes important, but only as a mechanism by which nation-states negotiate power'.[28]

Postmodern critical theory suggests that international relations have moved to a new evolutionary stage that is 'beyond Westphalia'. To that end, Ryngaert puts forward that the 'carving up of the world, as notably sanctioned by the Peace of Westphalia (1658), is historically contingent and politically constructed, and may therefore be subject to change in light of contemporary understandings of international law and society'.[29]

With that said, 'sovereignty has been central to our understanding of the states system and is the fundamental principle enunciated in the charter of

25 Croxton, 'The Peace of Westphalia of 1648' 571 (emphasis added); See also Hinsley, *Sovereignty* (2nd edn) 275–277; Eberhard Straub, *Pax et Imperium: Spaniens Kampf um seine Friedensordnung in Europa zwischen 1617 und 1635* (Schoningh 1980) 20–24.

26 Jack L. Goldsmith and Eric A. Posner, *The Limits of International Law* (Oxford University Press 2005); Anne-Marie Slaughter Burley, 'International Law and International Relations Theory: A Dual Agenda' (1993) 87 *American Journal of International Law* 205; Gralf-Peter Calliess and Peer Zumbansen, *Rough Consensus and Running Code: A Theory of Transnational Private Law* (Hart Publishing 2010).

27 Paul Schiff Berman, *Global Legal Pluralism: A Jurisprudence of Law beyond Borders* (Cambridge University Press 2012) 98.

28 Ibid.

29 Cedric Ryngaert, 'Subsidiarity and the Law of Jurisdiction' (2014) 2, online at: http://unijuris.sites.uu.nl/wp-content/uploads/sites/9/2014/12/Jurisdiction.pdf

the United Nations'.[30] So, it is unimaginable what would happen to the State system if sovereignty were no longer its organizing principle.[31] Yet 'the subject, scope and very sources of the Westphalian conception of international regulation, particularly its conception of international law' are contested today.[32] In fact, it is argued that the boundary between domestic or municipal law and international law is more fluid because international law 'applies directly to individual and to other legal persons within a State, so more and more international law depends very largely on incorporation into the local domestic law and application and enforcement by local, domestic courts'.[33] Thus, the territorial sovereignty of the State, according to Jennings, is 'now more rather than less an essential part of the structure of modern international law'.[34] He goes on to identify the challenging task of reconciling this position 'with the need for a considerable modification of that sovereignty if we are to develop and improve the ways in which the international community is able to perform governmental functions internationally'.[35]

Of course internal sovereignty was 'reduced' almost immediately. If a dictator should begin to slaughter his own citizens on sovereign territory, an international response is certain to follow, challenging such heinous 'internal' acts as a matter of 'external' (international) concern. Also, sovereignty has undergone significant changes since the Second World War. According to Schermers,

> Under international law we are most confronted with the idea that sovereignty of a State means that the State has unlimited power and is subjected to only those rules of international law which it has expressly accepted ... This aspect of sovereignty has seriously weakened during the second half of the twentieth century.[36]

War crimes of the Second World War give credence to this observation. Take for instance the Nuremburg trials in 1945. The International Tribunal at Nuremberg 'laid down, for the first time in history, that when *international rules* that protect basic humanitarian values are in conflict with *state laws*,

30 This is also found in Article 3(1) of the UN Charter, which reads 'the Organization is based on the principle of the sovereign equality of all its Members'. See Croxton, 'The Peace of Westphalia of 1648' 569–591.

31 See Croxton, 'The Peace of Westphalia of 1648'.

32 Ibid. See for instance Hedley Bull, *The Anarchical Society* (Macmillan 1977) 122–155.

33 Jennings, 'Sovereignty and International Law' 41.

34 Ibid.

35 Ibid.

36 Henry Schermers, 'Different Aspects of Sovereignty' in Gerard Kreijen (ed.), *State, Sovereignty, and International Governance* (Oxford University Press 2002) 185.

every individual must transgress the state laws (except where there is no room for "moral choice")'.[37]

Schermers goes on to explain:

> A second aspect of sovereignty concerns international solidarity. The more each State is full master of its own territory the less other States will feel responsible for what happens in these other sovereign States. When a government is fully sovereign over the internal matters of its State, it is also fully responsible for whatever happens in that State. Other States bear no responsibility. Also this side of sovereignty is weakening.[38]

This is evidenced by the emergence of international human rights law and international humanitarian law after the Second World War, beginning with the Universal Declaration on Human Rights 1948. Also, it is said that 'few states have ever exercised complete or absolute sovereignty within their own territorial boundaries, as the practice of diplomatic immunity highlights'.[39] In sum, 'the practice, as opposed to the doctrine, of sovereign statehood has always readily adapted to changing historical realities'.[40]

Van Staden and Vollaard consider, additionally, that other forces and developments have 'eroded and continue to erode pillars of the Westphalian system of sovereign States [and] alternative systems of political authority that may supersede territorial systems of rule'.[41] Jayasuriya tells us: 'The critical point is to note that the very notion of sovereignty is to be unbundled from its link with territory, models of sovereignty are embedded in specific social and economic structures and as these structures change, so does the form of sovereignty'.[42] This will be discussed below in greater detail.

The term jurisdiction stems from the Latin '*juris-dicere*', or to declare the law; '*juris-dare*' is to make it. In the words of Beale, jurisdiction is 'the power of a sovereign to affect the rights of persons, whether by legislation, by executive decree, or by the judgment of a court'.[43] The law of jurisdiction,

37 Held *et al.*, *Global Transformations* 72 referring to Antonio Cassese, *Violence and Law in the Modern Age* (Polity Press 1988) 132.

38 Schermers, 'Different Aspects of Sovereignty' 185.

39 Held *et al.*, *Global Transformations* 9 referring to Saskia Sassen, *Losing Control? Sovereignty in an Age of Globalization* (Columbia University Press 1996).

40 Held *et al.*, *Global Transformations* 9 referring to Sean D. Murphy, *Humanitarian Intervention: The United Nations in an Evolving World Order* (University of Pennsylvania Press 1996).

41 Alfred Van Staden and Hans Vollaard, 'The Erosion of State Sovereignty: Towards a Post-Territorial World?' in Gerard Kreijin (ed.), *State, Sovereignty, and International Governance* (Oxford University Press 2002) 166.

42 Kanishka Jayasuriya, 'Globalization, Law and the Transformation of Sovereignty: The Emergence of Global Regulatory Governance' (1999) 6(2) *Indiana Journal of Global Legal Studies* 431–432.

43 J. H. Beale, 'The Jurisdiction of a Sovereign State' (1923) 36 *Harv. L. Rev.* 241.

then, 'is doubtless one of the most essential as well as controversial fields of international law, in that it determines how far, *ratione loci*, a State's laws might reach'.[44] 'Jurisdiction sets the original terms for the existence of law, and then for its entry and exit'.[45] Importantly, there also exist jurisdiction-specific rules of procedure and evidence, and interpretations of key concepts found in international treaties; for example, how should the word 'accident' be interpreted in international conventions limiting airline liability.[46]

In civil aviation, aircraft, passengers and cargo rarely tend mostly to move between two or more territories of sovereign States. Thus, in international civil aviation, on a single journey one is most likely to find oneself in two or more different jurisdictions, and therefore subject personally (or *in rem*) to different laws. Thus, one major challenge for the law of jurisdiction in practice is that, in the international system, jurisdiction over a single event may be claimed concurrently by more than one State.[47] Where a non-state actor is involved, as Shaffer summarizes:

> Private international law concurrently provides rules and standards to govern situations in which more than one state asserts jurisdiction over a transaction or event involving nonstate actors. Thus, the concepts of public and private *international law* are both state-centric, addressing the relations between nation-states and between national legal systems, as reflected in the term 'international'.[48]

But nation-states are, according to Anderson, just 'imagined communities'.[49] If this is true then, 'nation-state bonds are neither natural nor inevitable; they are merely one particular way of imagining community among many'.[50] Why are nation-state communities privileged over others? Berman reminds us that:

> Although nation-states have become the dominant form of organizing space in the contemporary world, there are other ways of imagining community and constructing identity ... Thus, we need to look at nation-state sovereignty against the backdrop of alternative transnational, international,

44 Ryngaert, *Jurisdiction in International Law* (Oxford University Press 2008) 6.
45 Kaushal, 'The Politics of Jurisdiction' 759–792.
46 Brian F. Havel and Gabriel S. Sanchez, *The Principles and Practice of International Aviation Law* (Cambridge University Press 2014) 14.
47 Ryngaert, *Jurisdiction in International Law* 135.
48 Gregory Shaffer, 'Transnational Legal Ordering and State Change' in Gregory Shaffer (ed.), *Transnational Legal Ordering and State Change* (Cambridge University Press 2010) 3.
49 Benedict Anderson, *Imagined Communities: Reflections on the Origins and Spread of Nationalism* (rev edn, Verso 2006) 6, see also 74–90 on 'the nation-state as an imagined community'.
50 Berman, *Global Legal Pluralism* 62.

> or subnational identities, as well as possible ways of imagining community that are not based on physical territory at all.[51]

The so-called 'rule of reason'[52] in the law of jurisdiction provides the way forward, though it is questionable whether this is international law *per se* or simply a principle of non-binding international comity. In either case, the rule evidences one way in which 'the international community has resorted to post-realist, second-level principles of jurisdiction, such as "reasonableness", or "subsidiarity", to limit jurisdictional overlap'.[53] This is particularly true insofar as '[d]ifferent States may point to territorial conduct or effects of one and the same situation, and on that basis exercise jurisdiction over that situation … [and therefore] arbitrating principles may be called for'.[54] This leads to the extraterritorial effect of one State's laws. Ryngaert sums up the problem:

> A State's actions – jurisdictionally speaking the extension of the geographical reach of a State's law – are normally a function of the substantive interest to be protected by the law. In the dominant neo-realist view, when foreign-based activities are seen to threaten the interests of the State and its subjects, or to undermine the integrity of domestic regulation, States may have an incentive to geographically extend the writ of their laws to address the foreign source of this threat.
>
> [The] level of foreign protest … will depend … international consensus regarding the object and goal of regulation, the existence of safety-valves allowing equivalent foreign regulation to be taken into account, and obviously the political and economic costs of acceptance or protest. [And that] foreign protest is indeed the test for the legality of a State's jurisdictional claim.[55]

The landmark U.S. case, *Heller* v. *United States*,[56] provides an opportunity to examine the judicial separation between sovereignty and jurisdiction. 'If there is a distinction between sovereignty – the legal personhood of a nation – and jurisdiction – the rights and powers of a nation over its inhabitants –

51 Berman, *Global Legal Pluralism* 90 referring to Akhil Gupta and James Ferguson, 'Culture, Power, Place: Ethnography at the End of an Era' in Akhil Gupta and James Ferguson (eds), *Culture, Power, Place: Explorations in Critical Anthropology* (Duke University Press 1997) 17.

52 Restatement of Foreign Relations Law (3d) of the United States, para 401.

53 Ryngaert, 'Jurisdiction', 5–6.

54 Ryngaert, *Jurisdiction in International Law* 43.

55 'Jurisdiction', 4–5.

56 *Heller* v. *United States* [1985] 776 F2d 92 (3rd Cir).

then jurisdiction embodies the nation-state's power to exclude'.[57] However, according to Kaushal,

> Sovereignty and jurisdiction, the political and the legal, are tightly intertwined. On the one hand, sovereignty is the precondition for jurisdiction.[58] Jurisdiction is borne of sovereignty and continually dependent upon it, which means that every extension of jurisdiction is, to some extent, also an extension of sovereignty. Every jurisdictional act implicates the state, its reach, its content, and its rules ... On the other hand, in an era of juridification in which even the defining sovereign acts of declaring war and using force are legal acts, jurisdiction is sometimes the ultimate manifestation of sovereignty.[59]

Kaushal's work focuses on the 'overlooked political aspects of jurisdiction both from within (jurisdiction studies) and from without (sovereignty studies)'.[60] There are three main streams of jurisdiction in contemporary scholarship, which is also its 'multivocality'; 'it looks different in different places and has different meanings in different circumstances': (1) jurisdiction as territory, (2) jurisdiction as community, (3) jurisdiction as governance.[61]

The prevailing view is that the law of jurisdiction has a 'territorial bias'.[62] 'Jurisdiction is not only or always territorial, but territorial jurisdiction is the most familiar and predominant form of jurisdiction'.[63] It is therefore appropriate that we consider the long-standing link between territory and jurisdiction. It was interpreter Bartolus of Sassaferrato who linked *territorium* with jurisdiction. As Elden explains, Bartolus 'is taking the notion of land, or land belonging to an entity, as the thing to which jurisdiction applies, thus providing the extent of rule. The *territorium* then is not simply a property of the ruler; nor is jurisdiction simply a quality of the *territorium*. Rather, the *territorium* is the object of rule itself'.[64] Kaushal observes that

57 Kaushal, 'The Politics of Jurisdiction' 770.

58 Ibid., 790 referring to Costas Douzinas, 'The Metaphysics of Jurisdiction' in McVeigh (ed.), *Jurisprudence of Jurisdiction* (Routledge 2007).

59 Kaushal, 'The Politics of Jurisdiction' 790.

60 Ibid., 791.

61 Ibid., 762; 'Jurisdiction can be a territorial space (this side of the border is Michigan; that side is Ontario), a status (Canadian nationality; EU citizenship), a technical legal doctrine (the 'real and substantial connection' test), a political concept of legitimate authority (John Locke's jurisdiction based on tacit consent), an expression of the reach of sovereign law (international law rules on extraterritoriality), and a preliminary inquiry into law's attachment (a court's capacity to hear the case)', ibid., 762.

62 Ryngaert, 'Jurisdiction', 6; this idea can be linked to the concept of territorial sovereignty discussed elsewhere in this chapter.

63 Kaushal, 'The Politics of Jurisdiction' 765.

64 Ibid., 766 citing S. Elden, 'Territory: Part I' in J. A. Agnew and J. S. Duncan (eds), *The Wiley-Blackwell Companion to Human Geography* (Wiley-Blackwell online 2011) 265.

this 'marked the shift from the *personality* of law to the *territoriality* of law'.[65] 'Rule has become increasingly depersonalized. It has become rationalized, normalized, more a matter of routine and role than personal traits'.[66]

So, there are 'territorial jurisdictions', which with the 'emergence of maps changed the organising modality of the state so that "legal authority could follow territory"'.[67] Ryngaert tells us: 'It is crucial to understand that territoriality only became dominant in the 16th century, when cartographic detail allowed modern rulers to establish efficient bureaucracies ... Notably the view of Baldus de Ubaldis (1327–1400) that territory and jurisdiction go together "as mist to a swamp."'[68]

A problem with this process, however, as identified by Cormack and later applied by Kaushal, is that 'legal authority is not always modelled on or secondary to territorial authority'.[69] Yet, according to Ryngaert, 'Participants in international affairs, as well as international lawyers ... have perceived the law of jurisdiction to operate on the basis of the binary code territorial/extraterritorial with territorial jurisdiction being seen as valid, and extraterritorial as suspect, if not outright unlawful'.[70]

First, taking jurisdiction as territory, and the so-called 'territoriality principle'[71] as the most basic international law principle of jurisdiction, Kaushal notes that jurisdiction 'is theoretically infinite, but when it is linked to territory, it becomes finite [however] territorial jurisdictions are not simply contiguous silos. They develop and conflict'.[72] Thus, 'jurisdiction obtains acts that have been committed within the territory'.[73] However, as Ryngaert admits, the territoriality principle 'may sometimes create more problems than it solves. Whilst serving as the basic principle of jurisdictional order, it is open to diverging interpretations, and it could justify assertions that might be

65 Kaushal, 'The Politics of Jurisdiction' 766 (emphasis added).

66 Caporaso, 'Changes in the Westphalian Order' 22.

67 Kaushal, 'The Politics of Jurisdiction' 760–767 citing R. Thompson Ford, 'Law's Territory (A History of Jurisdiction)' (1999) 98 *Michigan Law Review* 843. Ford argues that there are administrative, synthetic jurisdictions and natural, organic jurisdictions; Kaushal identifies that Ford misses the political community (Kaushal, 'The Politics of Jurisdiction' 768).

68 Ryngaert, 'Jurisdiction' 2 citing Baldus, 'on Codex' in *Iuriusconsulti Omnium* (1577) vol. 7, *fol* 70v; Stuart Elden, *The Birth of Territory* (University of Chicago Press 2013) 231.

69 Kaushal, 'The Politics of Jurisdiction' 768 citing B. Cormack, *A Power to Do Justice: Jurisdiction, English Literature, and the Rise of the Common Law, 1509–1625* (University of Chicago Press 2007).

70 Ryngaert, 'Jurisdiction' in Orakhelashvili 2.

71 See Ryngaert, *Jurisdiction in International Law* Ch. 3 'the Territoriality Principle', for a comprehensive explanation of the development of the territoriality principle.

72 Kaushal, 'The Politics of Jurisdiction' 769.

73 Ryngaert, *Jurisdiction in International Law* 42.

based on very tenuous territorial links'.[74] Such connecting factors 'may have to give way to substantive justice approaches, which employ (State) jurisdiction as an instrument to bring about a more just world', of which international criminal law conventions are prime examples.[75] By the same token, 'regulatory law has followed suit by seemingly tying the legitimacy of a jurisdictional assertion to substantive projects of the international community, such as combating climate change, while paying lip-service to a weak territorial nexus'.[76] In this regard, Ryngaert also observes that 'jurisdiction is often exercised via trade or market-based mechanisms [and] [s]ince these measures impose a condition to obtain territorial access, they are nominally premised on the territorial principle, although one cannot gainsay that they aspire to protect public goods rather than territorial interests alone'.[77]

With that said, application of the territoriality principle in practice is not always obvious. In Kaushal's view, 'Territory and jurisdiction are conjoined in the body of the sovereign state. The modern order of sovereign statehood has added substance to territorial jurisdiction. Territory is the physical space upon which sovereignty is exercised; it is so closely allied to sovereignty and political power is conceived as inherently territorial'.[78]

Territory is 'not just the limit of the jurisdiction but its very definition'.[79] But what is territory then in the context of civil aviation? On airspace and outer space, Kelsen wrote in 1949:

> The territory of a State is usually considered as a definite portion of the earth's surface. This idea is incorrect. The territory of the State, as the territorial sphere of validity of the national legal order, is not a plane, but a space of three dimensions. The validity as well as the efficacy of the national legal order extends not only in width and length but also in depth and height ... Many writers assume that the entire space above and below the State territory (as part of the surface of the earth) belongs to the territorial state without regard to the extent of its effective control. This view, however, is not compatible with the general principle of effectiveness.[80]

74 Ibid., 43; Ryngaert argues that the U.S. assertion of jurisdiction in cases involving transnational securities fraud stray from the original criminal law 'constitutive elements test' (ibid., 42).

75 Ryngaert, 'Jurisdiction' 7, providing the example of criminal law conventions.

76 As was the judgment of CJEU in *The Queen on the Application of: International Air Transport Association, European Low Fares Airline Association v. Department for Transport* (C-344/04) [2006] ECR I-403.

77 Ryngaert, 'Jurisdiction' 7.

78 Kaushal, 'The Politics of Jurisdiction' 766.

79 Ryngaert, 'Jurisdiction' 3 citing Elden, *The Birth of Territory* 232.

80 Kelsen, *General Theory of Law and State* as cited in Cooper, 'Sovereignty in Space' 58.

According to Oduntan, a State may exercise quasi-territorial jurisdiction and personal jurisdiction over aircraft that have been granted legal personality, and over passengers, in foreign airspace; however, there remain significant challenges here, specifically as regards the control of aircraft, criminal acts and trespass.[81] But, as we have learnt, territorial jurisdiction may not benefit us in matters of global concern such as navigation, safety and security. It also causes us problems in the economic arena, such as in price-fixing cartels. Here, '[t]he rhetoric of territoriality and extraterritoriality dominates the discourse about conflicts of legislative jurisdiction'.[82]

Another hurdle of territorial jurisdiction, as mentioned above, is that the model is historically contingent. In an increasingly interconnected world, the practice of centring the law of jurisdiction on the principle of territoriality is clouded 'with doubts being raised about the viability of territoriality in our interconnected world'.[83] The risk here is what Ryngaert calls 'thin justice'. Referring to Ratner, he continues:

> Rooted as it is in a 'negative community' of common practices rather than common goals, the law of jurisdiction has not concerned itself with the potential under-regulation of global governance challenges, such as … the mitigation of climate change. This failure to engage with substantive issues … is characteristic of a modern international law that delimits sovereign powers and emphasizes State consent but 'defer[s] substantive resolution elsewhere'.[84]

Thus, it can be said that 'jurisdiction is on a path to become *just a tool* used to realize predefined goals of the *international community*'.[85] I would concur with Ryngaert, for reasons that hopefully will become clearer below.

Next, this leads us to consider the scholarship on 'jurisdiction as community' as an alternative, in the context of what Beneviste calls 'the speaking of the sovereign law of the community'.[86] In this construct, jurisdiction is a 'mode of organising and controlling collective life',[87] the way in which authority and power are organized and articulated in a community. 'Jurisdiction is also a manifestation of the liberal project of distinguishing between

81 See Oduntan, *Sovereignty and Jurisdiction in the Airspace and Outer Space.*

82 Hannah L. Buxbaum, 'Territory, Territoriality, and the Resolution of Jurisdictional Conflict' (2009) 57 *The American Journal of Comparative Law* 669–670 referring also to the *Justizkonflikt* on the 'disjunctures in the debate about jurisdictional reach' of aspects of European and U.S. civil procedure, in particular the collection of evidence.

83 Ryngaert, 'Jurisdiction' in Orakhelashvili 8.

84 Ibid., 6 citing Steven Ratner, *The Thin Justice of International Law* (Oxford University Press 2015).

85 Ibid., 9 (emphasis added).

86 Kaushal, 'The Politics of Jurisdiction' 761 citing E. Benveniste, *Indo-European Language and Society* (London: Faber and Faber 1973) 7.

87 Kaushal, 'The Politics of Jurisdiction' 763.

law and politics, by virtue of which politics is subordinated to legal rules that allocate, distribute, and discipline power'.[88]

As Kaushal puts it:

> For metaphysical jurisdiction, the union of sovereignty and jurisdiction is a constant. Jurisdiction depends upon a sovereign community for both justification and form. It is this articulation that brings law into existence and allows law's emergence as law. Jurisdiction contains the 'motif of a declaration that gives now and prospectively reproduces the power of law as always linked with a polity and a politics'.[89]

The political aspect of authority and community, however, as a means of organizing the two, can be problematic. Kaushal refers us to the work of Brown, who 'critically rearticulates the political with emphasis on the power/authority part of the union' of authority and community.[90] Brown describes the political as the 'distinct problematic of the values and powers binding collectivities'.[91] These 'political possibilities are not leashed to the form of the state and collective life must contend with the weakening of sovereign forms and the discovery of other modalities of power'.[92] Thus, the question is not so much about whether a community is able to assert jurisdiction, but to borrow Berman's words, 'whether other communities are willing to give deference to the judgment rendered and enforce it as if it were their own'.[93]

In this 'jurisdictional community', as Kaushal terms it,

> The state is still the primary organising category for understanding political and legal authority and it remains the primary institutionalized form for collective coexistence. The political is one of several ways of organising community and authority, but when the political is aligned with sovereignty and jurisdiction, it sits at the apex of that multiplicity.[94]

Therefore it must be remembered that '[t]here is no jurisdiction that is not state granted, approved, or tolerated'.[95] This has been said to 'signal a return

88 Ryngaert, 'Jurisdiction' 4.
89 Kaushal, 'The Politics of Jurisdiction' 781 citing Douzinas, 'The Metaphysics of Jurisdiction' 21.
90 Kaushal, 'The Politics of Jurisdiction' 764 referring to Wendy Brown, 'At the Edge' in Stephen K. White and J. Donald Moon (eds), *What is Political Theory?* (London: Sage Publications 2004).
91 Kaushal, 'The Politics of Jurisdiction' 764 citing Brown 'At the Edge' 103, 117.
92 Ibid.
93 Kaushal, 'The Politics of Jurisdiction' 772 citing Berman *Global Legal Pluralism*, Ch. 7.
94 Kaushal, 'The Politics of Jurisdiction' 764 on what later is referred to as 'jurisdictional community'.
95 Ibid., 772.

to the modern notion that politics is subject to law, and that only those political projects that survive the legality challenge can claim legitimacy'.[96]

The third and final area of jurisdiction scholarship is jurisdiction as governance. This relates to areas that are beyond national jurisdiction.[97] International aviation is by its very nature an excellent exemplification. Buxbaum tells us: 'The use of territoriality as a mechanical standard used to link particular conduct with a particular country's law – rightly rejected – must be distinguished from the use of territoriality as an expression of a specific understanding about fairness and legitimacy in cross-border regulation'.[98] Citing Berman's research, she claims that the 'cosmopolitan jurisdictional model would reject the construction of community as "a geographically determined territory circumscribed by fixed boundaries," instead of bringing into view the multiple interests and affiliations that define our sense of community'.[99] For instance, the U.S. Congress when assessing the reach of U.S. law, 'avoids extending this reach when this would create a "serious risk of interference with a foreign nation's ability independently to regulate its own commercial affairs"'.[100] As regards this approach, which 'already minimizes the importance of territory in determining legislative scope', Buxbaum adds that this would 'encourage the actors making jurisdictional decisions to replace a focus on internal domestic policy with a broader focus: to expand the "idea of a government's self-interest … [and] to include an interest in being a cooperating member of the global community"'.[101] This means that what we have witnessed in jurisdictional law as

> [d]ividing the world into compartments, as Mann put it, is no longer a satisfactory or even a viable way to conceive of regulating the global economy. It ignores the diffusion of both the conduct that must be regulated and also the means by which regulatory authority is asserted in the global economy. Yet methodological frameworks seeking a basis in transgovernmental communities, or in community values, must integrate the relevant values that are sometimes expressed through invocations of territorialism. The task will be to generate a conversation about what lies behind claims of 'territoriality' and 'extraterritoriality', thereby creating more specific awareness of what is being contested – not only the power

96 Ryngaert, 'Jurisdiction' 5.

97 David Freestone, 'International Governance, Responsibility and Management of Areas beyond National Jurisdiction' (2012) 27 *Int'l J. Marine & Coastal L.* 191.

98 Buxbaum, 'Territory, Territoriality, and the Resolution of Jurisdictional Conflict' 674.

99 Ibid.

100 Ryngaert, 'The Concept of Jurisdiction' in Orakhelashvili, 66 citing *F Hoffmann-La Roche Ltd* v. *Empagran SA* [2004] 315 F 3d 338, 2359–2367.

101 Buxbaum, 'Territory, Territoriality, and the Resolution of Jurisdictional Conflict' citing Paul Schiff Berman, 'Towards a Cosmopolitan Vision of Conflict of Laws: Redefining Governmental Interests in a Global Era' (2005) 153 *U. Pa. L. Rev.* 1819, 1880.

> of particular actors to regulate certain conduct, but the shape of the *global regulatory community*.[102]

In short, the emerging global regulatory community is accepted in this book as an example of a possible new paradigm for global governance of civil aviation.

'Airspace' sovereignty and its dynamic evolution

Returning now to the concept of airspace sovereignty,[103] as recognized in the Convention on International Civil Aviation ('Chicago Convention') 1944, it can be said that *this* version of State sovereignty is an instance of 'extreme' sovereignty, or even 'ultra' sovereignty. It is important to note the historical context of the agreement, and how it reflects the balance of State power in the 1940s. Without a doubt, 'sovereignty in aviation has a relatively strong military background', thus it 'plays a central role in aviation'.[104] Indeed, post-war 'reliance on sovereignty served as a tool to safeguard national airspace and security';[105] this signals the sheer military and political, and in parallel economic, importance.

Recalling from Article 1 of the Chicago Convention:

> The High Contracting Parties recognize that every State has complete and exclusive sovereignty over the airspace above its territory.

From this, '[i]t stands to reason that a State can enforce the provisions of this convention or of its own national legal order against the aircraft of another State only within that part of the airspace over which it has effective control. The validity of any legal order cannot extend beyond this sphere'.[106]

102 Buxbaum, 'Territory, Territoriality, and the Resolution of Jurisdictional Conflict' 675 referring to Frederick A. Mann, 'The Doctrine of Jurisdiction in International Law' (1964) 111 *Recueil des Cours* 1–162 (emphasis added); Klaus Vogel, 'Intervention' in *Territoriale Grenzen der Staatlichen Rechtsetzung* 18 (Walter Rudolf & Walter S. Habscheid eds. 1973) 83: 'noting that while international law prohibits only the exercise of sovereign acts on the territory of another state, states increasingly meet their regulatory ends not through "official" sovereign acts but through more *indirect* routes'. (emphasis added).

103 'Airspace sovereignty is delimited *ratione loci* in respect of the space above national territories and not *ratione materiae* in respect of the air, which may at any given time, be filling this space' (Oduntan, *Sovereignty and Jurisdiction in the Airspace and Outer Space* 205–206).

104 Pablo Mendes de Leon, 'The Dynamics of Sovereignty and Jurisdiction in International Aviation Law' in Gerard Kreijen (ed.), *State, Sovereignty, and International Governance* (Oxford University Press 2002) 483.

105 Ibid., 484.

106 Kelsen, *General Theory of Law and State* as cited in Cooper, 'Sovereignty in Space' 62.

As regards Article 1 of the Chicago Convention, Mendes de Leon argues that the words 'complete and exclusive' sovereignty do not 'enhance or qualify the sovereignty of contracting States', and that it can be argued that the drafters essentially meant 'complete and exclusive jurisdiction and control'.[107] As an aside, it is argued that jurisdiction, then, is 'not exclusively an attribute of the sovereign State'. It follows that jurisdiction could be taken as an 'alternative' to sovereignty insofar as it may be an alternative to sovereign States as the regulators of international civil aviation.[108]

In any case, the remainder of the Chicago Convention moves away from exclusive sovereignty to limit the sovereignty of sovereign States in certain respects. Sole reliance on Article 1 would of course also make subsequent provisions redundant. 'Article 1 of the Chicago Convention confirming the principle of sovereignty applies *only* as the basis of and subject to treaty obligations giving up national competencies, in the exercise of sovereign powers by States'.[109]

Coming back to the point made earlier on the importance of territory, now through the lens of airspace sovereignty we are also able to observe that the two are related as expressed in Article 1 of the Chicago Convention. Territory is further defined in the Convention in Article 2:

> For the purposes of this Convention the territory of a State shall be deemed to be the land areas and territorial waters adjacent thereto under the sovereignty, suzerainty, protection or mandate of such State.

The drafters of the Chicago Convention thus appear to have approached 'territory' from two positions: (1) recognizing that a State has sovereignty over the airspace above its territory; *and* (2) recognizing that a State's territorial sovereignty is in fact that which it exercises over its land areas and territorial waters. But why did the forefathers of international air law choose the words 'complete and exclusive sovereignty over the airspace'? Is this a question of interpretation? Was it perhaps the wish of the drafters to encapsulate something more along the lines of '(complete and exclusive) jurisdiction and control over the airspace' as we have seen suggested above?

Diederiks-Verschoor and Kopal remind us that in international air law, a distinction is recognized between the airspace above the national territory, the territorial waters and the high seas. Consequently, 'State sovereignty extends to the airspace above the national territory and the territorial waters' but does not include a right of innocent passage for aircraft as is the case for

107 Mendes de Leon, 'The Dynamics of Sovereignty and Jurisdiction in International Aviation Law' 486.

108 Ibid., 495.

109 Ibid., 486.

foreign vessels in territorial waters.[110] Mendes de Leon sums up the state of affairs: 'International air law takes the concept of "sovereignty" as the legal basis for rule- and policy-making powers in international air transport. Contracting States of the Chicago Convention are "sovereign" in air transport matters'.[111] He continues that 'the term *territory* under the Chicago Convention is defined by reference to "sovereignty" in Article 2 of the Convention and insofar as Fifth Freedom of the Air rights are territory based'.[112]

Writing in 1945, Kelsen says:

> [It] does not necessarily follow ... that the entire space above and below the surface belongs to the territory of the State concerned. It is quite possible that the airspace as well as the subsoil which is beyond the effective control of the territorial State has the character of no State's land. It seems, however, that, according to general international law, the other States have no right to occupy this space even if they have the technical ability to do so. The only way to characterize these parts of the space in conformity with the principle of effectiveness is to assume an exclusive right of the territorial State to occupy, that is to say, to extend according to the progress of its technical means, the efficacy of its legal order to those parts of the airspace and subsoil which before were beyond its effective control.[113]

On applying the doctrine of effectiveness to territory, Cooper considers Nepal and the highest peaks of the Himalayas as case-in-point: does Nepal exercise effective control over the entirety of its land areas? With reference to the limits to this 'airspace' jurisdiction, he continues: 'The proposal [on effective control] would create rights in space which would extend far upward for the strong State, but would be almost non-existent for the weak. It would probably be in violation of the basic principle of "equality of opportunity" between States which is implicit in the preamble to the Chicago Convention'.[114]

As this book considered in Chapter 1, the protective tendencies of States after the First and Second World Wars were driving forces of this special formulation (then retention) of convention text. Protectionism had intensified further by the time ICAO convened a conference in Geneva in November 1947, with a view to developing a multilateral agreement on the exchange of commercial rights in international civil air transport. The

110 Diederiks-Verschoor and Kopal, *An Introduction to Space Law* 38; see Article 12 in conjunction with Annexes 2, 6, 11 and 12 of the Chicago Convention.

111 Mendes de Leon, 'The Dynamics of Sovereignty and Jurisdiction in International Aviation Law' 488.

112 Ibid., 489.

113 Cooper, 'Sovereignty in Space' 58, 62 citing Kelsen, *General Theory of Law and State*.

114 Cooper, 'Sovereignty in Space' 62.

Geneva Conference delivered a resolution that the multilateral agreement 'would impose no obligations on its parties to enter into route agreements, entry into route agreements remaining entirely discretionary with the parties concerned'.[115] There was only one dissenting vote. At this Goedhuis observes, 'It is difficult to imagine a greater demonstration of separateness, of unbridled self-assertion, of a narrower nationalistic approach'.[116]

It should be remembered that when the Geneva Conference took place, it did so in an international political environment characterized by growing tensions between the West and the East. Goedhuis argues that an 'ultra-sovereignty fetish' developed during the subsequent Cold War, producing a 'period in which the undervaluation of international law was at its height'.[117] In fact, it was at the Academy of International Law just a year later that Jean-Jacques Rousseau concluded on the topic: 'que jamais les Gouvernements n'ont autant invoqué la souveraineté qu'aujourd'hui et sur un ton qui laisse loin derrière lui les plus véhémentes affirmations des Chancelleries de l'Europe monarchique ou impériale'.[118]

According to Held *et al.*, 'The First and Second World Wars led to a growing acknowledgement that international governance could not rely on the balance of power if the most extreme forms of violence against humanity were to be outlawed, and the growing interconnectedness and interdependence of nations recognized'.[119]

But what was the main driving force behind such extreme protectionism in civil aviation? The principal interest of States would clearly have been safety, but economic interests must also have featured prominently, especially as regards the extent to which a State could exploit its own aviation services: 'This was the reason which led the delegates to indulge in a concept of sovereignty which had originally been considered atavistic'.[120] At Chicago in 1944, the U.S. delegation advocated for 'freedom of air', whereas the UK delegation, fearful of the post-war production strength of U.S. manufacturers and the prospect of their market domination, argued for regulation of sovereign airspace under subsequent bilateral air services agreements (ASAs). The UK and U.S. were 'diametrically opposed as regards the regulation of the *economic* side of civil aviation'.[121] In real terms this translates into national airspace treated as *de jure* closed.

115 Goedhuis, 'The Air Sovereignty Concept' 214.

116 Ibid.

117 Ibid.

118 'Governments have never invoked more the sovereignty issue than today, and in a tone that leaves far behind the most vehement assertions of the chancelleries of the monarchical or imperial Europe' (ibid., 214–215).

119 Held *et al. Global Transformations* 62.

120 Goedhuis, 'The Air Sovereignty Concept' 215.

121 Mendes de Leon, 'The Dynamics of Sovereignty and Jurisdiction in International Aviation Law' 484.

Of course global air transport has evolved considerably since the Second World War, which evidences that the idea of *absolute* sovereignty, in times of peace, has been abandoned; in war times, this is rolled back. Goedhuis wrote in 1955: 'In the last few years, the idea has been gaining ground that no healthy development of world air transport is possible on the basis of absolute sovereignty'.[122] But he also recognized that hypothesizing the future of air transport was risky: 'One of the reasons why prophesies in the field of air relations are so risky is that aviation, economically as well as technically, is still in an experimental stage'.[123] Amidst this seeming uncertainty, he forecasted:

> One thing is certain and that is that the future regime of the air will be influenced decisively by the attitude of the United States who operate more than half of the total world air transport. Now the conflicting currents of thought regarding the limitation of air sovereignty are reflected more clearly in the aviation policy of the US than in that of any other country.
>
> ...
>
> In a country wishing to operate aviation services on a world-wide basis these tendencies are of course detrimental – but a state, especially a state the aviation of which is competitively the strongest in the world cannot expect other states to be liberal if its own attitude towards foreign air services is restrictive. In the aviation field, just as in every other field of human activities, one cannot – perhaps unfortunately – have it both ways.[124]

In the exercise of sovereignty ...

This next section considers the ways in which the *exercise* of sovereignty may be described according to specialisms, or in the words of Mendes de Leon, how it can be 'qualified and requalified'.

> Sovereignty of a State is subject to a dynamic evolution in the *exercise* of that sovereignty. In international aviation, the exercise of sovereignty is qualified and 'requalified' according to trends pertaining to arrangements within a State, that is with *autonomous* entities, as well as between States and international or supranational organizations, and is also subject to liberalization of air services and privatization of providers of such services.[125]

122 Goedhuis, 'The Air Sovereignty Concept' 216.
123 Ibid., 216.
124 Ibid., 216, 220.
125 Mendes de Leon, 'The Dynamics of Sovereignty and Jurisdiction in International Aviation Law' 486 (emphasis added).

Here, Mendes de Leon draws a distinction between autonomy and sovereignty, with reference to the *Lighthouses in Crete and Samos*[126] case – Crete at the time was autonomous but still under Turkey's sovereignty – not affecting that sovereignty is indivisible.[127] In other rulings sovereignty has been declared indivisible as it means independence. Taking from the *Island of Las Palmas*[128] case: 'Sovereignty in the relations between States signifies independence … Territorial sovereignty … involves the exclusive right to display the activities of a State'.[129]

For the convenience of discussing State sovereignty through the lens of international aviation, this project recognizes two descriptions of the exercise of sovereignty: first recognizing *technical* sovereignty, then *economic* sovereignty.

The first, technical sovereignty, takes from the apparent shift from territorial to functional sovereignty as identified in jurisdictional studies. On this point Van Staden and Vollaard state: 'The juxtaposition of various systems of policy making, each of them focused on different tasks, implies that sovereignty is no longer territoriality based and, consequently, no longer embracing a wide range of human activities. It pertains to specific societal sectors'.[130]

On the one hand, the nature of sovereignty becomes specialized around particular *policy areas* rather than the *territory* of the sovereign State. For instance, pooled sovereignty, which refers to the pooling of sovereignty by a group of States, produces the 'exercise of joint but at the same time fragmented authority. It is "joint" because it is exercised by a group of national governments; it is "fragmented" because it applies only to particular policy fields'.[131] The most commonly cited example of pooled sovereignty is the European Union vis-à-vis its 'Euro-polity'. Ruggie identifies the EU as the '"first truly post-modern international political form" in which exclusive control over territory is losing its position as the core feature of sovereignty'.[132] In turn, sovereignty becomes *non-territorial.* But so far there has been no realization of viable alternatives to State sovereignty; thus, the

126 *Lighthouses in Crete and Samos, France* v. *Greece*, ICGJ 322 (PCIJ 1937).

127 Mendes de Leon, 'The Dynamics of Sovereignty and Jurisdiction in International Aviation Law'.

128 *Island of Las Palmas* Case *(or Miangas), United States* v. *Netherlands*, Award (1928) II RIAA 829 ICGJ 392.

129 Mendes de Leon, 'The Dynamics of Sovereignty and Jurisdiction in International Aviation Law' 486.

130 Van Staden and Vollaard, 'The Erosion of State Sovereignty' 180.

131 Ibid., 180; see also The World Bank, 'Open Skies for Africa: Implementing the Yamoussoukro Decision' (2010) available online: https://siteresources.worldbank.org/EXTAIRTRANSPORT/Resources/515180-1262792532589/6683177-1285016043773/OpenSkiesForAfrica.pdf

132 Van Staden and Vollaard, 'The Erosion of State Sovereignty' 166 citing John Gerard Ruggie, 'Territoriality and Beyond: Problematizing Modernity in International Relations' [1993] *Int'l Org.* 174.

default position remains for territorial sovereignty as supreme and exclusive authority within a State's territory. Nonetheless, '[n]on-territorially based governance, for example in the form of "regimes", or "global public policy networks"', according to Van Staden and Vollaard, 'cannot replace the sovereign State'.[133] Albeit 'territory and size are no longer considered to determine economic wealth and national power', we are also witnessing a seemingly phenomenal emergence of 'virtual States'.[134]

The EU is also a good example of how *territorial* sovereignty can be transformed into *functional* sovereignty;[135] the EU – vis-à-vis pooled, non-territorial governance – is neither nation nor State; it has no territory. It is dependent of course on its Member States. In keeping with Van Staden and Vollaard: '[N]on-territorial governance will survive only, if it is embedded within a secure legal and political framework compelling States to abide by the standards of conduct and committing them to maintain regional or world order'.[136] This is because political authority is rooted in peoples' consent and loyalty.[137] The EU integration process itself 'raises doubts on the applicability of the concept of territorial sovereignty'.[138]

So, are non-territorial forms of political authority a viable alternative to territorial governance? The realists seem to have reservations. They 'regard security and territorial authority as two sides of the same coin',[139] which perhaps explains why in the EU context that despite post-Lisbon changes putting the European Parliament and the Council of Ministers on equal footing, and the elevation of the former so-called 'Third Pillar' on justice and home affairs to the supranational level, security remains intergovernmental in nature. National security vis-à-vis EU common security and defence policy has not been elevated. This serves as a 'reminder of the obstinacy national governments demonstrate in defending their sovereignty on matters of life and death'.[140]

Before considering technical sovereignty and economic sovereignty, each concept taken in turn, a distinction must first be made between sovereignty on the one hand, and national competencies, on the other; the competencies are part of the sovereignty. In the words of Mendes de Leon, 'States do no give up sovereignty, but transfer national competencies to, or share those

133 Ibid., 180.
134 Ibid., 166.
135 Ibid., 180.
136 Ibid., 182.
137 Brus, 'Bridging the Gap between State Sovereignty and International Governance' 22.
138 Van Staden and Vollaard, 'The Erosion of State Sovereignty' 166; A recent example is the European Commission proposal on 'outer EU borders', which would still require supervision of national territories under the authority of the Member States in question.
139 Ibid., 182.
140 Ibid.; see also A. Van Staden, 'Same Bed, Same Dreams? Europe's Search for Autonomy in International Security' (2000) 3 *Bologna Center J. Int'l Aff.* 17.

competencies with, other institutions, for instance, supranational organizations, *in the exercise* of their sovereign powers'.[141]

For international aviation, transfers in technical areas are customary practice. The most recent ICAO proposals to develop fair competition safeguards, common principles on consumer protection and a global market-based mechanism for international aviation emissions, all indicate movement into the economic area, too. It is argued that this transfer or sharing of national competencies, as an exercise of a State's sovereign powers, builds, or at least provides an opportunity to build, functional or quasi-functional sovereignty for international institutions.

Technical (functional) sovereignty

It is undisputable that the creation of and adherence to universal technical rules on air navigation is *a practical necessity*; there are a number of other 'functional-type' areas as well. 'Because of the need for a unified framework for the technical side of air transport operations, national competencies have been transferred to ICAO[142] in the areas of safety, security, immigration, facilitation, and the environment in which ICAO is the central regulator'.[143] This is done vis-à-vis ICAO and the international SARPs.[144]

The caveat is that 'contracting States are free to decide whether or not, and, if so, how they implement ICAO standards in their national laws ... [and they] can file differences'.[145] Whilst under Article 37 of the Chicago Convention ICAO SARPs are binding for all ICAO Member States, it is possible that a Member State may be unwilling or unable to comply with a specific SARP; this may be for a particular period of time or indefinitely. In the case of intended non-compliance, the State in question, typically via the national civil aviation administration, is obliged to 'give notice' to ICAO Council by 'filing a difference' under Article 38 of the Chicago Convention. The cost of implementation, difficulty in comprehending or interpreting the Annex material, or difference of interpretation between States tend to be cited as the main reasons for non-compliance.[146]

141 Mendes de Leon, 'The Dynamics of Sovereignty and Jurisdiction in International Aviation Law' 486.

142 They could also be transferred to a supranational organization, as is the case for some of these areas in the EU (author's note).

143 Mendes de Leon, 'The Dynamics of Sovereignty and Jurisdiction in International Aviation Law' 485.

144 On sovereignty, the Chicago Convention requirement for States to provide air navigation services and facilities, see J. Naveau, 'Droit de l'air et nationalisme historique' (1990) 15 *Annals of Air and Space Law* 183.

145 Mendes de Leon, 'The Dynamics of Sovereignty and Jurisdiction in International Aviation Law' 485.

146 See ICAO, 'Annex 9: Compliance Issues', (24 March 2015) available online at: www.icao.int/APAC/Meetings/2015%20FAL/4.Day2.1200-1230.Annex9Compliance Issues.2015March04.pdf

The major problem with the filing of differences, however, is that 'ICAO has no enforcement or sanction mechanism at its disposal, [thus] ICAO has very limited supranational legislative powers. Enforcement of ICAO standards and the imposition of sanctions must be handled by contracting States of the Chicago Convention (Art 12)'.[147]

As regards the involvement of non-state actors in the development of and adherence to international SARPs, within the Chicago System non-state and private actors remain heavily if not entirely dependent on sovereign States to negotiate, agree and enforce policy. 'Though sovereign States may delegate the right to set standards to functionally-recognized governing bodies, non-State actors still rely largely on territorially organized state policy and military to enforce compliance with the standards'.[148]

It follows that States are *responsible* for civil aviation. Mendes de Leon says:

> Although this convention is a very flexible instrument, in that its provisions are broadly formulated, it consistently entrusts States with responsibility for aviation-related tasks. It remains to be seen whether this system will respond to the needs of the twenty-first century. Several authorities are competing for competencies in aviation matters. *The question is whether 'sovereignty' is and should remain the basis for regulating international civil aviation.*[149]

It should be remembered that, devastatingly, the Cold War gave rise to many incidents of alleged or actual unauthorized aerial transgressions and intrusions, resulting in the downing of civilian airliners. In 1953, Lissitzyn suggested that a rule for international customary law could be inferred from State practice: 'In its efforts to control the movements of intruding aircraft the territorial sovereign must not expose the aircraft and its occupants to unnecessary or unreasonably great danger – unreasonably great, that is, in relation to the reasonably apprehended harmfulness of the intrusion'.[150]

There are too many tragic examples to cover here; only a few examples of alleged intrusions are provided below. In 1955, a civilian aircraft *en route* from Vienna, Austria to Tel Aviv, Israel via Istanbul, Turkey strayed into Bulgarian airspace was shot down.[151] In 1960, a United States U2 reconnaissance aircraft was shot down over the USSR. Then, in 1978 and 1983, two Korean Air Lines (civilian) aircraft were shot down over the USSR.[152]

147 Ibid.

148 Van Staden and Vollaard, 'The Erosion of State Sovereignty' 182.

149 Mendes de Leon, 'The Dynamics of Sovereignty and Jurisdiction in International Aviation Law' 494 (emphasis added).

150 Oliver J. Lissitzyn, 'The Treatment of Aerial Intruders in Recent Practice and International Law' (1953) 47 *AJIL* 559, 586.

151 Milde, *International Air Law and ICAO* 51.

152 Ibid., 50–55; see also Chrystel Erotokritou, 'Sovereignty Over Airspace: International Law, Current Challenges, and Future Developments for Global Aviation' (2012) 4(5) *Student Pulse*, online at: www.studentpulsse.com/a?id=645

The 1983 incident, which fortunately did not end in a total loss of human life, led to the subsequent amendment of the Chicago Convention, inserting Article 3bis,[153] which arguably did not establish a new *principle* but rather reflects the way in which the rule evolved a principle of customary international law to refrain from the use of force against civilian aircraft in interception situations.[154] This also marked 'in principle, [a] change in legal direction of modern state'.[155] However, there are possible issues with interpretation of Article 3bis of the Chicago Convention. For example, the text refers to 'weapons', not 'force'; and the expression 'in flight' is used rather than a situation in which an aircraft is recaptured 'on the ground' after a hijacking. For other situations, special international conventions are now in place, e.g. the 1963 Tokyo Convention on Offences and Certain Other Acts Committed on Board Aircraft; this permits interference in certain situations.

On a related point, Shaw tells us that the dispute resolution provision in Article 82 of the Chicago Convention 'provides for the abrogation of all inconsistent obligations and understandings among ICAO members and it is a moot point whether this means that article 3 *bis* (when in force) would override the Tokyo provisions,[156] although it should be noted that the Tokyo Convention deals only with offences committed on board the aircraft'.[157] Also, Article 25 of the Chicago Convention provides that, for aircraft in distress, States will offer assistance, on the condition that the distress situation must be made known to intercepting forces. Ultimately, the doctrine of self-defence may be employed, in situations involving terrorism such as the tragic events of September 11th, or for argument's sake, the Korean airliner allegedly believed by the Soviets to have been a U.S. spy plane; proportionality must be exercised.[158]

While it is commonplace for States to impose limitations on flights operated by foreign aircraft in national airspace,[159] nowadays, it is arguably

153 The first part paragraph of Article 3bis reads: '(a) The contracting States recognize that every State must refrain from resorting to the use of weapons against civil aircraft in flight and that, in case of interception, the lives of persons on board and the safety of aircraft must not be endangered. This provision shall not be interpreted as modifying in any way the rights and obligations of States set forth in the Charter of the United Nations'.

154 Milde, *International Air Law and ICAO* 50–58; see also Bin Cheng, *General Principles of Law as Applied by International Courts and Tribunals* (Cambridge University Press 2003); Bin Cheng, 'The destruction of KAL flight KE007, and Art 3bis of the Chicago Convention' in Van Gravesande and Van der Veen Vonk (eds), *Air Worthy* (Kluwer Law and Taxation Publishers 1985) 47–74.

155 Held *et al.*, *Global Transformations* 72.

156 Cheng, 'The destruction of KAL flight KE007' 49 (note in original).

157 Shaw, *International Law* 476.

158 Ibid., 476–479.

159 I. Diederiks-Verschoor, *An Introduction to Air Law* (6th revised edn, Kluwer Law International 1997) 12–14; Article 17 of the Chicago Convention provides that an aircraft takes the nationality of the registration State. The conditions for registration are a matter for national law.

within a responsibility framing[160] in the context of safety and security regulation that is comparatively 'low politics' when compared to, say, economic regulation. With respect to the former, one can easily comprehend potential problems associated with technical competencies and resources to facilitate air navigation and safety measures within a State's sovereign airspace. There are numerous examples of situations in which one State's airspace for historical reasons was, or still is, effectively controlled by another State. Take for instance the Southeast Asia region of Malaysia, Indonesia and Singapore. Since 1946, Singapore's Flight Information Region (FIR) has included some of the airspace over the southern part of Malaysia and above Indonesia's Riau and Natuna Islands in the South China Sea, which means Singapore manages the airspace.[161] Also, the upper airspace over Togo and Benin, nestled along the Gulf of Guinea between Ghana and Nigeria, has historically been designated under the Accra FIR. Under a new agreement signed in 2016, Ghana now manages the terrestrial airspace and the oceanic sector while the Togolese and Beninese airspace is managed from Lomé (Togo).[162]

There are also examples of airspace extensions. For instance, the U.S. claims 'responsibility' for international airspace navigation in so-called air defence identification zones (ADIZs), which are beyond U.S. territorial sovereignty. Requirements on 'foreign aircraft' are loosely based on Article 11 of the Chicago Convention.[163] Additional issues are presented for the airspace over exclusive economic zones (EEZs), where States may exercise sovereign rights but not claim exclusive sovereignty.[164] Finally, the EU is an example of cross-border, flexible use of airspace.[165] Extensions of airspace or responsibility for airspace may also yield an extension of national political space.

160 Or in the words of Joanne Scott, a 'responsibility-based frame' (Joanne Scott, 'The Geographical Scope of the EU's Climate Responsibilities' (2015) 17(1) *Cambridge Yearbook of European Legal Studies* 92–120).

161 Sections of airspace within the Kuala Lumpur FIR are also under control of Singapore Area Control (ACC) (Civil Aviation Authority of Singapore, 'ENR 2.1 Air Traffic Services Airspace' (18 November 2010), online at: www.caas.gov.sg/caasWeb2010/export/sites/caas/en/Regulations/Aeronautical_Information/AIP/enroute/enr2/ENR2.1.pdf).

162 See Dominic Andoh, 'Airspace dispute resolved', *B&FT Online* (17 February 2016), online at: http://thebftonline.com/business/aviation/17388/airspace-dispute-resolved-.html

163 Anthony Aust, *Handbook of International Law* (Cambridge University Press 2010).

164 I. Diederiks-Verschoor, *An Introduction to Air Law* (8th rev. edn, Kluwer Law International 2006) Ch. 2; P. P. Heller, 'Flying over the Exclusive Economic Zone' [1978] *ZLW* 15–17; E. Cuadra, 'Air Defense Identification Zones: Creeping Jurisdiction in the Airspace' (1978) 18 *Virginia Journal of International Law* 485.

165 Which dates back to Commission Regulation (EC) 2150/2005 of 23 December 2005 laying down common rules for the flexible use of airspace, OJ L342/20; see Diederiks-Verschoor, *An Introduction to Air Law*, 8th edn 96; notwithstanding issues with implementation of Single European Sky 2 (SES2) and EUROCONTROL.

Economic (functional) sovereignty

Whilst the parties to the Paris and Chicago Conventions 'were and are concerned with the regulation of safety and security in civil aviation, [they] did not treat air transport as an economic activity'.[166] Mendes de Leon says this changed in Europe following the *French Merchant Seamen* case, which concerned vessels used in the context of an economic activity.[167] Market liberalization for aviation began in the European Union in the mid-1980s, following deregulation in the United States in 1978.[168]

To date, there has been no transfer of national competencies to the international level where economic matters are concerned. Mendes de Leon argues this is '[i]n light of reliance on the principle of sovereignty', as States continue to 'determine who flies in their national airspace, and, if so, under what terms and conditions'.[169] As we established above, State sovereignty extends to the airspace above a State's national territory and above its territorial waters.[170] For scheduled international air services, States exchange (economic) traffic rights[171] with other States by way of negotiated treaties: ASAs.[172] Under the International Air Services Agreement, as discussed, the Chicago System effectively provides two Freedoms of the Air. The International Air Transport Agreement today is of little importance.[173] So, what resulted was the extensive proliferation of bilaterals and multilaterals.[174] The ASAs developed first as restrictive agreements – for example U.S.–UK Bermuda Agreement of 1946, which was denounced by the UK in 1976 and

166 Mendes de Leon, 'The Dynamics of Sovereignty and Jurisdiction in International Aviation Law' 491.

167 Case 167/73, *Commission* v. *France* (Re French Merchant Seamen) [1974] ECR 359, [1974] CMLR 216.

168 Steven Truxal, *Competition and Regulation in the Airline Industry: Puppets in Chaos* (Routledge 2012).

169 Mendes de Leon, 'The Dynamics of Sovereignty and Jurisdiction in International Aviation Law' 485 (including an applicable competition regime, regimes for taxes and charges, and access to infrastructures and air as laid down in ASAs).

170 With respect to air law jurisdiction over the high seas, Article 12 of the Chicago Convention applies, in conjunction with Annexes 2, 6, 11 and 12. The law applicable is the law of the state of aircraft registration notwithstanding issues around military usage of shared airspace. See Diederiks-Verschoor, *An Introduction to Air Law*, 8th edn 32–33. It should also be noted that, in the law of the sea, 'the coastal State may *adopt* laws and regulations relating to innocent passage through the territorial sea in respect of a considerable number of activities, but it may only *enforce* those laws (whether criminally or civilly) in limited circumstances', Ryngaert 'The Concept of Jurisdiction' in Orakhelashvili 60 (emphasis added).

171 This is taken on the presumption that traffic rights have commercial value.

172 Chicago Convention, Art 6.

173 It can be said that whereas an international convention on freedom of overflight exists, it is not universally accepted. See Lee, 'Revisiting Freedom of Overflight in International Air Law' 351–370.

174 According to ICAO, there are 3000 ASAs in force today (ICAO, 'Database of World's Air Services Agreements', online at: www.icao.int/sustainability/pages/Doc9511.aspx).

renegotiated as Bermuda II in 1977 – or in more recent times, quite liberal agreements – for example the EU–Canada Air Transport Agreement 2009.[175] As Shaw points out: 'The Chicago Conference system was to some extent undermined by the growth of bilateral agreements as the means to regulate international air transport, but many common principles may be discerned in such agreements based as they are upon the Bermuda model'.[176]

It is put forward that the Chicago System of negotiated traffic and landing rights for passenger, mail and cargo can be argued to be antiquated; it is coming under stress owing to developments in technology. Furthermore, in an era of economic liberalization and intense globalization since the Second World War, there has been a 'growing preference of national governments to relax legal constraints on the international trade of goods and capital, implying a weakening hold by these governments over the transaction flows within their territories'.[177] Ryngaert calls this a 'paradox of liberalism' and questions: 'how can a positive freedom (right to act) and negative freedom (the right to be free from outside interference) be simultaneously guaranteed? Inevitably, such freedoms will have to be balanced against each other'.[178] Traditionally, one State does not interfere in another State's economic affairs – such as antitrust or securities law and regulation. Yet, in these and other areas, 'Multilateral treaties have been creating co-operation and even integration of States within certain policy fields on a regional and global scale. Indeed, this trend of governance across territorial borders is predominantly present within economic issue-areas'.[179] Examples include the EU and the Association of Southeast Asian Nations (ASEAN) on the one hand, and the International Monetary Fund (IMF) and the World Bank on the other hand.[180]

As far as developed countries are concerned, globalization of the economy, the growth of regional institutions such as those mentioned above and the emergence of international regulatory regimes reveals that the conventional notion of State sovereignty has limited efficacy.[181] According to Van Staden and Vollaard: 'At the root of the claim that State sovereignty declines and that, for this reason, the very concept of territoriality bound political authority is growing obsolete lies, first and foremost, in the belief that the forces of market integration and economic globalization are beyond the control of national governments'.[182] This underscores the earlier discussion on territorial sovereignty and its limitations.

175 The EU cites this agreement as 'so far the most ambitious air transport agreement between the EU and a major partner in the world' (European Commission, 'International Aviation: Canada Transport'. Available online at: http://ec.europa.eu/transport/modes/air/international_aviation/country_index/canada_en.htm).

176 Shaw, *International Law* 467.

177 Van Staden and Vollaard, 'The Erosion of State Sovereignty' 167.

178 Ryngaert, 'Jurisdiction' 4.

179 Van Staden and Vollaard, 'The Erosion of State Sovereignty' 167.

180 Ibid.

181 Jayasuriya, 'Globalization, Law and the Transformation of Sovereignty' 426.

182 Van Staden and Vollaard, 'The Erosion of State Sovereignty' 167.

That is why a State's 'exclusive jurisdiction over its territory', according to Jayasuriya, needs rethinking, but what then might be the ramifications of fragmentation of sovereignty?[183] The 'emergent system of global governance depends on a fundamental reconstitution of our conventional Westphalian-inspired ideas of sovereignty and Statehood'.[184] He suggests that 'what these regulatory regimes essentially achieve is to expose the limitations of the Westphalian assumption of mainstream international relations and law, namely that territory is the central component of State sovereignty, thereby conjuring up a legal world composed of interacting unitary States'.[185] Citing the work of Zaring, Jayasuriya continues: 'From an international law perspective, many regulatory regimes fail to pass muster because international organizations are considered to be "organizations composed of states and constituted by formal treaty."'[186]

In the light of recent developments and ongoing realities in international society and international law, it is undeniable that the role of State sovereignty appears to be changing.[187] Thus, it can be said that a formidable challenge to the Westphalian framework is mounting, if we have not already observed some major changes in terms of territory, public authority and sovereignty.[188]

Citing the proliferation of international law, Krisch gives a caution about fragmentation:

> Expressed through a proliferation of treaties and regimes, institutions as well as courts and quasi-courts, this fragmentation not only appears as the flipside of the growth in strength and breadth of international law, but also seems to pose a threat to its unity and coherence.
>
> ...
>
> Conflicts between obligations had always existed and were the logical result of an order of sovereigns: 'Because of the spontaneous, decentralized and unhierarchical nature of international law-making – law-making by custom and by treaty – lawyers have always had to deal with heterogeneous materials at different levels of generality and with different normative force'.[189]

183 Jayasuriya, 'Globalization, Law and the Transformation of Sovereignty' 426.
184 Ibid.
185 Ibid., 428.
186 Ibid. citing David Zaring, 'International Law by Other Means: The Twilight Existence of International Financial Regulatory Organizations' (1998) 33 *Tex. Int'l L.J.* 281, 285.
187 Brus, 'Bridging the Gap between State Sovereignty and International Governance' 7; Brus queries whether this is a paradigmatic change or a developmental change.
188 Caporaso, 'Changes in the Westphalian Order'.
189 Nico Krisch, 'Pluralism in Postnational Risk Regulation' in *Beyond Constitutionalism: The Pluralist Structure of Postnational Law* (Oxford University Press 2010) 199 citing a Report of the Study Group, *Fragmentation*, para 484. For more on fragmentation of international law, see e.g. M. Koskenniemi and P. Leino, 'Fragmentation of International Law: Postmodern Anxieties?' (2002) 15 *Leiden Journal of International Law* 553–579.

It is often difficult to locate the *ultimate* authority in the competition between internal and external 'authorities'.[190] 'The competition between different levels of law is also a competition between different collectives' rights to make law, between competing claims for law-making authority'.[191] This 'pluralism of competing collectives', noting differences between States and non-State actors that underlie this competition in an increasingly pluralist world,[192] is 'not only a legal, technical affair, but is also based on intense social contestation about the locus of authority and the right collective for decision-making on matters of food safety and the environment'.[193] Krisch queries whether a more 'tightly integrated, hierarchically organized, "constitutionalist" structure [could help] to overcome the difficulties of cooperation'.[194]

This exposes international law's fragmentation; the same goes for international air law, too. There is a 'multitude of regulatory regimes and international dispute settlement systems, the jurisdiction of which may be partly overlapping or at least in conflict with other specialised fields of international law and policy'.[195] A report published by the International Law Commission finds that there is 'no homogenous, hierarchical meta-system realistically available to do away with such problems [of coordination at the international level]'.[196] Instead, it would seem most prudent to recognize that 'the unity of global law', in the words of Fischer-Lescano *et al.*, 'is no longer structure-based ... but is rather process-based, deriving simply from the modes of connection between legal operations, which transfer binding legality between even highly heterogeneous legal orders'.[197]

190 Krisch, 'Pluralism in Postnational Risk Regulation' refers in his discussion to cases brought before the Court of Justice of the European Union relating to the UN charter, UN sanctions, UNCLOS and disputes over genetically modified organisms vis-à-vis the WTO. A notable case is Case C-308/06 *Intertanko* [2008] ECR I-04057 on the UN Convention on the Law of the Sea (UNCLOS) and EU legal order. He says, 'UNCLOS, like the WTO Agreements, has often been heralded as an example of increasing legalization – and especially judicialization – of international affairs: the International Tribunal for the Law of the Sea, even though it does not at present attract a great number of cases, certainly represents an important element in the move towards dispute settlement by permanent judicial institutions' (Krisch, 'Pluralism in Postnational Risk Regulation' 189).

191 Krisch, 'Pluralism in Postnational Risk Regulation' 189.

192 Mark A. Pollack and Gregory C. Shaffer, *When Cooperation Fails* (Oxford University Press 2009).

193 Krisch, 'Pluralism in Postnational Risk Regulation' 206.

194 Ibid., 220.

195 Ramses A. Wessel and Jan Wouters, 'The Phenomenon of Multilevel Regulation: Interactions between Global, EU and National Regulatory Spheres' (2007) *International Organizations Law Review* 282–283.

196 Ibid., 283 citing Martti Koskenniemi, 'Fragmentation of International Law: Difficulties arising from the diversification and expansion of International Law' (Report of the Work of the Study Group of the International Law Commission, U.N. Doc. A/CN.4/L.682 2006) para 484.

197 Andreas Fischer-Lescano, Gunther Teubner and Michelle Everson, 'Regime-Collisions: The Vain Search for Legal Unity in the Fragmentation of Global Law' (2004) 24 *Mich. J. Int'l L.* 999, 1007–1008.

Returning again to the *economic* aspect of this book's narrative, we take competition law as an example for which territoriality – *objective* territoriality – has been relied upon as the so-called 'effects doctrine'. The example given above in which territoriality challenges jurisdictional law is price-fixing, but there exist other equally plausible infringements of antitrust legislation as well.[198] If a cartel is global – with the involvement of actors in different jurisdictions and with worldwide effects – there is all the more difficulty in determining which is the 'territorial State'. Ryngaert provides several good examples including the worldwide *Vitamins*[199] cartel which led to the *Empagran*[200] litigation in U.S. courts[201] and the U.S. Restatement (Third) of U.S. Foreign Relations Law (1987). 'Ultimately, the rule of reason aims at identifying the State with the strongest connection, in terms of contacts or interests, with the situation'.[202] Ryngaert continues:

> The ongoing dispute between the United States and European countries regarding the desirability of a multilateral antitrust regime ... reflects different assumptions about the virtue of territorial sovereignty as the foundation of a global network. The current preference of Germany (and the European Union generally) for bringing antitrust regulation under the WTO [World Trade Organization] umbrella is consistent with its vision of sovereign equality. Conversely, the United States, accustomed to addressing the issue of regulatory conflict primarily as a matter of domestic interest and policy, may continue to prefer bilateral and ad-hoc cooperation and coordination efforts.[203]

Another semi-recent example involving international aviation is the inclusion of aviation activities in the EU's Emissions Trading System (ETS).[204] 'The requirements of the territoriality principle have also been considered to be met where foreign airlines were obliged to surrender emissions allowances in

198 For an example of a global price-fixing cartel in international aviation, see Commission Decision C (2010) 7694 final relating to a proceeding under Article 101 TFEU, Article 53 of the EEA Agreement and Article 8 of the Agreement between the European Community and the Swiss Confederation on Air Transport (Case COMP/39258 – *Airfreight*); see also Steven Truxal and S. Harris, 'Airfreight: Regulatory Environment Encourages or Imposes Price Co-ordination?' (2013) 78(3) *Journal of Air Law & Commerce* 541–584.

199 *Re Vitamins Antitrust Litigation* 120 F 2d 58 (D.D.C. 2000).

200 *Hoffmann* v. *Empagran* (n 60).

201 Ryngaert, 'The Concept of Jurisdiction' in Orakhelashvili 62, 63, 65.

202 Ibid., 63, 64; see also *Kiobel* v. *Royal Dutch Petroleum Co*, 621 F 3d 111 (2nd Cir 2010), 133 S Ct 1659 (2013), and Alien Tort Statute regarding U.S. 'cases that touch and concern' the U.S. (Ryngaert, 'The Concept of Jurisdiction' 61).

203 Buxbaum, 'Territory, Territoriality, and the Resolution of Jurisdictional Conflict' 672 referring to Kevin C. Kennedy, 'Competition Law and the World Trade Organisation' (2001) 33 *Geo. Wash. Int'l L. Rev.* 585, 14–17.

204 European Commission, 'Reducing emissions from aviation'. Available online at: http://ec.europa.eu/clima/policies/transport/aviation/index_en.htm

respect of non-territorial air mileage on the ground that the relevant aircraft departed from, or landed at, a territorial airport'.[205]

Ryngaert tells us that such 'liberal interpretations of territoriality in economic and environmental law have given rise to substantial international tension', citing blocking laws such as the U.S. Federal law prohibiting U.S. airlines from participating in the ETS[206] and related threats of legal action at the WTO.[207] This book returns to the EU ETS and international aviation emissions in Chapters 3 and 4.

Non-territorial governance as an alternative?

As we understand from the discussion above, one State's claim of jurisdiction over a specific matter may come under challenge. Where international supervision of a State court's assertion of jurisdiction is lacking, 'it is almost inevitable that the exercise of jurisdiction is prone to subjective, even parochial interpretations'.[208]

Nonetheless, experience has shown that regulators and courts in one State are capable of successfully establishing dialogues with their counterparts in other States through intergovernmental networks[209] to create what Krisch and Kingsbury coin as the emergence of a 'global administrative space' vis-à-vis global administrative law and global governance.[210] In this global governance space, of regulation and administration, it is recognized that the strict divide between international and national is breaking down as the administrative functions of regulation take place through complex interaction between officials and institutions on different levels.[211] The 'great divide' of internal/external, national/international is thus challenged.[212] In the field of antitrust law, for instance, 'the institutionalized contacts and dialogues, setting out duties of consultation, information-sharing, positive comity, and conditional reciprocity, between transatlantic regulators have surely contributed to the decrease of regulatory conflicts, although the substantive convergence of antitrust laws may also be an explanatory

205 Ryngaert 'The Concept of Jurisdiction' in Orakhelashvili 56.
206 S. 1956, European Union Emissions Trading Scheme Act of 2011 (2012) Pub.L. 112–200.
207 Lorand Bartels, 'The Inclusion of aviation in the EU's ETS: WTO law considerations' (2012) ICTSD online, available at: www.ictsd.org/bridges-news/biores/news/the-inclusion-of-aviation-in-the-eu%E2%80%99s-ets-wto-law-considerations
208 Ryngaert, 'The Concept of Jurisdiction' in Orakhelashvili 64.
209 A. M. Slaughter, 'Governing the Global Economy through Government Networks' in M. Byers (ed.), *The Role of Law in International Politics* (Oxford University Press 2000) 177.
210 N. Krisch and B. Kingsbury, 'Global Governance and Global Administrative Law in the International Legal Order' (2006) 17 *Eur. J. Int'l L.* 1.
211 Ibid.
212 Clark, *Globalization and International Relations Theory.*

factor'.[213] This book will return to competition rules and antitrust law relating to international aviation in Chapter 3.

Non-territorial (global) governance can thus serve as an alternative to existing systems that are at times polycentric, overlapping, fragmented and conflicting, and also *competing* for authority. Citing the telecommunications sector as a case study for non-territorial governance, Held *et al.* link the regulatory regime as 'global' in the sense that it

> represents a type of functional political space which transcends national territorial boundaries and which articulates, in this case, a sense of political community not anchored in a territorial logic *per se*, but rather in a transnational community of interests whose commonality resides in members' positions as providers, consumers or regulators of international telecommunications services.[214]

In the wider debates over the actual or perceived status of the Westphalian system then, the global telecommunications regime and its 'infrastructure mediates the Westphalian order of states and rearticulates political interests, structures and outcomes'.[215]

Another means of non-territorial governance is through global public policy networks.[216] Van Staden and Vollaard propose that these could serve as foundation for future global policies:

> These networks refer to alliances of government agencies, international organizations, corporations, and elements of civil society such as non-governmental organizations, professional associations, or religious groups. By taking private actors as *partners* in the framing and implementation of policies of public sector agencies, both the legitimacy and the effectiveness of these policies may be increased.[217] Private actors not only have a stake in the outcome and often possess better information than public actors, but also have a boundless range of activity … [and ultimately] gain a greater voice in international decision-making.[218]

Increasingly, political accountability moves beyond (traditional) State responsibility as principal–agent relationship, to include non-state actors and private actors in the mix through partnerships, which multiplied become networks. While private actors gain a greater voice as Van Staden

213 Ryngaert, 'The Concept of Jurisdiction' in Orakhelashvili 65.

214 Held *et al.*, *Global Transformations* 62.

215 Ibid., 62.

216 W. H. Reinicke, 'The Other World Wide Web: Global Public Policy Networks' (1999–2000) 117 *Foreign Pol'y* 44–45.

217 W. H. Reinicke, 'Global Public Policy' (1997) 76 *Foreign Pol'y* 132.

218 Van Staden and Vollaard, 'The Erosion of State Sovereignty' 177 (emphasis added).

and Vollaard point out, this author would add that they must also be prepared to accept the associated responsibility if they 'want a seat at the table'. Many non-State actors are 'bigger' and more financially powerful than many States, yet jurisdiction remains 'tightly bound to the state'.[219]

This responsibility framing, or responsibility balancing, proves particularly challenging in practice, however, especially in highly complex industries, in which one tends to witness a shift from command-and-control regulation to more process-oriented regimes. In their research, Mills and Koliba examine the tragic explosion of the *Deepwater Horizon* oil rig in the Gulf of Mexico in April 2010 when 'over 205 million gallons of oil[220] had been discharged into the Gulf of Mexico and over 650 miles of coastline habitat were covered in oil'.[221] They apply the 'governance network accountability framework' developed by Koliba *et al.*[222] to the disaster 'to identify the dominant accountability frames (democratic, market, and collaborative)'.[223] In the case of *Deepwater Horizon*, they identify high political (democratic) accountability on the one hand and the need for elected officials to rely on expertise of private actors on standards and compliance for associated risks. On the other hand they found market demands were also at play.

It is easy to see why there has been a proliferation of scholarship on the accountability of non-state actors and private actors, particularly in the areas of human rights and the environment.[224] As non-state actors play an ever-increasing role within a diminishing hierarchical legal environment, they also assume a correlative duty.[225] The State, in the words of Brown, nonetheless

219 Kaushal, 'The Politics of Jurisdiction' 765; consider for instance global oil companies or banks.

220 Maureen Hoch, 'New Estimate Puts Gulf Oil Leak at 205 Million Gallons' (2010), online at: www.pbs.org/newshour/rundown/2010/08/new-estimate-puts-oil-leak-at-49-million-barrels.html (note in original).

221 Russell M. Mills and Christopher J. Koliba, 'The Challenge of Accountability in Complex Regulatory Networks: The Case of the *Deepwater Horizon* Oil Spill' (2015) 9 *Regulation & Governance* 77–91, 78.

222 Christopher J. Koliba, Russell M. Mills and Asim Zia, 'Accountability in Governance Networks: An Assessment of Public, Private, and Nonprofit Emergency Management Practices Following Hurricane Katrina' [2011] *Public Administration Review* 71, 210–220.

223 Mills and Koliba, 'The Challenge of Accountability in Complex Regulatory Networks' 78.

224 Richard A. Higgott, Geoffrey R. D. Underhill and Andreas Bieler (eds), *Non-State Actors and Authority in the Global System* (Routledge 2000); on non-State actors as standard setters, see Anne Peters *et al.* (eds), *Non-State Actors as Standard Setters* (Cambridge University Press 2009).

225 Elena Pariotti, 'International Soft Law, Human Rights and Non-State Actors: Towards the Accountability of Transnational Corporations?' (2009) 10(2) *Human Rights Review* 139–155.

'remains a unique and uniquely vulnerable object of political accountability'.[226]

Subsidiarity as an alternative?

Next, let us consider subsidiarity in the law of jurisdiction as a variation on the jurisdictional rule of reason discussed above. The *précis* of subsidiarity is that, where one State is better placed to exercise jurisdiction, other States should refrain 'unless the latter State's failure to do so harms the *global interest*, and multilateral regulation and supervision are absent'.[227] The State ultimately exercising jurisdiction thereby acts as what König calls a 'trustee of mankind'.[228]

In considering the protection of the environment as one example of a matter of global interest, Ryngaert tells us that one State may exercise subsidiary jurisdiction 'to compensate the primary jurisdiction State's failure to provide minimum levels of environmental protection and enforcement'. In the example of the EU's ETS, greenhouse gas emissions harm the global interest, and at the same time, there may be a further impetus for the EU to advance European values, to set global standards, and to protect trade interests, beyond EU jurisdiction. The conflict over inclusion of aviation activities in the EU ETS arose in part because this 'positive dimension' of subsidiarity is challenged by the 'negative dimension', which led to protest over 'foreign regulation' interference with the latter State's *domaine réservé*:[229]

> For economic reasons, certain States may indeed be disinclined to strictly enforce environmental norms or protect environmental values, whereas other States, may favor a high level of environmental protection and enforcement, be inclined to *extend* their domestic regulation and enforcement to foreign economic operators who are subject to lax rules in their home State. Often, these bystander States may do so to protect environmental values globally or extraterritorially, but also to level the international playing field so as to ensure that domestic operators [are] not put at a competitive disadvantage as a result of strict domestic environmental regulation.[230]

226 Wendy Brown, 'Power after Foucault' in J. S. Dryzek, B. Honig and A. Phillips (eds), *The Oxford Handbook of Political Theory* (Oxford University Press 2006) 65.

227 Ryngaert, 'The Concept of Jurisdiction' in Orakhelashvili 67 (emphasis added).

228 On trustees of the international community, see D. König, 'The Enforcement of the International Law of the Sea by Coastal and Port States' (2002) 62 *ZaöRV* (*Zeitschrift für ausländisches öffentliches Recht und Völkerrecht*) 1, 15.

229 Ryngaert, 'Subsidiarity in the Law of Jurisdiction' 16–17.

230 Ibid., 17 (emphasis added).

Subsidiarity in the law of jurisdiction is commonplace in the maritime world. In short, seagoing vessels fly two flags, representing the vessel's flag State and port State. When the vessel is within the territorial jurisdiction of the port State, that State exercises so-called port States jurisdiction. Ryngaert provides numerous examples of instances in which port States jurisdiction is exercised for activities that a vessel's flag State fails to address, such as pollution, fishing on the high seas or labour standards.[231] The port State thus 'protects the *international* interests in the face of flag State regulatory failure'.[232] The relevant law of the sea, the UN Convention on the Law of the Sea 1982 (UNCLOS), provides in Article 218(1):

> When a vessel is voluntarily within a port or at an off-shore terminal of a State, that State may ... institute proceedings in respect of any discharge from that vessel *outside* the internal waters, territorial sea or exclusive economic zone of that State in violation of applicable international rules and standards established through the competent international organization or general diplomatic conference.[233]

The problem with the exercise of port State jurisdiction in the global interest is that, as we have seen above in the example of the EU ETS, it may be that the port State is incentivized by domestic or regional economic reasons rather than acting altruistically for the greater good. The risk is that the port/coastal State's interests are 'just masqueraded as common interests ... [which] may legally be questionable'; are they a 'smokescreen'?[234] It follows that there may be a greater frequency of this type of subsidiarity in the law of jurisdiction 'the more the underlying substantive norm which the port State wishes to enforce rises to the level of a truly *international norm*'.[235] In effect, port/coastal States may be seen to act as enforcers of international law.

> When a given port State's regulation protects goods that are as such *not* protected by international regulation, this does not mean that port State

231 E.g. ITLOS, Case at International Tribunal for the Law of the Sea (ITLOS) concerning the conservation and sustainable exploitation of swordfish stocks in the South-Eastern Pacific Ocean, *Chile* v. *European Community* (2000) 40 ILM 475; Barents Sea 'Loophole' Agreement 1999; see Ryngaert, 'Subsidiary and the Law of Jurisdiction' 18; see also Maria Gavouneli, *Functional Jurisdiction in the Law of the Sea* (Martinus Nijhoff Publishers 2007).

232 Ryngaert, 'Subsidiarity' 18.

233 Convention on the Law of the Sea, Part XII, 'Protection and Preservation of the Marine Environment', online at: www.un.org/Depts/los/convention_agreements/texts/unclos/part12.htm (emphasis added).

234 Ryngaert, 'Subsidiarity' 20; See M. Hakimi, 'Unfriendly Unilateralism' (2014) 55 *Harvard Int'l L. J.* 105, 125.

235 Ryngaert, 'Subsidiarity and the Law of Jurisdiction', 24 (emphasis added).

> jurisdiction over such goods is necessarily internationally unlawful. But it may well mean that the unilateral measures taken to enforce such a regulation cannot be as far-reaching, unless perhaps … the port State can somehow objectively establish that the international community unjustifiably fails to protect the goods the former wishes to protect unilaterally. Concerns remain, however, over abuse of port State jurisdiction to advance national rather than global interests.[236]

In his work, Ryngaert focuses on 'whether, and if so how, international trade law, and WTO law in particular, accommodates the exercise of subsidiary jurisdiction by bystander States or the EU aimed at protecting the environment or raising environmental standards elsewhere'.[237] In the cases brought before the WTO that were unquestionably characterized by struggles between economic and environmental interests, there has sometimes been a higher standard put on free trade and other times on environmental interests.[238]

So, is there a future for subsidiarity in the law of jurisdiction? Ryngaert concludes:

> For subsidiarity to remain a viable procedural tool for 'reconciling competing norms' and 'encourag[ing] dialogue among multiple jurisdictions', jurisdictional applications of subsidiarity should find a middle ground between 'apology' and 'utopia'. Bystander States and regional organizations should not shrink from their responsibilities to strive for the realization of global justice by applying judicial or regulatory avoidance techniques, but neither should they foist their own interpretations of global justice onto others who may have legitimate reasons to follow rival interpretations.[239]

By the same token, recognizing the environment as a global public good[240] through the 'exercise of universal civil jurisdiction risks trampling on a foreign nation's prerogative to "regulate its own commercial affairs", and could adversely affect "much needed direct foreign investment" in host countries'.[241] One possible solution is what Mannens calls 'shared sovereignty'.[242] Brus tells us that, 'As the shift towards the social function of

236 Ibid., 24–25.
237 Ibid., 25.
238 E.g. *Tuna/Dolphin* (1991, 1994) and *Shrimp/Turtle* cases (1998), respectively.
239 Ryngaert, 'Subsidiarity and the Law of Jurisdiction' 31.
240 Hans Lindahl, 'A-Legality: Postnationalism and the Question of Legal Boundaries' (2010) 73 *Modern L. Rev.* 30.
241 Ryngaert, 'The Concept of Jurisdiction' in Orakhelashvili 67, referring to UK and Netherlands arguments in *Kiobel* v. *Royal Dutch Petroleum*, 133 S Ct 1659 (2013) litigation on question of U.S. jurisdiction.
242 Wolf Mannens, 'Shared Sovereignty? Minority Claims and the Effectiveness of State Authority', in Kreijen (ed.), *State, Sovereignty, and International Governance* (Oxford University Press 2012).

the State is undeniably related to the development of international standards, the international community shares the burden of dealing with conflictuous situations ... by using its collective authority'.[243] Somek warns us, however:

> When authority becomes transnationally shared, things are no longer looking up for sovereignty. The belief in state power ruling supremely over a territory is scarcely sustainable. There is both much penetration of state power by private actors and increasing preponderance of international cooperation ... sovereign states acting by themselves lack the capacity to address challenges of a transnational kind. Attempting to go it alone merely indicates myopia.[244]

Conclusion

Berman explains that the 'nation-state, socially constructed and historically contingent, is only one way of parsing the modern world'.[245] His work on global legal pluralism 'seeks to grapple with the complexities of law in a world where a single act or actor is potentially regulated by multiple legal or quasi-legal regimes'.[246] The 'nation-state community is constructed and contingent; it is neither the most logical nor the most practiced form of community in a globalised, transnational world'.[247] As Hooghe and Marks put it, 'Territorial jurisdictions are intended to be, and usually are, stable for several decades or more, though the allocation of policy competencies across levels is flexible'.[248] Berman suggests that 'if territorial location is of less significance now than it once was, we increasingly face normative questions about whether legal rules based on territory are desirable'.[249] However, Berman justifies this:

> this is not to say that territory is unimportant, but it is difficult to deny that we are increasingly affected by activities and decisions that take place

243 Brus, 'Bridging the Gap between State Sovereignty and International Governance' 8.

244 Alexander Somek, 'Any Further Bids on Popular Sovereignty?', abstract of keynote address at Transnational Law Institute Conference 'Transnational Sovereignties: Constellations, Processes, Contestations' King's College London 2016; see Alexander Somek, 'Accidental Cosmopolitanism' (2012) 3(4) *Transnational Legal Theory* 371–392; Alexander Somek, 'The Individualisation of Liberty: Europe's Move from Emancipation to Empowerment' (2013) 4(2) *Transnational Legal Theory* 258–282.

245 Berman, *Global Legal Pluralism* 89.

246 Ibid., 4.

247 Kaushal, 'The Politics of Jurisdiction' 771.

248 Liesbet Hooghe and Gary Marks, 'Types of Multi-Level Governance' in Henrik Enderlein, Sonja Wälti and Michael Zürn (eds), *Handbook on Multi-level Governance* (Edward Elgar 2010) 17.

249 Berman *Global Legal Pluralism* 91.

> far from us in a spatial sense. Such deterritorialized effects have always been present to some extent, of course. One need only look at the history of empire to realize that the strings of governance were often pulled by far-off rulers. But at least in the premodern world such political arrangements, perhaps because of the slow pace of transportation and communications, rarely meant strong centralized control of distant realms. Rather, the social construction of space was organized around many centers, with a patchwork of overlapping and incomplete rights of government.[250]

Resnik succinctly sums up the state of affairs when she says, 'Legal borders, like physical ones, are permeable, and seepage is everywhere'.[251] At the same time, our globalized world is experiencing significant, contemporary changes and transnational challenges. This calls urgently for a re-examination of the doctrines of sovereignty and jurisdiction. Our very experience with real world events makes evident that the foundations of jurisdiction are shifting to the extent that 'in postmodern times it is becoming an instrument to realize international community goals of substantive justice'.[252] Thus it can be said that '[i]n reality, jurisdiction is a site for political struggle regarding the allocation of power among the participants in the international society'.[253] The 'notion of global politics' suggests that political 'space can no longer be conceived as coterminous with the boundedness of the territorial nation-state: politics and governance spill across national boundaries'.[254]

A way of theorizing the interaction between international law and politics in the global system is to apply the notion of a what Krasner calls the 'international regime',[255] which refers to 'a set of implicit or explicit principles, norms, rules, and decision-making procedures around a particular set of issues in a range of international policy areas'.[256] Jayasuriya criticizes Krasner's analysis on regulatory cooperation of international regimes, claiming it 'is still trapped within the basic confines of the Westphalian paradigm of

250 Berman *Global Legal Pluralism* 91. 'Noting that premodern states were not based principally on territorial sovereignty and that, instead, medieval Europe was in some ways an archetype for nonexclusive territorial rule; its "patchwork of overlapping and incom - plete rights of government … [was] inextricably superimposed and tangled"' (Ruggie, 'Territoriality and Beyond' 149).

251 Judith Resnik, 'Foreign as Domestic Affairs: Rethinking Horizontal Federalism and Foreign Affairs Preemption in Light of Translocal Internationalism' (2007) 57 *Emory L.J.* 31, 64.

252 Ryngaert, 'Jurisdiction' 1.

253 Ibid., 1–2.

254 Held *et al.*, *Global Transformations* 62.

255 With its origins in the work of Kenneth W. Abbott, 'Modern International Relations Theory: A Prospectus for International Lawyers' (1989) 14 *Yale J. Int'l L.* 335.

256 Stephen D. Krasner, *International Regimes* (Cornell University Press 1983) 2.

sovereignty, and as such is not able to encompass within its framework some of the fundamental changes in the architecture of international law'.[257] There are forces at play that 'continue to erode pillars of the Westphalian system of sovereign States ... [so one must consider] alternative systems of political authority that may supersede territorial systems of *rule*'.[258]

Thus, in the words of Buxbaum, a reshaping of the law of jurisdiction is needful: 'The "borderless" nature of some activities, the near-global nature of others – all of this seems to demand regulatory solutions freed from territorial underpinnings ... the multidisciplinary retheorization of territory and power in the global age supports and promotes the development of "global" theories of jurisdiction'.[259]

In the context of civil aviation, Mendes de Leon questions the future of sovereignty in our increasingly interdependent world. 'States share jurisdiction in aviation matters with or transfer such jurisdiction to, to begin with, supranational organizations. In the future, international and supranational organizations, whether on a global or on a regional level, will play their own role in aviation-related matters, with less involvement of States acting individually'.[260] This author attempts to develop this line of thinking later.

This chapter has examined the scholarship on sovereignty and jurisdiction as a means to challenge classic international law thinking, premised on the contractual nature of international law and consent-based law making. The 'contractual model of regime formation is underpinned by the Westphalian model in which sovereignty is linked with exclusive territorial jurisdiction'.[261] There is a Westphalian bias in the Chicago System; this international regime is inter-governmental with State members, thus it represents a contractual model of inter-State relationships in which the treaty (Chicago Convention and Annexes) is central.[262] Krisch reminds us that '[t]he consensual structure of the international legal order, with its strong emphasis on sovereign equality of states, has always been somewhat precarious'.[263] The Westphalian principle of exclusivity also extends into the domestic arena.[264] Yet, owing to the 'combined force of economic globalization and environmental concerns', we are witnessing a serious challenge to *this* doctrine of State sovereignty.[265]

257 Jayasuriya, 'Globalization, Law and the Transformation of Sovereignty' 431.

258 Van Staden and Vollaard, 'The Erosion of State Sovereignty' 166 (emphasis added).

259 Buxbaum, 'Territory, Territoriality, and the Resolution of Jurisdictional Conflict' 668.

260 Mendes de Leon, 'The Dynamics of Sovereignty and Jurisdiction in International Aviation Law' 494.

261 Jayasuriya, 'Globalization, Law and the Transformation of Sovereignty' 431 citing Ruggie, 'Territoriality and Beyond'.

262 Jayasuriya, 'Globalization, Law and the Transformation of Sovereignty' 430 referring to Abram Chayes and Anoonia Handler Chayes, 'On Compliance' (1993) 4 *Int'l Org.* 174, 172.

263 Krisch, 'The Decay of Consent'.

264 Caporaso, 'Changes in the Westphalian Order'.

265 Van Staden and Vollaard, 'The Erosion of State Sovereignty' 181.

Could it be that economic power is the new 'transnational heir of sovereignty' in today's globalized world?[266] What we observe is the 'process of [sovereignty's] gradual transformation in the context of the emergence of international governance'.[267] Against this, Brus forecasts:

> States will remain the most important actors in international law and international relations, but they will have to adapt to the changing circumstances in the present international society. On the one hand it means being part of a continuous process of developing norms of the international community which determine the degree of freedom that sovereign States enjoy in inter-State relations and, as a relatively new element, in the conduct of their internal affairs.[268]

For international aviation, Havel advocates that a plurilateral agreement may be the only means truly to globalize the sector: 'Until the restrictive precepts of the Chicago Convention are rolled back, in the United States *and* among America's aviation trading partners, no authentic globalization of the international aviation system will be possible'.[269]

When embracing a post-sovereignty era, one must be cautious however. Pluralist norms can be shaped through global legal discourses – constitutional, legislative and administrative – about how to authorize and when to limit State officials' actions.[270] Scheuerman identifies emergency situations, *inter alia* environmental disasters, financial crises, epidemics and refugees, in which international organizations, having developed political and legal mechanisms, are often well-equipped to take action.[271]

Though, relating *emergency* action to actions taken for the common good, we witness as Hooghe and Marks put it: 'The diffusion of authority in new political forms has led to a profusion of new terms: multi-level governance, multi-tiered governance, polycentric governance, multi-perspectival governance, FOCJ[272] (functional, overlapping and competing jurisdictions),

266 Maria Rosaria Ferrasrese, 'Governance: A Soft Revolution with Hard Political and Legal Effects' (2014) 1(1) *Soft Power* 35–58.

267 Brus, 'Bridging the Gap between State Sovereignty and International Governance' 21.

268 Ibid., 21–22.

269 Brian F. Havel, *Beyond Open Skies* (Wolters Kluwer 2009) 5; See also Goedhuis 'The Air Sovereignty Concept' 216, 220.

270 Judith Resnik, 'Globalization(s), Privatization(s), Constitutionalization, and Statization: Icons and Experiences of Sovereignty in the 21st Century' (2013) 11(1) *International Journal of Constitutional Law* 162–199.

271 William Scheuerman 'Cosmopolitanism and the World State' (2013) 40(3) *Review of International Studies* 419–441; William Scheuerman, 'From Global Governance to Global Stateness' in P. Strik (ed.), *The Concept of the State in International Relations: Philosophy, Sovereignty and Cosmopolitanism* (Edinburgh University Press 2015).

272 As coined by Bruno Frey and Reiner Eichenberger, *The New Democratic Federalism for Europe. Functional, Overlapping, and Competing Jurisdictions* (Cheltenham: Edward Elgar 1999) (author's note).

fragmegration, the post-national state, consortio, and condominio, to name but a few'.[273]

Indeed, new forms of governing have been created though the centralization and disbursement of authority. For instance, '[t]he last two decades has also seen the creation of a large number of transnational regimes, some of which exercise real supranational authority. At the same time, public/private networks of diverse kinds have multiplied from the local to the international level'.[274] Hooghe and Marks clarify:

> The core belief is that governance must operate at multiple scales in order to capture variations in the territorial reach of policy externalities. Because externalities arising from the provision of public goods vary immensely – from planet-wide in the case of global warming to local in the case of most services – so should the scale of governance. Multi-level governance is necessary to internalize spillovers across jurisdictions while tailoring policy to local circumstances.[275]

They continue: 'However, beyond the presumption that governance has become (and should be) multi-jurisdictional, there is no agreement on how multi-level governance should be organized'.[276] Cox 'foresaw consequently that "[g]lobalization transforms the bases of state authority from within and produces a multilevel post-Westphalian order in which the state remains important but only one among several levels of authority"'.[277]

Mills and Koliba identify that '[t]he shift from traditional command and control oversight to process oriented regulatory regimes has been most pronounced in highly complex industries, such as aviation and deepwater oil drilling, where the intricate and technical nature of operations necessitates risk-based regulatory networks based largely on voluntary compliance with mutually agreed upon standards'.[278] Before moving on to the next chapters, it is useful to note that international aviation offers an opportune case study to explore the relatively new concepts of 'global law' and 'transnational law'.

There has been a proliferation of scholarship in these areas, too, but they do not always offer clear conceptualizations. Shaffer provides a helpful critique. *Global law*,[279] on the one hand, 'posits, by its name, that universal

273 Hooghe and Marks, 'Types of Multi-Level Governance' 17.

274 Ibid.

275 Ibid.

276 Ibid.

277 Van Staden and Vollaard, 'The Erosion of State Sovereignty' 167 citing Robert W. Cox, 'Globalization, Multilateralism and Social Choice' (1990) 13(1) *Work in Progress* 2; see also Held *et al.*, *Global Transformations* and Caporaso, 'Changes in the Westphalian Order'.

278 Mills and Koliba, 'The Challenge of Accountability in Complex Regulatory Networks'.

279 Walker, *Intimations of Global Law*.

legal norms are being created and diffused globally in different legal domains that may or may not involve agreements between states'.[280] He tells us that 'the Kingsbury project on "global *administrative* law" chose the title on the presumption that regulatory structures are under pressure to respond to global demands "that have a common normative character, specifically an administrative law character. The growing commonality of these administrative law-type principles and practices is building a unity between otherwise disparate areas of governance"'.[281] Held *et al.* say that global law 'is meant a domain of law different in kind from the law of states and the law made between one state and another for the mutual enhancement of their geopolitical interests'.[282]

On the other hand, Shaffer tells us that:

> The concept of *transnational law* has been developed to address legal norms that do not clearly fall within traditional conceptions of national and international law, but are not necessarily global in nature ... generally is comprised of legal norms that apply across borders to parties located in more than one jurisdiction ... encompasses public and private international law ... From a narrow perspective, transnational law is composed only of rules 'which regulate actions or events that transcend national frontiers ... which do not wholly fit into such standard categories' of public and private international law.[283]

Transnational law is thus increasingly used not only as a source of law, but also a *subject* of law: 'transnational law applying to transnational situations'.[284] Sassen adds that the

> emergent formalization of a complex, multisited institutional order ... signals that such formalizations are possible outside the sphere of law of the national state. At its most developed this is becoming a form of

280 Shaffer, 'Transnational Legal Ordering and State Change' 3 referring to Elizabeth H. Boyle and John W. Meyer, 'Modern Law as a Secularized and Global Model' (1998) 49 *Soziale Welt* 275–294 and John Braithwaite and Peter Drahos, *Global Business Regulation* (Cambridge University Press 2000).

281 Benedict Kingsbury, 'The Concept of Law in Global Administrative Law' (2009) 20 *European Journal of International Law* 3.

282 Held *et al.*, *Global Transformations* 70; see also David Held, *Democracy and the Global Order: from the Modern State to Cosmopolitan Governance* (Stanford University Press 1995) Ch. 10, also referring to global humanitarian law and the wider discourse on 'cosmopolitan law'.

283 Shaffer, 'Transnational Legal Ordering and State Change' 4 citing Philip Jessup, *Transnational Law* (Yale University Press 1956) (emphasis added).

284 Shaffer, 'Transnational Legal Ordering and State Change' 5.

> global law.[285] At its most elementary it consists of a variety of partial and autonomous systems of rule for governing specialized sectors.[286]

Again, this supports this book's view that international civil aviation is an appropriate case study of the wider debate.

285 See Gunther Teubner, 'Societal Constitutionalism: Alternatives to State-Centered Constitutional Theory' in Christian Joerges, Inger-Johanne Sand and Gunther Teubner (eds), *Transnational Governance and Constitutionalism* (Hartford: Hartford Publishing 2004) (note in original).

286 Sassen, *Territory, Authority, Rights* 224.

3 Economic and environmental regulation

Introduction

This chapter considers economic and environmental regulation of international (civil) aviation within the broader context of the large-scale, emerging economic and environmental concerns of the global neighbourhood.[1] It is posited that the Chicago System challenges the ability of States to address problems that are of a transnational nature. As we will see, in spite of there being relevant national and regional laws 'on the books', international economic and environmental regulation are incoherent or lacking. This provides impetus for introduction of the transnational law approach to civil aviation as a lens through which to theorize the emergence of a complex global governance regime for global aviation. 'Global aviation' refers to the globalized aviation sector.

As a starting point, we acknowledge that there are complex, global problems facing society today. For the purpose of this project, two contemporary challenges are selected: fair competition safeguards and consumer protection (economic) and greenhouse gas emissions and climate change (environmental).[2] These represent two key areas in which one can witness the greatest cumulative pressure for change. For some States, protection of the environment appears to take political priority; for others, economic considerations prevail. Even so, we accept that there is a strong interface between

1 This refers to market regulation and environmental standards, rather than operational and safety issues. The premise is that the reach by one State in the area of international aviation often extends beyond its national territory. As identified earlier, there are also parallels with international human rights and humanitarian law regimes. A 'substantial majority of states [post-Second World War] either supported or acquiesced in the development of a comprehensive international human rights regime. The contemporary human rights regime consists of overlapping global, regional and national institutions and conventions' (Held *et al.*, *Global Transformations* 67).

2 In the competition area, the Organisation for Economic Co-operation and Development (OECD) identifies and works in seven areas: abuse of dominance and monopolization, cartels and anti-competitive agreements, mergers, liberalization and competition intervention in regulated sectors, pro-competitive policy reforms, regulatory reform and competition policy; see OECD, 'Competition', online at: www.oecd.org/competition

the environment and international trade.[3] While the push factor for one government or another may be different, from either perspective both would likely nod in agreement on the need for change. 'Global' aviation may provide the much needed 'lift' to governments of all persuasions. Further to this, it is Daley's view that 'the vital economic and social benefits of the air transport industry should not be lost – and in fact they should be distributed far more widely and equitably – but that the environmental impacts of air transport nevertheless require urgent and effective management'.[4]

In the first part of this chapter, this author considers the increasingly important aspects of economic regulation, in particular market regulation, State aid and consumer protection, as they impact on and implicate the global aviation sector. It is argued that these areas are global public goods.

European Union law and policy in these areas will be identified as providing high standards in terms of strict regulation and compliance. Two Gulf States – United Arab Emirates and Qatar – are discussed alongside China as examples of two of the fastest growing regions in global aviation. These examples are also selected in the light of concerns voiced recently by U.S. and European carriers over alleged lax regimes in the relevant regions and that this, coupled with State-ownership and subsidies make it difficult for the Western carriers to compete on the global market. Thus, there is a perceived divergence in the regulatory regimes, which this chapter explores in the light of the ongoing investigations in the U.S. and EU. The incorporation of 'fair competition clauses' in future open skies agreements along with global competition law are taken into account as possible ways forward.

The second part of this chapter looks at the relationship between international aviation and the environment, specifically in the context of limitation and reduction of greenhouse gas (GHG) emissions from aviation and the respective impact GHG emissions are understood to have on global climate change.[5] From the start, this author takes the position that the environment is a global public good. The experience of globalization prompts a rethinking on the complex, multi-scalar nature of climate change governance. The EU Emissions Trading System (ETS) is considered as an example of global environmental leadership that appears to be the catalyst, or at least accelerator, of the emerging global governance regime for environmental regulation of aviation vis-à-vis market-based measures, as this book examines again in Chapter 4.

3 See e.g. N. Jaspers and R. Falkner, 'International Trade, the Environment, and Climate Change' in R. Falkner (ed.), *The Handbook of Global Climate and Environmental Policy* (Oxford: John Wiley & Sons 2013).

4 Ben Daley, *Air Transport and the Environment* (Farnham: Ashgate 2010) 16.

5 The focus here is on GHG emissions from aircraft engines. This author is mindful, however, that a range of other pollutants from aviation contribute to climate change, including contrails, airport and ground transportation emissions.

Economic regulation

International civil aviation is projected to continue experiencing steady growth in demand by an annual average of between 4.1 per cent and 4.6 per cent through 2034.[6] The strongest region for growth in aviation is the Middle East, with Africa close behind. According to IATA's latest *Passenger Forecast*, 'Eight of the ten fastest-growing markets in percentage terms will be in Africa with Central African Republic, Madagascar, Tanzania, Burundi and Kuwait making up the five fastest-growing markets'.[7]

Looking forward to the markets expected to grow fastest over the next two decades, IATA reports that the 'Middle East will grow strongly (4.9 per cent) and will see an extra 237 million passengers a year on routes to, from and within the region by 2034. The UAE, Qatar and Saudi Arabia will all enjoy strong growth of 5.6 per cent, 4.8 per cent, and 4.6 per cent respectively. The total market size will be 383 million passengers'.[8] Also, the five fastest-increasing markets in terms of passenger numbers will be (in descending order): China, the U.S., India, Indonesia and Brazil.[9] Most of these of course signal a dramatic shift in high demand for air connectivity in key emerging markets. However, in international passenger markets, the Middle East carriers are far ahead of others in terms of passenger traffic growth (13 per cent) and increased capacity (11.9 per cent).[10]

In the first part of this chapter, this author presents four case studies on market regulation in: the EU, United Arab Emirates, Qatar and China. The UAE, Qatar and China are selected owing to the substantial growth in these States as regards 'global' aviation including infrastructure. EU market regulation including consumer protection is also covered for comparison.

Airlines operate within a global economy. This book posits throughout that the airline business is no longer inter-national; it is resoundingly global in nature. It also notes that in the globalized economy, one tends to find layered and at times overlapping authorities in the area of economic regulation. Traditionally, market regulation, antitrust and securities in particular are areas reserved for national law and policy. In practice, one State should therefore refrain from interfering with the economic regulation of actors in another State. However, given the global nature of the marketplace, there is a risk of overlapping, inconsistent or conflicting regulation of a single actor at multiple levels, which can lead to a state of confusion for the actor and inefficiency in the system of regulation. This is particularly true for

6 International Air Transport Association (IATA), 'IATA 20 Year Passenger Forecast', online at: www.iata.org/publications/Pages/20-passenger-forecast.aspx; Airbus, 'Global Market Forecast 2015–2034: 'Flying by Numbers', online at: www.airbus.com/company/market/forecast

7 IATA, 'IATA 20 Year Passenger Forecast'.

8 Ibid.

9 Ibid.

10 IATA, 'Strong Demand for Air Travel Rises in 2014' (5 February 2015), online at: www.iata.org/pressroom/pr/Pages/2015-02-05-01.aspx

global private and quasi-private (i.e. State-controlled) actors, such as international airlines. This section aims to identify some of the layers and overlap as evidence of the problem in which an airline business registered in one State is subject to foreign competition laws.

First let us look at market regulation and enforcement, or lack thereof, against unfair trade practices and anti-competitive behaviour in the global aviation sector. Krisch argues that, '[i]n an increasingly liberalized and globalized economy, market regulation and enforcement are key goods'; thus they are accepted here as 'global public goods'.[11] This is supported by the fact that the nature of infringements of competition law and antitrust are increasingly transnational in nature.[12] It is also recognized that there are two aspects to antitrust: regulatory and non-regulatory. Statute-based regulatory laws are applied domestically even if privately enforced, whereas non-regulatory laws, e.g. on damages for antitrust infringements, reflect the political economy and sovereignty of a State.

There are two main perspectives on unfair trade practices. The first perspective this book identifies is the EU as a system of rigorous market regulation for air carriers and high level of consumer protection for passengers. We examine the EU and its high regulatory threshold for economic regulation through strict rules in particular jurisdictions that may put domestic or regional operators at a competitive disadvantage on the global market.

The second perspective this book investigates is how airlines face growing economic concerns such as discrimination vis-à-vis unfair play and/or a lack of a 'level playing field' on global markets owing to State subsidies and relatively lax rules in particular jurisdictions. It follows that an inequality of regulation and/or compliance ensues locally. Given the global nature of aviation, the (local) inequality projects onto the global market; its effects are felt globally. The impact on some major airlines, it is argued, is felt through loss of market share.

Case study: European Union

External Aviation Policy

The European Union's current External Aviation Policy is managed in close cooperation and coordination between the EU and its 28 Member States.[13] With that said it should be noted that following the 2002 'open skies' judgments the EU has assumed exclusive competence with respect to conducting

11 Krisch, 'The Decay of Consent' 12.

12 Although the subject is beyond the scope of this book, the same can be said of securities violations.

13 As this book takes a globalist approach to civil aviation, the development of the internal market for aviation services following three liberalization packages is purposefully excluded from our discussion. For a detailed examination of the liberalization of the EU sector, see Truxal, *Competition and Regulation in the Airline Industry*.

aviation relations with trading partners, so-called 'third countries'.[14] Whereas individual (sovereign) Member States negotiated bilateral air services agreements with third countries in the past, this authority is now exercised by the EU; in essence, the European Commission. At its core, EU External Aviation Policy has three main objectives:

(i) creating consumer benefits (which suggests a strong continued focus on market opening);
(ii) safeguarding competitiveness, which suggests stronger EU-level measures to insist on ownership and control reform, reductions of the regulatory burden and an international level playing field (all difficult to secure at Member State level); and
(iii) wider public policy objectives going beyond traffic rights (the EU approach will therefore seek to ensure overriding public safety, security and environmental goals)[15]

From the above we are able to glean that the principal aim of the EU's policy is to maintain very high standards across all areas of European aviation. The European Commission states: 'In the interest of European citizens and businesses, it is crucial to maintain high EU standards for safety, security, the environment, social issues and passenger rights'.[16] It also underlines that the

14 See Case C-466/98 *Commission* v. *United Kingdom* [2002] ECR I–9427; Case C-467/98 *Commission* v. *Kingdom of Denmark* [2002] ECR 9519; Case C-468/98 *Commission* v. *Kingdom of Sweden* [2002] ECR 9575; Case C-469/98 *Commission* v. *Republic of Finland* [2002] ECR 9627; Case C-471/98 *Commission* v. *Kingdom of Belgium* [2002] ECR 9681; Case C-472/98 *Commission* v. *Grand Duchy of Luxembourg* [2002] ECR 9741; Case C-475/98 *Commission* v. *Republic of Austria* [2002] ECR 9797; Case C-476/98 *Commission* v. *Federal Republic of Germany* [2002] ECR 9855. In these decisions, so-called 'nationality clauses' were deemed to infringe ex-Article 43 of EC Treaty as they were inconsistent with the single European market for air transport. SeeTreaty on the Functioning of the European Union (TFEU) (consolidated version) [2012] OJ C326/1, 26 October 2012, Arts 3, 4.

15 Communication from the Commission to the European Parliament, The Council, The European Economic and Social Committee and the Committee of the Regions, 'The EU's External Aviation Policy: Addressing Future Challenges', COM(2012) 556 final, online at: http://ec.europa.eu/transport/modes/air/international_aviation/doc/com_2012_556_fr.pdf

16 European Commission, 'Commission presents a new Aviation Strategy for Europe', Press Release IP/15/6144 (7 December 2015), available online at: http://europa.eu/rapid/press-release_IP-15-6144_en.htm. On safety, see European Commission, 'The European Aviation Safety Policy', online at: http://ec.europa.eu/transport/modes/air/safety/index_en.htm; on security, see European Commission, 'Aviation Security', online at: http://ec.europa.eu/transport/modes/air/security/index_en.htm; on the environment, see European Commission, 'Environment', online at: http://ec.europa.eu/transport/modes/air/environment/index_en.htm; on social issues, see European Commission, 'Social Dimension', online at: http://ec.europa.eu/transport/modes/air/internal_market/social_dimension_en.htm; on passenger rights, see Europa, 'Passenger rights', online at: http://europa.eu/youreurope/citizens/travel/passenger-rights/index_en.htm

same high standard is to be projected, and thus effectively exported, externally:

> EU's external aviation policy and initiatives should promote and defend European interests more vigorously and continue to promote and share European values, standards and best practices on a collaborative basis. It should aim at the highest possible standards to be applied in the industry, through regulatory cooperation and convergence. These goals will not be achieved without coordinated EU-level negotiations with key partners.[17]

Yet, a major hurdle to the liberalization of aviation globally has been the common practice of incorporating ownership and control clauses in air services agreements, as mentioned earlier.[18] According to the European Commission,

> ownership and control regimes remain fundamentally stuck where they were negotiated in 1944 in the Chicago Convention. The difficulties encountered as a result of current ownership and control provisions are significant and require negotiations with partner countries and highly complex governance structures. Inevitably this means that the full benefits of consolidation cannot be achieved. Alliance members cooperate more and more closely to offer customers a seamless integrated global multi-hub network service.[19]

On the same topic the European Commission published a brief progress report in 2016:

> Just three months after its adoption by the European Commission, the Aviation Strategy is starting to deliver its first results. The Council has yesterday authorised the European Commission to open negotiations with China and Japan in view of concluding Bilateral Air Safety Agreements (BASA). Such agreements enhance air safety worldwide and contribute to the global competitiveness of the European aviation industry by cutting red-tape and facilitating exports.[20]

Thus we can understand why the EU has set the negotiation of new external aviation agreements with its 'global partners' as a key priority.[21]

17 COM (2012) 556 final.

18 See also Isabelle Lelieur, *Law and Policy of Substantial Ownership and Effective Control of Airlines* (Ashgate 2003).

19 COM (2012) 556 final.

20 European Commission, 'Aviation: EU to launch negotiations with China and Japan for new safety agreements' (Transport 2016), online at: http://ec.europa.eu/transport/modes/air/news/2016-03-08-china-japan-safety-agreements_en.htm

21 European Commission, 'External Aviation Policy: Global Partners – Transport', online at: http://ec.europa.eu/transport/modes/air/international_aviation/external_aviation_policy/global_partners_en.htm

Competition rules

This section briefly outlines the EU competition rules to evidence the EU's clear, *ex ante* rules relating to agreements between undertakings and prohibited abuse of dominance on a relevant market.

Articles 101 and 102 of the Treaty on the Functioning of the European Union (TFEU) are the two most important competition policy provisions and form the main body of European competition law.[22] Article 101(1) TFEU prohibits

> all agreements between undertakings, decisions by associations of undertaking and concerted practices which may affect trade between Member States and which have as their objective or effect the prevention, restriction or distortion of competition within the common market, and in particular those which:
>
> a) directly or indirectly fix purchase or selling prices or any other trading conditions;
> b) limit or control production, markets, technical development, or investment;
> c) share markets or sources of supply;
> d) apply dissimilar conditions to equivalent transactions with other trading parties, thereby placing them at a competitive disadvantage;
> e) make the conclusion of contracts subject to acceptance by the other parties of supplementary obligations which, by their nature or according to commercial usage, have no connection with the subject of such contracts.[23]

Such agreements are void under Article 101(2) TFEU. However, Article 101(3) TFEU provides that the provisions of Article 101(1) may be declared 'inapplicable' if the agreement, decision or concerted practice

> contributes to improving the production or distribution of goods or to promoting technical or economic progress, while allowing consumers a fair share of the resulting benefit, and which does not:
>
> a) impose on the undertakings concerted restrictions which are not indispensable to the attainment of these objectives;
> b) afford such undertakings the possibility of eliminating competition in respect of a substantial part of the products in question.[24]

22 Alongside the EC Merger Regulation: Council Regulation (EC) 193/2004 of 20 January 2004 on the control of concentrations between undertakings (the EC Merger Regulation) [2004] OJ L24/2.

23 TFEU (n 14) Title VII (ex. Title VI), s1, Art 101(1) (a–e).

24 TFEU, Art 101(3) (a–b).

It should also be noted that the European Council conferred on the European Commission the power to grant exemptions from Article 101(1) TFEU prohibitions.[25]

Article 101(1) TFEU prohibits unjustifiable price-fixing as incompatible with the internal market of the EU; this applies to all industries.[26] In the case of *Ahmed Saeed*,[27] the Court of Justice of the European Union confirmed that price-fixing agreements between airlines were automatically void unless they had been granted an exemption under Article 101(3). 'The *Ahmed Saeed* case is quite an important one in this area as it raised by the Court the need to distinguish between price-fixing and a "consultation" on tariffs to determine application of ex. Article 81(3) TEC (now Article 101(3) TFEU) to the actual circumstances in the industry'.[28] In short,

> Consultations on tariffs or fares are common, worldwide practice in the airline industry. These consultations are held on a bilateral or multilateral 'conference' basis. The major international conference for scheduling and fares is held biannually (June and November) under the framework of IATA. 'As many as 300 airline companies are members of the association and these represent more than 98 percent of all international scheduled air traffic'.[29]

However, it should be noted that the European Commission decided[30] to end a previous block exemption under Article 101(3) TFEU for IATA tariff conferences. 'As a result, IATA and individual carriers must now ensure that their agreements are compatible with the EU competition rules'.[31]

25 Regulation 17 [1959–1962] OJ Spec. Ed. 87, Art 9; Noting the consumer welfare benefits arising from e.g. airline alliances operating under this exception and also U.S. antitrust immunity. See Truxal, *Competition and Regulation in the Airline Industry*.

26 Truxal, *Competition and Regulation in the Airline Industry*; TFEU Art 101(1)(a).

27 Case 66/86, *Ahmed Saeed Flugreisen and Silver Line Reisebüro GmbH* v. *Zentrale zur Bekämpfung unlauteren Wettbewerbs E.V.* [1989] ECR 803, [1990] 4 CMLR 102, involving price-fixing. Travel agents obtained and sold tickets from outside their Member State at a discounted rate constituting abuse as there was no distinction between inter - national flights. The problem with this case was that there was at the time no implementing legislation to achieve applicability of Article 101(3) to the air transport sector within a Member State. This led to Council Regulation (EC) 411/2004 on the intra and extraterritorial powers of the Commission with respect to air transport ([2004] OJ L68).

28 Truxal, *Competition and Regulation in the Airline Industry* 75–76.

29 Ibid.; figures taken from the IATA website, www.iata.org/whatwedo/scheduling/schedules_conference.htm

30 See European Commission, 'Competition: Commission ends block exemption for IATA passenger tariff conferences for routes between the EU and non-EU countries', Press release IP/07/973, Brussels (29 June 2007).

31 Truxal, *Competition and Regulation in the Airline Industry*, 92–93.

Article 102 TFEU provides that 'any abuse by one or more undertakings in a dominant position within the common market or in a substantial part of it shall be prohibited as incompatible with the common market insofar as it may affect trade between Member States'.[32] It should be noted that this Article includes no provision for exemptions.[33]

State aid

Whilst it is not the aim of this book to critique or discuss EU State aid legislation and case law in detail, it is nevertheless important to note the origins and current status of this area of EU law. The historical context of the State subsidies and the development of 'subsidy control' coincide conveniently with the same post-First World War timeframe captured by this book.

Locating the origins of subsidies generally, Piernas López tell us: 'Protectionism and subsidies increased substantially with the beginning of the First World War, and even more so in the aftermath of the Great War. Massive subsidies were granted for multiple purposes, including commercial credit, shipbuilding, rail and air transport, exports, and housing'.[34] After the Second World War,

> subsidies in Europe achieved the dimension that they still have today. Several reasons justify this development; the need to rebuild national industries and infrastructure after the War, the influence of the Marshall Plan, which required the establishment of a national distribution network of funds, different national planning experiences, and the ideological movement towards a more interventionist State model.[35]

In his work, Piernas López provides a definition of State subsidy and traces the evolution of the practice by way of comprehensive discussion and analysis. To sum up the European story, he says the

> EEC [European Economic Community] Treaty had therefore to be respectful to the economic sovereignty of Member States inasmuch as

32 TFEU, Title VII (ex. Title VI), s1, Art 102.

33 See for instance the divergent outcomes in the Virgin Atlantic/British Airways conflict over BA's granting of loyalty discounts to travel agents. The CJEU upheld the European Commission's decision that British Airways abused its dominance on the UK market for the purchase of travel agent services by rewarding loyalty (Commission Decision 2000/74 of 14 April 1999, OJ L30/1, 4 February 2004) while in the U.S. it was held that Virgin did not suffer harm (257 F.3d 256 (2nd Cir. 2001).

34 Juan Jorge Piernas López, *The Concept of State Aid Under EU Law: From Internal Market to Competition and Beyond* (Oxford University Press 2015) 24.

35 Ibid., 25.

> this sovereignty did not impinge upon one of the fundamental objectives of the EEC Treaty. In the same vein, the Rome Treaties were not meant to replace *national aid* by *European aid*. As a result, some criteria seemed necessary, even at the level of the definition of aid, to distinguish between general measures, to be tackled *ex-post*, from selective advantages, to be tackled *ex-ante*, and even among the latter in order to exclude those measures that were not liable to distort competition or trade. Finally, both the Report and the negotiations made clear that only the Commission could be entrusted with the task of deciding on the acceptability of State aids, as this decision could not be left to the partisan will of Member States.[36]

Under Articles 107 to 109 TFEU, the Commission has the power to deal with State aid that distorts or threatens to distort competition in the internal market.[37] Article 107(1) TFEU provides that:

> Save as otherwise provided in this Treaty, any aid granted by a Member State or through State resources in any form whatsoever which distorts or threatens to distort competition by favouring certain undertakings or the production of certain goods shall, in so far as it affects trade between Member States, be incompatible with the internal market.[38]

Thus State aid is a priori incompatible with the internal market. Whilst Article 107(1) TFEU does not define 'aid', the CJEU

> has clarified that this notion requires the following criteria to be met: First, there must be an intervention by the State or through State resources. Second, the intervention must be liable to affect trade between Member States. Third, it must confer an advantage on the recipient. Fourth, it must distort or threaten to distort competition. The Court of Justice has also clarified that the advantage conferred must be selective as it has to favour 'certain undertakings or the production of certain goods'. This article has not been modified since its introduction in the European Economic Community Treaty of 1957, save for the draftsman substituting the phrase 'internal market' in place of 'common market'.[39]

36 Ibid., 43 (emphasis added).

37 See also European Commission, 'State Aid procedures', online at: http://ec.europa.eu/competition/state_aid/overview/state_aid_procedures_en.html

38 TFEU Art 107(1); OJ C115/91, 9 May 2008.

39 Piernas López, *The Concept of State Aid Under EU Law* 3.

The EU has a comprehensive State aid regulatory regime.[40] State aid is tightly regulated and rules on unlawful interventions tend to be strictly enforced; firms are regularly ordered to pay back subsidies and favourable loans provided by the Member States in question.[41] Following implementation of the EU internal aviation market's final aviation 'liberalisation package' 1993, a wave of cases involving States aid granted by individual Member States to their flailing airlines include *Sabena*,[42] *Iberia*,[43] *Aer Lingus*,[44] *TAP Air Portugal*,[45] *Air France*,[46] *Olympic Airways*[47] and *Alitalia*.[48] For reference, a major case involving an airport is *Charleroi*.[49]

For policymakers and regulators in the EU, the challenge in this area has been to work towards a goal of competitive neutrality[50] while previously State-owned and controlled national flag-carriers of each Member State have been privatized and opened to foreign direct investment.

The injection of public money into private enterprises is always controversial, even if done or allegedly undertaken 'in the public interest'.[51] The EU takes a hard line on State aid vis-à-vis detailed legislation and guidelines, investigation and enforcement powers, adding up to a very high overall level of scrutiny. The European Commission has published three sets of specialized guidance for granting of State aid to airports and airlines in 1994,

40 Noting that there have also been temporary rules established in response to the global economic and financial crisis, but not in transport. See European Commission, 'State Aid control', online at: http://ec.europa.eu/competition/state_aid/legislation/temporary.html

41 For a detailed examination of State aid to airlines and airports in the EU, see Truxal, *Competition and Regulation in the Airline Industry* 93–102.

42 [1991] OJ L300/48.

43 European Commission, 'XXII Report on Competition Policy' (1993) 269.

44 Commission Decision 94/118/EC of 21 December 1993 concerning aid to be provided by the Irish government to the Aer Lingus group [1994] OJ L54/30.

45 Commission Decision 94/698/EC of 6 July 1994 concerning increase in capital, credit guarantees and an exemption in favour of TAP [1994] OJ L279.

46 Commission Decision 94/653/EC of 27 July 1994 concerning the notified capital increase of Air France [1994] OJ 254.

47 Commission Decision 94/696/EC of 7 October 1994 on the aid granted by Greece to Olympic Airways [1994] OJ L273.

48 Case C26/2008 (ex. NN31/2008) – *Prêt de 300 millions d'euros à ALITALIA* ('Recovery of 300 million Euros from Alitalia'), 12 November 2008.

49 [2003] OJ C18/03. The Walloon Region of Belgium granted by private law contract 'infrastructure and operational aid'. In a landmark decision, some of the aid was declared compatible. Aid for the Dublin–Charleroi route, reduced fees at Charleroi for Ryanair and others and one-shot incentives for new routes were declared incompatible with the competition rules.

50 OECD, 'Competitive Neutrality: Maintaining a level playing field between public and private business' (2012), online at: www.oecd.org/competition/competitiveneutrality maintainingalevelplayingfieldbetweenpublicandprivatebusiness.htm

51 See Mike Feintuck, 'Regulatory Rationales Beyond the Economic: In Search of the Public Interest', in Robert Baldwin, Martin Cave and Martin Lodge (eds), *The Oxford Handbook of Regulation* (Oxford University Press, 2010).

2005 and 2014.[52] The *2014 Guidelines,* the most comprehensive to date, replace all previous versions. The change in the titles of each set of the above guidelines reflects the evolution of EU's State aid policy in the aviation sector with respect to airports and airlines.

In effect, the *2014 Guidelines* distinguish between start-up aid and operating aid. Whilst initial, start-up aid may be permitted on the basis that this form of injection tends to provide benefits to regional airports and to encourage airlines to begin operations on markets yet untested, operating aid is viewed as a general rule as a distortive form of aid, which may only be permitted under very exceptional circumstances. Small, regional airports may receive operating aid during the period of transition from public to private financing as a case in point. The intended outcome is that once private finance is in place to support regional airports, public funding will in time become less necessary. For airlines, start-up aid may be provided during and beyond this transitional period, particularly on new and untested routes to mitigate the risk for airlines to some degree. Typically, operating on any new route first requires a sound business case to be prepared, but in untested markets this will be quite difficult to establish.

The *2014 Guidelines* set out the European Commission's latest approach to assessing compatibility of aid to airports and airlines vis-à-vis a series of so-called 'compatibility conditions'. For the purposes of the current study, we consider only the conditions on State aid to airlines. The four relevant compatibility conditions are:

(1) contribution to a well-defined objective of common interest;[53]
(2) need for State intervention;
(3) appropriateness of the aid measure and;
(4) incentive effect.

Subject to fulfilment of the above conditions, State aid may be provided to airlines amounting to no more than 50 per cent of eligible costs for a maximum of three years (the start-up period). Member States must make all injection plans public, and the aid is not to be combined with other forms of support.[54] The *2014 Guidelines* thus aim to create an open and transparent system of monitoring, in which there is a duty on each Member State also to keep records.

52 See European Commission, 'Community guidelines on the application of Articles 92 and 93 of the EC Treaty and Article 61 of the EEA Agreement to State aids in the aviation sector', [1994] OJ C350/5; European Commission, 'Guidelines on financing of airports and start-up aid to airlines departing from regional airports', Commission Communication of 9 December 2005, [2005] OJ C312/1; and European Commission, 'Guidelines on State aid to airports and airlines', Communication from the Commission of 4 April 2014, [2014] OJ C99/03.

53 This refers to aid of social dimension under TFEU, Art 107(2)(A).

54 This takes into account tax relief or exemption rulings, noting that State aid is interpreted widely here.

Consumer protection

For most jurisdictions, it can be said that air passengers, carriers and shippers are addressed at international law under the Convention for the Unification of Certain Rules for International Carriage by Air 1999, commonly known as the Montreal Convention. The Montreal Convention has been ratified by 103 of the 191 Member States of the International Civil Aviation Organi - zation (ICAO) plus the EU (including all of the 28 Member States of the EU). The Montreal Convention modernizes and consolidates the Warsaw Convention 1929.[55]

The first key provision for our purposes is Article 17(2) of the Montreal Convention on air carrier liability in the event of lost or damaged baggage. It provides:

> The carrier is liable for damage sustained in case of destruction or loss of, or of damage to, checked baggage upon condition only that the event which caused the destruction, loss or damage took place on board the aircraft or during any period within which the checked baggage was in the charge of the carrier. However, the carrier is not liable if and to the extent that the damage resulted from the inherent defect, quality or vice of the baggage. In the case of unchecked baggage, including personal items, the carrier is liable if the damage resulted from its fault or that of its servants or agents.

The relevant limits to air carrier liability are set out in Article 22 of the Montreal Convention.

If the passenger and/or his baggage are delayed, or a shipper's cargo is delayed, the injured party may have a claim under Article 19 of the Montreal Convention:

> The carrier is liable for damage occasioned by delay in the carriage by air of passengers, baggage or cargo. Nevertheless, the carrier shall not be liable for damage occasioned by delay if it proves that it and its servants and agents took all measures that could reasonably be required to avoid the damage or that it was impossible for it or them to take such measures.

The Contracting Parties to the Montreal Convention also agree that the international law is to operate in exclusivity. Article 29 of the Montreal Convention provides:

55 Convention for the Unification of Certain Rules Relating to International Carriage by Air, as amended and supplemented by The Hague Protocol of 28 September 1955, the Guadalajara Convention of 18 September 1961, the Guatemala Protocol of 8 March 1971, and the four additional Montreal Protocols of 25 September 1975 ('the Warsaw Convention', originally signed at Warsaw on 12 October 1929).

> In the carriage of passengers, baggage and cargo, any action for damages, however founded, whether under this Convention or in contract or in tort or otherwise, can only be brought subject to the conditions and such limits of liability as are set out in this Convention without prejudice to the question as to who are the persons who have the right to bring suit and what are their respective rights. In any such action, punitive, exemplary or any other non-compensatory damages shall not be recoverable.

In practice, the exclusivity of the Montreal Convention has been called into question in the EU, where regional legislation provides rights to air passengers via 'direct effect'. In fact, aviation was the first sector in the EU to benefit from passengers' rights legislation following Directive 90/314/EEC ('the Package Travel Directive')[56] and Regulation (EEC) 295/91 ('the Denied Boarding Regulation'),[57] the latter of which was repealed by Regulation (EC) 261/2004. Subsequently, the EU created a series of passenger rights for other modes of transport.[58] Since it came into force in early 2005, the EU law on air passenger rights has been topical and contentious.[59]

According to Recital 1 of Regulation 261/2004: 'Action by the Community in the field of air transport should aim, among other things, at ensuring a high level of protection for passengers. Moreover, full account should be taken of the requirements of consumer protection in general'.[60] This is also consistent with Articles 12 and 169 TFEU on

56 Council Directive 90/314/EEC of 13 June 1990 on travel, package holidays and package tours [1990] OJ L158/59; see also 'Commission Working Document on the Council Directive 90/314/EEC of 13 June 1990 on travel, package holidays and package tours', Brussels, 26 July 2007. The Package Travel Directive was one of eight directives covered by the 'Review of the Consumer Acquis'. In light of the outcome of the consultation on the Green Paper and the input to the consultation in this working document, the Commission will consider the need for a reform of the Directive.

57 Regulation (EEC) 295/91 of 4 February 1991 establishing common rules for a denied-boarding compensation system in scheduled air transport [1991] OJ L36/5.

58 EU passenger rights legislation also exists for sea/waterways, coach transport and rail travel.

59 For a comprehensive study on air passenger rights, see Michal Bobek and Jeremias Prassl (eds), *Air Passenger Rights: Ten Years On* (Bloomsbury 2016).

60 Regulation (EC) 261/2004 of the European Parliament and of the Council of 11 February 2004 establishing common rules on compensation and assistance to passengers in the event of denied boarding and of cancellation or long delay of flights, and repealing Regulation (EEC) 295/91 [2004] OJ L46/1.

promoting interests of consumers and ensuring a high level of consumer protection.[61]

Regulation 261/2004 established a set of minimum rights for air passengers, complementing, according to the Court, existing international law on air passenger rights under the 1999 Montreal Convention,[62] which entered into force in relation to the EU in 2004.[63] The Montreal Convention features an unlimited liability regime for carriers on injury or death of passengers. Regulation 261/2004 goes a step further to provide more adequately for protection in the case of denied boarding (over-booking), delays and cancellations, and to ensure that compensation payments are 'standardised and immediate'.[64]

The following is an abridged list of what are the relevant provisions of Regulation 261/2004:

- definitions (Article 2);
- scope: 'flight' (Article 3);
- denied boarding (Article 4);
- cancellation (Article 5);
- reimbursement: a gratis return flight to the point of departure or transport by some other means to their destination (Article 8);
- compensation (Article 7) (staggered; from EUR 250 for flights of 1500 kilometres or less, up to EUR 600 for flights of over 3500 kilometres);
- 'Right to care' (Article 9) (meals, refreshments, means of telecommunication and hotel accommodation if necessary);
- partial compensation in the event of downgrading (Article 10).

61 Other EU laws relating to air carrier liability include Council Regulation (EC) 2027/97 of 9 October 1997 on air carrier liability in the event of accidents [1997] OJ L285/1, 17 October 1997; Regulation (EC) 785/2004 of the European Parliament and of the Council of 21 April 2004 on insurance requirements for air carriers and aircraft operators [2004] OJ L138/1, 30 April 2004; Regulation (EC) 2111/2005 of the European Parliament and of the Council of 14 December 2005 on the establishment of a Community list of air carriers subject to an operating ban within the Community and on informing air transport passengers of the identity of the operating air carrier, and repealing Article 9 of Directive 2004/36/EC, [2005] OJ L344/15, 27 December 2005; Regulation (EC) 1107/2006 of the European Parliament and of the Council of 5 July 2006 concerning the rights of disabled persons and persons with reduced mobility when travelling by air [2006] OJ L204/1, 26 July 2006; Commission Implementing Regulation (EU) 295/2012 of 3 April 2012 amending Regulation (EC) 474/2006 establishing the Community list of air carriers which are subject to an operating ban within the Community[2012] OJ L98/13, 4 April 2012.

62 Convention for the unification of certain rules for international carriage by air (Montreal, 28 May 1999).

63 Council Decision 2001/539/EC of 5 April 2001 on the conclusion by the European Community of the Convention for the unification of certain rules for international carriage by air ('the Montreal Convention') [2001] OJ L194/38.

64 Case C-344/04, *The Queen on the Application of International Air Transport Association, European Low Fares Airline Association* v. *Department for Transport* [2006] ECR I-403.

The CJEU has on numerous occasions, in response to references made by national courts of Member States, interpreted the legislation's meaning and applicability. Nonetheless, the rights granted to air passengers under Regulation 261/2004 are, according to the CJEU, consistent with but additional to existing international law, in particular the Montreal Convention 1999.[65]

From the very start, critics from both sides – consumer groups and industry – have been vociferous in their concerns that the CJEU's interpretations of the rules, which at times appear to expand the scope of the Regulation and parliamentary intention, can be seen as lacking in certainty and therefore they promote confusion around air passenger rights and air carrier liability. The CJEU's varied interpretation and expanded jurisprudence have included such crucial matters as: compensation for flights cancelled owing to a 'technical failure'[66] or an airport strike,[67] or even following closure of airspace owing to the 'extraordinary circumstances' occasioned by a volcanic eruption;[68] time limits for passengers to bring claims;[69] the freedom to opt-in to flight cancellation insurance;[70] and more recently, air carrier liability for baggage containing personal property of one party checked in under another party's name;[71] and damage caused to an aircraft by mobile stairs.[72]

Recital 4 of Regulation 261/2004 provides: 'The Community should ... raise the standards of protection set by that Regulation both to strengthen

65 The CJEU have considered, for instance, the compatibility of passenger rights to compensation in the event of delay or cancellation of flights under the Common Rules with passenger rights under the Montreal Convention, whereby confirming its decision in Joined Cases C-581/10 and C-629/10, *Emeka Nelson, Bill Chinazo Nelson, Brian Cheimezie Nelson* v. *Deutsche Lufthansa AG* (C-581/10) and *The Queen, on the application of TUI Travel plc, British Airways plc, easyJet Airline Co. Ltd, International Air Transport Association* v. *Civil Aviation Authority* (C-629/10), 15 May 2012 (references for preliminary rulings). The CJEU's finding in *Sturgeon* was confirmed in Joined Cases *Nelson* and *TUI Travel and others*, 23 October 2012.

66 Case C-549/07, *Friederike Wallentin-Hermann* v. *Alitalia*, ECR 2008, P. I-11061, 2 December 2008; Case C-83/10, *Aurora Sousa Rodríguez and Others* v. *Air France SA*, 13 October 2011 (a preliminary ruling).

67 Case C-22/11, *Finnair Oyj* v. *Timy Lassooy*, 19 April 2012 (a preliminary reference).

68 Case C-12/11, *Denise McDonagh* v. *Ryanair Ltd*, 22 March 2012 (a preliminary reference).

69 Case C-139/11, *Joan Cuadrench Moré* v. *Koninklijke Luchtvaart Maatschappij NV (KLM)*, 22 November 2012 (a preliminary ruling).

70 Case C-112/11, *ebookers.com Deutschland GmbH* v. *Bundesverband der verbraucherzentralen und verbraucherverbände – verbraucherzentrale Bundesverband eV*, 19 July 2012 (a preliminary ruling). It should be noted that this case was brought on the interpretation of Regulation (EC) 1008/2008 of the European Parliament and of the Council of 24 September 2008 on common rules for the operation of air services in the Community [2008] OJ L293/3.

71 Case C-410/11, *Pedro Espada Sánchez and Others* v. *Iberia Líneas Aéreas de España SA*, 22 November 2012 (a preliminary ruling)

72 Case C-394/14, *Sandy Siewert and Others* v. *Condor Flugdienst GmbH*, 14 November 2014 (a preliminary ruling).

the rights of passengers and to ensure that air carriers operate under *harmonised* conditions in a liberalised market'.[73] There are serious challenges to this harmonization goal.[74]

The first challenge to Regulation 261/2004 arose early after its implementation in 2004, when the International Air Transport Association and the European Low Fares Airline Association each brought before the High Court of Justice of England and Wales, Queen's Bench Division (Administrative Court), judicial review proceedings against the UK Department for Transport relating to the implementation of Regulation 261/2004.[75]

In *IATA and ELFAA*, the two associations contested the validity of Regulation 261/2004 on a number of points covering Articles 5 to 7 of Regulation 261/2004. The CJEU confirmed the consistency of the Regulation with the Montreal Convention and, on examination, found no factors affecting the validity of Articles 5 to 7 of Regulation 261/2004. In this first-ever challenge to the Regulation, the CJEU thus rejected the arguments of IATA and ELFAA to the contrary.

The CJEU considered its interpretation of Regulation 261/2004 insofar as ensuring it did not conflict with the principles of proportionality, of an 'equitable balance of interests' referred to in the Montreal Convention[76] and of equal treatment and non-discrimination, or with Articles 16 and 17 of the Charter of Fundamental Rights of the European Union.[77] On equal treatment and non-discrimination, the CJEU held that Articles 5 to 7 of Regulation 261/2004 do not infringe the principle of equal treatment,[78] finding that 'different modes of transport, having regard to the manner in which they operate, the conditions governing their accessibility and the distribution of their networks, are not interchangeable as regards the conditions of their use'.[79] The CJEU held:

> Since the assistance and taking care of passengers envisaged by Article 6 of Regulation No 261/2004 in the event of a long delay to a flight constitute such *standardised and immediate compensatory measures*, they are not among those whose institution is regulated by the Convention. The system prescribed in Article 6 simply operates *at an earlier stage* than the system which results from the Montreal Convention.[80]

73 Recital 4, Regulation (EC) 261/2004 (60) (emphasis added).
74 Olena Bokareva, 'Air Passengers' Rights in the EU: International Uniformity versus Regional Harmonization' (2016) 41(1) *Air & Space Law* 3–24.
75 Case C-344/04, *The Queen on the Application of International Air Transport Association, European Low Fares Airline Association* v. *Department for Transport* [2006] ECR I-403.
76 Montreal Convention, Preamble.
77 [2000] C364/01, 18 December 2000.
78 *IATA and ELFAA* paras 93–99.
79 *IATA and ELFAA* para 96.
80 *IATA and ELFAA* para 46 (emphasis added).

In its *Emirates Airlines* judgment,[81] the CJEU gave a strict interpretation of the concept of a 'flight', which appears in Article 3(1) of Regulation 261/2004. In this case, the CJEU held that 'flight'

> must be interpreted as *not* applying to the case of an outward and return journey in which passengers who have originally departed from an airport located in the territory of a Member State to which the EC Treaty applies travel back to that airport on a flight from an airport located in a non-member country. The fact that the outward and return flights are the subject of a single booking has no effect on the interpretation of that provision.[82]

The *Emirates Airline* judgment clarifies that Regulation 261/2004 will apply to all passengers on flights departing from EU airports and passengers on flights departing from a third country for an EU airport, so long as compensation has not been provided by a third country and the airline in question is a Community Carrier.

In *Wallentin-Hermann*,[83] on reference from a Viennese Court, a family holding a confirmed booking on an Alitalia-operated flight from Vienna (Austria) to Brindisi (Italy) arrived at their destination four hours late owing to a 'complex engine defect in the turbine'. The defect was discovered the day before the flight and Alitalia was notified six hours before scheduled take-off. The family checked in on the day as normal but Alitalia cancelled the flight just five minutes prior to the scheduled departure. The CJEU offered a rigorous interpretation in *Wallentin-Hermann* of the exemption from the obligation to provide compensation and assistance to passengers in the event of cancellation caused by 'extraordinary circumstances' pursuant to Article 5(3) of Regulation 261/2004. The CJEU held that the words 'extraordinary circumstances' in Article 5(3) should be interpreted strictly: 'a technical problem in an aircraft which leads to the cancellation of a flight is *not* covered by the concept of "extraordinary circumstances"... unless that problem stems from events which, by their nature or origin, are *not inherent* in the normal exercise of the activity of the air carrier concerned *and* are beyond its actual control'.[84]

In other words, following *Wallentin-Hermann*, airlines may no longer rely on Article 5(3) 'exceptional circumstances' in the case of 'technical problems' that could have been avoided if all reasonable measures had been

81 Case C-173/07, *Emirates Airlines – Direktion für Deutschland* v. *Diether Shenkel*, ECR 2008, p. I-5237, 10 July 2008.

82 Ibid., para. 54.

83 *Friederike Wallentin-Hermann* v. *Alitalia.*

84 Ibid. (emphasis added); *See* Jochem Croon, 'Placing Wallentin-Hermann in Line with Continuing Airworthiness: A Possible Guide for Enforcers of EC Regulation 261/2004' (2011) 36(1) *Air and Space Law* 1–6.

taken. Technical problems which are normal or inherent in aviation will not exempt airlines; minimum maintenance will suffice as 'reasonable steps'.

Next came the CJEU judgment in the joined cases of *Sturgeon and Others*[85] and *Böck and Lepuschitz,* confirmed by the Grand Chamber of the CJEU in 2012 in *Nelson and Others.*[86] It is significant to note that *Sturgeon* was upheld by the Grand Chamber of the CJEU on appeal from the General Court.[87]

The facts in *Sturgeon and Others* were that Mr Sturgeon and his family booked a flight between Toronto (Canada) and Frankfurt (Germany) on airline Condor (registered in Germany). Following check-in, the flight was 'cancelled'. Affected passengers retrieved their checked baggage and were transported to a hotel. On the following day, passengers were returned to the airport, checked into another airline with same flight number as Condor and into different seats. The effect of all this was that the passengers arrived more than 25 hours late at Frankfurt. Condor argued the flight was not 'cancelled' but merely 'delayed', and thus Mr Sturgeon and others had no right of recourse under Regulation 261/2004. The case of *Böck and Lepuschitz* had similar facts. The passengers were delayed 22 hours in total. 'The background to *Sturgeon* was the airlines' tendency to not cancel long delayed flights but let passengers sit out the delay (in the *Sturgeon* cases twenty-two and twenty-five hours) in order to avoid having to pay them compensation under Articles 5 and 7 of the Regulation'.[88]

Important in both these cases was the concept of the passenger itinerary as evidence of *original* travel plans. In *Böck and Lepuschitz,* the Air France flight operated the aircraft it originally planned to use, appended the letter 'A' to the flight number, and the aircraft departed one day later than scheduled. Article 2(l) of Regulation 261/2004 provides a definition for 'cancellation': 'the non-operation of a flight which was previously planned and on which at least one place was reserved'. Thus, the flight was not 'cancelled' it was subject to a long delay. In *Sturgeon and Others,* the flight on which the passengers travelled in the end was not operated by Condor, though it had the same flight number, and seats were changed. In contrast to the Air France flight, the Condor flight was 'cancelled' according to the Article 2(l) definition of 'cancellation'.

The Court referred to its earlier judgment in *IATA and ELFAA,*[89] in which it also confirmed that the objective of Regulation 261/2004, 'is to strengthen protection for air passengers by redressing damage suffered by

85 Joined Cases C-402/07 and C-432/07, *Christopher Sturgeon and Others* v. *Condor Flugdienst GmbH* (C-402/07) and *Stefan Böck and Cornelia Lepuschitz* v. *Air France SA* (C-432/07), 19 November 2009 (a reference for preliminary rulings)

86 *Nelson and Others.*

87 In October 2012.

88 Cees van Dam, 'Air Passenger Rights after *Sturgeon*' (2011) 36(4/5) *Air and Space Law* 259–274, 259.

89 Ibid., paras 82, 85, 97 and 98.

them during air travel, [and that] situations covered by the regulation must be compared, in particular by reference to the type and extent of the various types of inconvenience and damage suffered by the passengers concerned'[90] to find ultimately that 'the situation of passengers whose flights are delayed should be compared with that of passengers whose flights are cancelled'.[91]

The CJEU thus interpreted Articles 5 to 7 of Regulation 261/2004 'as meaning that passengers whose flights are delayed may be treated, for the purposes of the application of the right to compensation, as passengers whose flights are cancelled'.[92] This cleared the way for the CJEU consequently to extend, on the principle of equal treatment, the Article 7 right to compensation, which applies to passengers on *cancelled* flights, to passengers on flights *delayed* for three hours or more, too, with the 'extraordinary circumstances' caveat, i.e. so long as the long delay was not 'caused by extraordinary circumstances which could not have been avoided even if all reasonable measures had been taken, namely circumstances beyond the actual control of the air carrier'.[93]

Crucially, the CJEU also ruled in *Sturgeon* that 'extraordinary circumstances' in Article 5(3) of Regulation 261/2004, in the absence of a clear definition or list in the legislation of circumstances that qualify for the exception, the phrase 'must be interpreted as meaning that a technical problem in an aircraft which leads to the cancellation or delay of a flight is not covered by the concept of "extraordinary circumstances" within the meaning of that provision, unless that problem stems from events which, by their nature or origin, are *not inherent in the normal exercise of the activity of the air carrier concerned and are beyond its actual control*'.[94]

Post-*Sturgeon*, whilst the position on cancellation and long delay has been clarified, it can be argued that the legislation remains ambiguous insofar as the Court's ruling on technical cancellations did not clarify it for an airline as it is perhaps rather difficult to define what is *inherent* in airline operations. Some scholars have commented that this is one case where airlines simply have to 'bite the bullet', but others boycotted the decision, at least at first.[95]

In the joined cases, *Nelson* and *TUI Travel and Others*,[96] the Amtsgericht Köln (Germany) and the High Court of Justice (England and Wales) sought clarification concerning the scope of the CJEU's Fourth Chamber's judgment in *Sturgeon and Others*.[97]

90 Ibid., para 49.
91 Ibid., para 50.
92 Ibid., para 50.
93 Ibid., para 50.
94 Ibid., para 50 (emphasis added).
95 See Bobek and Prassl (eds), *Air Passenger Rights*.
96 *Nelson and Others*.
97 *Sturgeon and Others*.

In the first of the two joined cases, *Nelson*, the dispute between passengers and the airline Lufthansa arose following a delay to the passengers' flight of more than 24 hours. In the second case, *TUI Travel*, the applicants, TUI Travel, British Airways, easyJet Airline and the International Air Transport Association (IATA) brought proceedings before the UK courts 'following the Civil Aviation Authority's refusal of their request not to impose on them an obligation to compensate passengers whose flights are delayed. That independent regulator, responsible for enforcing aviation regulation in the United Kingdom, had stated that it was bound to give effect to the ruling in *Sturgeon and Others*'.[98]

The airlines argued that *Sturgeon and Others* is 'inconsistent' in two respects: (1) with the *IATA and ELFAA* judgment;[99] and (2) with the Montreal Convention in terms of the 'standardised and immediate measures'. In response, the CJEU confirmed firstly in *Nelson* and *TUI Travel and Others* its previous ruling in *Sturgeon and Others* that passengers who have been subject to a long delay may[100] be compensated,[101] reiterating the principle of equal treatment.

Secondly, the CJEU clarified that there is no tension between the Montreal Convention and Regulation 261/2004. The Court referred to its earlier decision *IATA and ELFAA*, in which it found that nothing in the Montreal Convention indicates an intention by the Convention's authors

> to shield air carriers from any form of intervention other than those laid down by those provisions, in particular action which could be envisaged by the public authorities to redress, in a standardised and immediate manner, the damage that is constituted by the inconvenience that delay in the carriage of passengers by air causes, without the passengers having to suffer the inconvenience inherent in the bringing of actions for damages before the courts.[102]

98 CJEU, 'Judgment in Joined Cases C-581/10 *Nelson and Others* v. *Deutsche Lufthansa* AG and C-629/10 *TUI Travel and Others* v. *Civil Aviation Authority*' 23 October 2012) Press release No 135/12, available online: http://curia.europa.eu/jcms/upload/docs/application/pdf/2012-10/cp120135en.pdf, 1.

99 *IATA and ELFAA*.

100 Air passengers have the Art 7 of Regulation 261/2004 right to compensation where a flight is delayed by three hours or more unless that delay is the result of 'extraordinary circumstances'. See Recital 15 and Art 5(3) of Regulation 261/2004, by way of derogation from the provisions of Art 5(1) and the CJEU's interpretation in Cases C-294/10, *Andrejs Eglītis and Edvards Ratnieks* v. *Latvijas Republikas Ekonomikas ministrija*, 12 May 2011, and C-549/07 *Wallentin-Hermann* as to what should constitute 'extraordinary circumstances'.

101 *Nelson and Others* para 39.

102 Ibid.; references for a preliminary ruling under Article 267 TFEU from the Amtsgericht Köln (Germany) and the High Court of Justice of England and Wales, Queen's Bench Division (Administrative Court) (United Kingdom), made by decisions of 3 November and 10 August 2010 respectively, received at the Court on 13 and 24 December 2010, in the proceedings *Nelson and Others* para 46.

It should also be noted that although the questions referred related to Article 6 'standardised and immediate measures', the Court 'did not rule out that other measures' such as Article 7 compensation, 'may fall outside the scope of the Montreal Convention'.[103]

Momentously, the CJEU also held that 'loss of time', as it had examined previously in *Sturgeon and Others*,[104] 'constitutes an inconvenience' as covered by Regulation 261/2004, which must be redressed vis-à-vis compensation as provided for in the Regulation.[105] The Court said, 'it should be made clear that, like the inconveniences referred to in *IATA and ELFAA*, a loss of time cannot be categorised as "damage occasioned by delay" within the meaning of Article 19 of the Montreal Convention, and, for that reason, it falls outside the scope of Article 29 of that convention'.[106]

Namely, as Article 19 of the Montreal Convention provides:

> The carrier is liable for damage occasioned by delay in the carriage by air of passengers, baggage or cargo. Nevertheless, the carrier shall not be liable for *damage occasioned by delay* if it proves that it and its servants and agents took all measures that could reasonably be required to avoid the damage or that it was impossible for it or them to take such measures. (emphasis added)

Whilst the phrase 'damage occasioned by delay' is not defined in the Montreal Convention, Article 22 sets out the upper limit to consequential damage. It would seem *prima facie* that damage occasioned by delay would include the cost of toiletries, clothing and so on, rather than the 'inconvenience' associated with loss of time.

All the same, according to the CJEU, Article 19 of the Montreal Convention 'implies, in particular, that the damage arises as a result of a delay, that there is a causal link between the delay and the damage and that the damage is individual to passengers depending on the various losses sustained by them',[107] whereas the obligation for an air carrier to pay compensation under Regulation 261/2004

> does not arise from each actual delay, but only from a delay which entails a loss of time equal to or in excess of three hours in relation to the time of arrival originally scheduled … [and] whereas the extent of the delay is normally a factor increasing the likelihood of greater damage, the *fixed compensation* awarded under that regulation remains unchanged in that regard, since the duration of the actual delay in excess of three hours is

103 *Nelson and Others* para 47.
104 Ibid., paras 52, 61.
105 Ibid., para 48.
106 Ibid., paras 49, 55.
107 Ibid., para 50.

> not taken into account in calculating the amount of compensation payable under Article 7.[108]

Therefore the obligation to pay compensation is compatible with Article 29 of the Montreal Convention regarding basis of claims.[109] Coincidentally, it is worth nothing that the right to care obligation under Article 9 of Regulation 261/2004 does operate at an earlier stage than the Montreal Convention.[110]

Thus, in *Nelson* and *TUI Travel and Others*, the CJEU held that the requirement to compensate passengers is consistent with the Montreal Convention since 'the *loss of time* inherent in a flight delay constitutes an inconvenience which is not governed by the Montreal Convention. Consequently, the obligation to compensate passengers whose flights are delayed falls outside the scope of that convention, but remains ***additional*** to the system for damages laid down by it'.[111]

The CJEU recognized that the obligation on air carriers to pay compensation for long delays entails financial consequences. Nonetheless it was of the view that 'those consequences cannot be considered disproportionate to the aim of ensuring a high level of protection for air passengers'.[112] The Court went on to reiterate, citing the telecoms case of *Vodafone and Others*:[113] 'The importance of the objective of consumer protection, which includes the protection of air passengers, [which] may justify even substantial negative economic consequences for certain economic operators'.[114] And it stated finally that the provision is consistent with the principle of 'equitable balance of interests' referred to in the last paragraph of the preamble to the Montreal Convention, insofar as the 'standardised and immediate compensatory measures', which are provided for in Regulation 261/2004, 'include the obligation to provide care to passengers whose flight has been cancelled, [and] are not among those whose institution is governed by the Montreal Convention'.[115]

In *McDonagh*[116] the CJEU reiterated, referring to previous case law,[117] that air carriers are exempted from the obligation to pay Article 7 compensation when exceptional circumstances arise, but a passenger's Article 9 right to care remains in any case.[118] The CJEU ruled that Article 5 of Regulation 261/2004 'must be interpreted as meaning that circumstances such as the closure of part of European airspace as a result of the eruption of the Eyjafjallajökull

108 Ibid., para 54 (emphasis added).
109 Ibid., para 56.
110 See *Wallentin-Hermann* para 32 and *Nelson and Others* para 57.
111 CJEU, 'Judgment', 2 (emphasis added).
112 *Nelson and Others* para 76.
113 Case C-58/08 *Vodafone and Others* [2010] ECR I-4999, paras 53 and 69.
114 *Nelson and Others* para 81.
115 *McDonagh* para 52 referring e.g. to *Wallentin-Hermann* para 32.
116 *McDonagh*.
117 *Wallentin-Hermann* para 18 and *Nelson and Others* para 72.
118 *McDonagh*.

volcano constitute "extraordinary circumstances" within the meaning of that regulation which *do not release* air carriers from their obligation laid down in Articles 5(1)(b) and 9 of the regulation to provide care',[119] effectively for as long as the circumstances persist. However, the 'limit' of reimbursement shall be as is 'in the light of the specific circumstances of each case, proved necessary, appropriate and reasonable to make up for the shortcomings of the air carrier in the provision of care to that passenger, a matter which is for the national court to assess'.[120]

In *Timy Lassooy*[121] the Court reiterated that 'extraordinary circumstances' may relate only to 'a particular aircraft on a particular day' rather than the effect of an earlier flight on another. The CJEU held that the concept of 'denied boarding' in Articles 2(j) and 4 of Regulation 261/2004 'must be interpreted as relating not only to cases where boarding is denied because of overbooking but also to those where boarding is denied on other grounds, such as *operational reasons*', as in the present case.[122]

In *Sánchez*,[123] the CJEU interpreted Articles 17 and 22 of the Montreal Convention,[124] in which air carrier liability for the loss of or damage to passenger's baggage is capped at 1131 special drawing rights (SDRs) per person, not per item. In this case, the passengers, Mr Espada Sánchez, Ms Oviedo Gonzáles and their two children, both minors, boarded a flight from Barcelona (Spain) to Paris (France) operated by Iberia. The baggage of the family of four was packed into two suitcases, which were irretrievably lost after check-in.[125]

The applicants argued the application of Articles 17(2) and 22(2) of the Montreal Convention. In Article 22(2) of the Montreal Convention, it reads:

> In the carriage of baggage, the liability of the carrier in the case of destruction, loss, damage or delay is limited to 1000 Special Drawing Rights for each passenger unless the passenger has made, at the time when the checked baggage was handed over to the carrier, a special declaration of interest in delivery at destination and has paid a supplementary sum if the case so requires. In that case the carrier will be liable to pay a sum not exceeding the declared sum, unless it proves that the

119 Ibid., para 34.
120 Ibid., para 51.
121 *Finnair Oyj* v. *Timy Lassooy*.
122 Ibid. (emphasis added).
123 *Sánchez and Others*.
124 All EU Member States are signatories and the EU acceded to the Convention by Council Decision 2001/539. Substantive provisions of the Montreal Convention were adopted in Council Regulation (EC) 2027/97 as amended by Council Regulation (EC) 889/2002 on air carrier liability in the event of accidents [2002] OJ L140/2.
125 *Sánchez and Others* para 13.

sum is greater than the passenger's actual interest in delivery at destination.[126]

Article 3(3) of the Montreal Convention provides: 'The carrier shall deliver to the passenger a baggage identification tag for each piece of checked baggage'. The CJEU held this could not be relied upon to support a contrary interpretation.[127]

What is significant about *Sánchez*, according to Prassl, is that the Court's 'assertion of jurisdiction to interpret the substantive rules of the Montreal Convention of 1999 presents a departure from the existing hybrid approach to the regulation of airline liability resulting from contracts of carriage by air, where a single regime is independently interpreted and applied by national courts'.[128]

As Regulation 261 applies to all flights operated by Community (or Union) carriers and to flights departing from an EU airport operated by non-EU carriers, the level of air passenger rights on flights to the EU are inconsistent. If both Regulation 261 and the Montreal Convention apply to a particular flight, which they often do, it is clear from the above discussion that, by placing the onus on the airline in the event of an unforeseen event, the EU law provides a significantly higher level of consumer protection and *prima facie* quicker access to assistance, compensation and rebooking. If only the Montreal Convention applies to the flight, the claimant must first have a founded claim to avail himself of his rights at international law.

On top of this, as we have seen from the interaction between EU law and international law in the area of passenger rights and lost baggage, there is significant room for interpretation of the law by national courts. Crucial in today's competitive business climate, there is also concern amongst EU carriers that this imbalance creates a disadvantageous situation in terms of airline liability, and the Regulation should therefore be extended to apply to all flights to and from the EU irrespective of the airline's flag of registration. In response to airlines' concerns around the cost of compliance with Regulation 261, a major reform including more than 500 legisative amendments was proposed in March 2013.[129] Work is ongoing in this

126 The limit now stands at SDR 1131, which is roughly equivalent to USD1600. Interestingly, Art 22(5) provides limited liability where fault is presumed, unlimited liability where fault is proved.

127 Jeremias Prassl, 'Case C-410/11 Pedro Sanchez v. Iberia: Shared Baggage, Single Interpretation' (*Eutopia law*, 3 December 2012), online at: https://eutopialaw.com/2012/12/03/case-c-41011-pedro-sanchez-v-iberia-shared-baggage-single-interpretation/; see also Bokareva, 'Air Passengers' Rights in the EU'.

128 Prassl, 'Case C-410/11 Pedro Sanchez v. Iberia'.

129 European Council, 'Strengthening air passenger rights in the EU', online at: www.consilium.europa.eu/en/policies/air-passenger-rights/

area.[130] This book returns to consumer protection in the context of successful development by ICAO of global core principles for national and regional air passenger rights regimes.

Case study: The Gulf (United Arab Emirates and Qatar)

Next we consider the civil aviation sectors in the Gulf States of United Arab Emirates and Qatar. The UAE is a federation of six Emirates (Abu Dhabi, Dubai, Sharjah, Umm al-Quwain, Fujairah and Ajman), established formally in December 1971 when the long-standing British–Trucial Sheikhdoms treaty expired allowing for full independence.[131] The Emirate of Qatar declared its independence from Britain as an independent State in September of the same year.[132]

Dubai International Airport began operations in 1960; Abu Dhabi opened in 1969. Relatively small-scale operations lasted until about the early 1990s, since which time the airports have serviced routes to numerous destinations with additional aircraft acquired by the two 'local' carriers, Emirates and Etihad, respectively.[133] In recent years, the airports of Dubai, Abu Dhabi and Doha have announced ambitious plans for expansion. Much work has already been undertaken to place these airports at the top of the global list for good customer service and high passenger numbers.[134] There has also been academic research published on various aspects of the rise of

130 One issue holding up the process is the question of application of the proposed new regulation to Gibraltar.

131 U.S. Department of State, 'United Arab Emirates', Background Notes Series (online) (Washington: Superintendent of Documents, 29 December 2011).

132 For a good discussion on the legal system of Qatar, see Ahmed Aly Khedr, 'A Guide to Qatar's Legal System' (GlobaLex, New York University, July 2009), available online at: www.nyulawglobal.org/globalex/Qatar.html; for legal scholarship related specifically to Qatar in this area, see J. E. Peterson, 'Qatar and the World: Branding for a Micro-State' (2006) 60(4) *Middle East Journal* 732–748.

133 Nadia Khan, 'Historical Overview: The 40-year Rise of UAE Aviation', *Arabian Supply Chain* (7 Feb 2012), available online at: www.arabiansupplychain.com/article-6943-historical-overview-the-40-year-rise-of-uae-aviation/4/.

134 For a critique on the achievability of these plans, see Marion Murel and Frankie O'Connell, 'Potential for Abu Dhabi, Doha and Dubai Airports to Reach their Traffic Objectives' (2011) 1 *Research in Transportation Business & Management* 36–46.

the Gulf carriers on the global market,[135] including the development of the likes of Dubai from a regional hub to a tourist destination.[136]

For the purposes of this study, we examine the regulatory environment in the UAE and Qatar in light of the fact that Emirates Airlines and Etihad Airlines are each 100 per cent State-owned, and Qatar Airways is 50 per cent State-owned.[137]

United Arab Emirates: competition law

In comparison to EU competition law, as regards Articles 101–102 TFEU, it would appear that the United Arab Emirates have enacted legislation that introduces competition regulations with similar requirements. The relevant legislation is Federal Law No. 4 2012 on the Regulation of Competition.[138] Article 5 of Federal Law No. 4 prohibits restrictive agreements; it provides:

> 1. Agreements which have as their subject or objective the abuse, restriction or prevention of competition shall be prohibited, in particular the agreements that aim to:
>   a. fixing, directly or indirectly, purchase or sale prices of goods or services by causing increase, reduction, or fixing of prices, thereby adversely affecting Competition
>   b. determining the terms and conditions of sale, purchase, or performance of services, or any similar transaction.
>   c. collusion in bids or proposals in tenders, practices, and other supply offers.
>   d. freezing or limiting production, development, distribution or marketing, and other investment aspects.
>   e. conspiracy not to purchase from certain organization or organizations, limiting sale or supply to certain organization or organizations, and preventing or obstructing its/their ability to carry out its/their business.

135 John F. O'Connell, 'The Rise of the Arabian Gulf Carriers: An Insight into the Business Model of Emirates Airline' (2011) 17(6) *Journal of Air Transport Management* 339–346; Wolfgang Grimme, 'The Growth of Arabian Airlines from a German Perspective: A Study of the Impacts of New Air Services to Asia' (2011) 17(6) *Journal of Air Transport Management* 333–338; S. Nataraja and A. Al-Aali, 'The Exceptional Performance Strategies of Emirates Airlines' (2011) 21(5) *Competitiveness Review* 471–486; Murel and O'Connell, 'Potential for Abu Dhabi, Doha and Dubai Airports to Reach their Traffic Objectives'.

136 Guilherme Lohmann *et al.*, 'From Hub to Tourist Destination: An Explorative Study of Singapore and Dubai's Aviation-Based Transformation' (2009) 15(5) *Journal of Air Transport Management* 205–211.

137 ICAO, 'List of Government-owned and Privatized Airlines (unofficial preliminary compilation)', online at: www.icao.int/sustainability/documents/privatizedairlines.pdf

138 Federal Law No. 4 of 2012 on the Regulation of Competition, online at: http://ejustice.gov.ae/downloads/latest_laws/federal_law_4_2012_en.pdf

f. restricting the freedom of supply of goods or services to the Relevant Market, or removing goods or services from the Relevant Market, including hiding or unlawfully storing goods or services, abstaining from dealing in goods and services, or creating a sudden oversupply that leads to circulating the goods and services at fake prices.

2. Subject to the provisions of the above Federal Law No. 18 of 1981, restrictive Agreements among Organizations, which prejudice, restrict, or prevent Competition, shall be prohibited, including the agreements that are aimed at:
   a. market sharing, or allocation of clients on the basis of geographical areas, distribution centers, customer quality, seasons, periods of time, or any other basis that adversely affects Competition.
   b. taking any measures to obstruct the entry of any Organizations to the market, excluding any Organizations from the market, or obstruction of accession to any existing agreements or joint ventures.

3. Save for Sub-clause (a), Clause (1), and Sub-clause (a), Clause 2, the provisions of this Article shall not apply to low-impact agreements in which the total share of the Organizations which are parties to these agreements do not exceed the percentage set by the Council of Ministers of the total transactions in the Relevant Market. The Council of Ministers, based on proposal of the Minister, may increase or reduce this percentage according to the economic situation requirements.[139]

Registered commercial agency agreements are excluded even if they contain anti-competitive restrictions.[140]

On abuse of a dominant position, Article 6 of Federal Law No. 4 reads:

1. No Organization of a Dominant Position in the Relevant Market, or in a substantial or influential part thereof, may carry out any acts or actions that lead to the abuse of this position in order to

139 Ibid.

140 Zubair Mir *et al.*, 'The New UAE Federal Competition Law Federal Law No 4 of 2012 Concerning Regulating Competition' (Herbert Smith Freehills LLP competition briefing, February 2013) 1, online at: www.herbertsmithfreehills.com/-/media/Files/PDFs/2013/The%20new%20UAE%20Federal%20Competition%20Law%20%20Federal%20Law%20No%204%20of%202012%20concerning%20regulating%20competition%20%2012%20February%202013.pdf; see Federal Law No. 18 of 1981.

prejudice, restrict, or prevent Competition, particularly those which have the following subjects or objectives:

a. directly or indirectly imposing prices or conditions for resale of goods or services;
b. selling goods or performing services at below cost price with the aim of obstructing the entry of competitive Organizations to the Relevant Market, excluding them, or exposing them to losses that make it hard for them to continue their business;
c. unjustified discrimination of customers of identical contracts in terms of prices of goods and services, or the terms of sale or purchase contracts;
d. forcing a customer not to deal with a competitive Organization.
e. Rejection, in whole or in part, of dealing under the usual commercial terms.
f. Unjustified abstention from selling or purchasing goods and services, or reducing or obstructing this dealing, thereby imposing a false price.
g. making the conclusion of a sale or purchase contract or agreement for goods or services conditional on the acceptance of obligations for dealing in other goods or services which by nature or under commercial use are unrelated to the subject of the original dealing or agreement.
h. disseminating, knowingly, false information about the products or their prices.
i. increasing or decreasing the available quantities of the product, thereby creating a forced deficit or oversupply of the goods in question.

2. The Dominant Position referred to in Clause 1 of this Article is realized when the share of any Organization exceeds the percentage prescribed by the Council of Ministers of the total transactions in the Relevant Market. The Council of Minister, upon a proposal by the Minister, may increase or decrease this percentage based on the economic situation requirements.[141]

Articles 7 to 9 of Federal Law No. 4 set out the procedures around organising 'economic concentration' as a result of mergers or acquisitions, under which transactions must be notified to the Ministry of Economy and may be implemented subject to prior approval.[142]

141 Federal Law No. 4 of 2012.
142 Ibid.

It is understood that this is the first UAE legislation on merger control, also insofar as it includes prohibitions on anti-competitive agreements and abuse of a dominant position; it also contains strict penalties.[143] Whilst the UAE now has, 'for the first time, a comprehensive competition law that covers the standard three pillars found in many competition regimes: rules dealing with restrictive agreements, abuse of a dominant position and merger control',[144] it is essential for our study to note that *inter alia*, land, sea and air transport sectors, transport by rail and related services are exempted from the scope of the legislation.

Just as in other jurisdictions, a firm may avail itself of the legislation and file a complaint with the Ministry of Economy if affected by anti-competitive agreements or conduct. In terms of penalties,

> Fines may not yet be at levels which provide a serious deterrent, but infringements bring a risk of reputational damage, particularly for international companies. Moreover, given cross-border co-operation among competition enforcement agencies, infringements picked up in the UAE may well lead to investigations by agencies elsewhere, and in jurisdictions where penalties may be more severe.[145]

In addition, it should be noted that other Middle East and Northern Africa jurisdictions, such as

> Egypt, Jordan, Kuwait, Qatar, Saudi Arabia and Syria already have some form of competition law in force. Fines in the new UAE law are comparable to those in other MENA jurisdictions, e.g. Saudi Arabia. But they are low compared with many jurisdictions in other regions. This may be changing though: Saudi Arabian authorities are considering replacing relatively low fixed-level fines with the more common turnover-based fines.[146]

No specific UAE legislation on State aid was located.

Qatar: competition law

The State of Qatar also has enacted competition legislation. There is additionally a specific law on air travel agencies. The relevant legislation is Law No. 19 of 2006 on the Protection of Competition and Prevention of

143 Freshfields Bruckhaus Deringer, 'United Arab Emirates: New Competition Law' (January 2013), online at: www.freshfields.com/uploadedFiles/SiteWide/Knowledge/UAE_new%20competition%20law.pdf

144 Mir *et al.*, 1.

145 Freshfields, 'United Arab Emirates' 4.

146 Ibid.

Monopolistic Practices, Qatar Economy and Commerce Minister's Resolution No. 61 of 2008 promulgating the Executive By Law of Law No. 19 of 2006 on Competition Protection and Monopolistic Practices Prohibition, Qatar Law No. 26 of 2006 regulating Air Travel Agencies and Executive Regulations thereof – Doha Qatar, and Qatar Decretal Law No. 15 of 2007 regulating the Marketing and Sale of Government-regulated products outside the State of Qatar.

Law No. 19 prohibits anti-competitive business practices in a similar way to European and U.S. jurisdictions. Enforcement of the law is delegated to a committee. The law

> does not apply to governmental acts or any acts of any entity controlled or supervised by the state. This effectively limits the applicability of the law to the private sector and it will not apply to existing monopolies controlled by the government, such as Mowasalat (which has a monopoly on taxis and buses in Qatar for 20 years from 2004) and Qatar Fuel (WOQOD, which has a monopoly on the sale and distribution of fuel and other petroleum products in Qatar for 15 years from 2003).[147]

No specific Qatar legislation on State aid was located.

UAE and Qatar: State aid allegations

In January 2015, the Partnership for Open and Fair Skies (POFS), a group comprising three major U.S. airlines and seven trade associations, published a strongly worded White Paper entitled 'Restoring Open Skies: The Need to Address Subsidized Competition from State-Owned airlines in Qatar and the UAE'.[148] The White Paper presents a case for why the U.S. government should 'roll back' its exchange of traffic and landing rights on the liberalized 'open skies' bilateral air services agreements between the U.S. and Qatar and U.S. and the UAE. This gave way to the 'the almost unprecedented proceeding that the U.S. Departments of Transportation, Commerce and State jointly opened in April 2015, inviting any and all interested parties to submit

147 Oxford Business Group, 'Rules of the Game: Legislation for Operating a Business' (*The Report: Qatar 2012*, 2012), online at: www.oxfordbusinessgroup.com/overview/rules-game-legislation-operating-business

148 The Partnership for Open and Fair Skies is a coalition composed of American Airlines, Delta Air Lines and United Airlines, along with the Air Line Pilots Association, Int'l, the Allied Pilots Association, the Airline Division of the International Brotherhood of Teamsters, the Association of Flight Attendants–CWA, the Association of Professional Flight Attendants, the Communications Workers of America and the Southwest Airlines Pilots' Association. The White Paper is available at: www.openandfairskies.com/wp-content/themes/custom/media/White.Paper.pdf

their views and comments openly, publicly, and "on the record"'.[149] The U.S. official dockets closed in August 2015; an investigation is ongoing.

In Europe, the European Commission adopted a new Aviation Strategy for Europe in December 2015, which boasts as its core objective to 'place the EU as a leading player in international aviation, whilst guaranteeing a level playing field'.[150] This has been interpreted as a move to negotiate 'a new European-wide air traffic agreement with Gulf states as a way of boosting European airlines against what some of them have termed unfair subsidies enjoyed by Middle East-based rivals'.[151]

Returning to the White Paper, in short, POFS alleges that the three major Gulf carriers – Emirates, Etihad and Qatar Airways – receive State aid that secures them an unfair advantage on the global market. The bilateral ASAs permits the airlines to transport passengers e.g. 'behind Qatar via Qatar and intermediate points to a point or points in the United States and beyond'.[152] The U.S. carriers allege they are losing, or fear they will lose, market share between U.S. and intermediary points, such as Europe. This makes for a very controversial situation for aviation; should the U.S. government re-examine its treaty arrangements with Qatar and the UAE?

In general State-aid allegations are not easy to prove without sound evidence; lack of transparency would of course make the task even more challenging. Whilst the White Paper has collated a significant amount of evidence from a variety of sources, including financial statements, it must be said that this author does not support or reject the allegations. Rather, this section of the book attempts to paint a picture of the current controversy in the spirit of apolitical and unbiased academic discussion.

In 2015, Doug Parker, CEO of American Airlines, stated: 'We believe there is now overwhelming evidence that the governments of Qatar and the UAE are violating the aviation trade agreements between the U.S. and those countries by providing enormous subsidies to [the three Gulf airlines] – subsidies in amounts that are unprecedented in the history of international trade'.[153] As an

149 Allan I. Mendelsohn, 'Unravelling Open Skies' (McGill University Institute for Air & Space Law, Occasional Paper Series No. 1, December 2015) 3–4, available online at: www.mcgill.ca/iasl/files/iasl/2016-occasional_paper_i_unravelling_open_skies-mendelsohn.pdf; see U.S. Department of State 'U.S. Department of State, Commerce, and Transportation Seek Stakeholder Input on Gulf Carrier Subsidy Claims' (Media Note, 10 April 2015), online at: www.state.gov/r/pa/prs/ps/2015/04/240582.htm

150 European Commission, 'Commission Presents a New Aviation Strategy for Europe'.

151 Julia Fioretti and Victoria Bryan, 'EU Seeks New Air Traffic Agreements in Gulf Carrier Battle' *Reuters* (London, 7 December 2015), available online at: www.reuters.com/article/us-eu-aviation-idUSKBN0TQ16D20151207

152 Air Transport Agreement between the Government of the United States of America and the Government of Qatar, Section 1 (3 October 2011), available online at: www.state.gov/e/eb/rls/othr/ata/q/qa/114294.htm

153 Bart Jansen, 'Emirates, Etihad Rebut U.S. Airlines' Charge' *USA Today*, 17 March 2015. Available online at: www.usatoday.com/wlna/todayinthesky/2015/03/17/gulf-carriers-etihad-emirates-subsidies-us-chamber-aviation-summit/24844191/

aside it is worth noting that UAE and Qatar are both members of the World Trade Organization. The WTO Agreement on Subsidies and Countervailing Measures defines a subsidy as a 'financial contribution' by a government that confers a 'benefit' on its recipient.[154] American Airlines, Delta Airlines and United Airlines claim that Emirates, Etihad and Qatar Airways[155] have received USD42 billion in subsidies since 2004. All three Gulf airlines strongly deny the allegations.

It should be noted in parallel that pressure is also mounting on governments of EU Member States and the EU institutions to respond to alleged shifting of international airline hubs away from Europe. The European Cockpit Association has stated publically:

> Qatar Airways is 100% owned by the Qatar state via the Qatar Investment Authority; Etihad Airways is 100% owned by the government of Abu Dhabi; and Emirates is wholly-owned by the Government of Dubai. As their financial situation lacks transparency, there are no guarantees that the governments are running their companies as 'private' entities. From a simple financial perspective, as long as the oil and gas revenues remain in the region, these companies will enjoy a huge 'war chest' and access to 'cheap' money to finance their further expansion. In addition, weak social legislation in their countries offers them the competitive advantage of a precarious workforce that cannot count on the respect of the basic standards set by the International Labour Organisation (ILO).[156]

What can be gleaned from the 55-page White Paper is that the governments of Dubai, Abu Dhabi and Qatar are pursuing economic development strategies that depend in large part on the continued expansion of the flow of international air passenger traffic through their hubs. The success of these strategies depends on the continued rapid growth of their respective airlines, Emirates, Etihad and Qatar Airways, which is the main reason subsidization appears possibly to be a common factor in the running of all three airlines. Each of the three airlines will be examined below in the light of the White Paper's allegations.

Beginning with Emirates, which is based in Dubai, the White Paper suggests that the financial statements of Emirates do not disclose all dealings agreed. This makes it difficult to quantify any subsidies that the airline(s) may

154 See the full text of the agreement at: www.wto.org/english/docs_e/legal_e/24-scm.pdf

155 Depending on the source, it is interesting that one finds 'the Big Three' referring to U.S. or the Gulf carriers.

156 European Cockpit Association, 'The Case for Fair Competition in Europe's Aviation: Why Action is Needed to Safeguard our Aviation's Future' 10, online at: www.eurocockpit.be/sites/default/files/the_case_for_fair_competition_in_eus_aviation_14_1125_online_f.pdf. The ownership of Qatar Airways, as claimed by the European Cockpit Association is disputed; see n.137 above.

or may not have received. The White Paper suggests, however, that the government of Dubai has injected at least USD218 million in capital, the make-up of which is USD137 million that it injected prior to 1995, USD7 million that it injected that fiscal year, USD23 million in 1996–97 (via transfer of a training college) and an additional USD51 million that it injected over a five-year period from 2001 to 2005 (at a time Emirates was claiming publicly that it was not subsidized).[157]

According to a study by Compass Lexecon, the money given to Emirates by the Dubai Airports Company for the construction of a terminal for its exclusive use amounted to USD7.8 billion alone.[158] The study also suggests that the airport could not have afforded the construction on its independent resources. The report also concluded that Emirates received an additional USD94 to 145 million subsidy in 2013 as a result of the government's decision to exempt transfer traffic from passenger charges. In total, the report identifies that the two subsidies amounted to between USD437 and 532 million in 2013 and 2.26 billion since 2004.

Moreover, the White Paper suggests that Emirates is paying its related parties on average just 15 per cent less than it would pay an unrelated party, which it is alleged translates into its receipt of a subsidy of USD330 million per year.

Yet, according to the White Paper, Emirates' founding decree specifically exempts the airline from the payment of such duties 'for all its imports of planes, equipment, spare parts and other materials that are necessary for its operations or to be sold on its planes or distributed for the sake of advertisement'.[159] It is argued in the White Paper that tax exemptions are subsidies. While there is a fine line between subsidies and tax breaks, it is not an agreed view amongst economists that the two are the same.[160]

In addition, the fact that Sheikh Ahmed Saeed Al Maktoum is in charge of many positions that are inter-connected allegedly creates a conflict of interest. To be exact, the White Paper explains that the Sheikh acts as:

> Chairman of Dubai Airports, the Chairman of Dnata (the monopoly ground handling operation at the Dubai airports), the Chairman of Dubai Duty Free (the monopoly duty-free operator at DXB), the Chairman of Dubai Aerospace Enterprise (which leases aircraft to Emirates), the Chairman of Dubai's low-cost carrier Flydubai, the Chairman of Dubai Airport Free Zone Authority, and the Chairman of Emirates NDB (the UAE's largest bank). He is also the President of the air

157 Partnership for Open and Fair Skies, 'Restoring Open Skies' 35–36.

158 Ibid., 17.

159 Partnership for Open and Fair Skies, 'Restoring Open Skies' 34; see Government of Dubai, Decree Number (2) 1985 concerning the establishment of a Corporation to be known as Emirates, Art 9.

160 Partnership for Open and Fair Skies, 'Restoring Open Skies' 4.

transportation regulator (the Dubai Civil Aviation Authority (DCAA)), the Second Vice Chairman of Dubai's Executive Council (which is responsible for formulating policies and strategies for the Emirate of Dubai), a Director of Dubai Aviation City Corporation, and the Chairman of Dubai's Economic Development Committee. As the son of the former ruler of Dubai, the brother of the former ruler of Dubai, and the uncle of Dubai's current ruler, he is also a member of the ruling family.[161]

The White Paper speculates that any one individual in such a wide range of powerful positions could easily provide benefits to a firm. It also discusses how Emirates' strategy is closely aligned with the strategic development objectives of its ultimate owner, the government of Dubai, as set out in the Dubai Strategic Plan 2015. The primary aim of the Plan is to achieve economic growth by expanding the aviation sector in which Emirates plays a significant role.[162] An example of this is the additional airport infrastructure that is financed by the government of Dubai. The White Paper states:

> The government is spending tens of billions of dollars to build that infrastructure, which is grossly in excess of the capacity needed to serve Dubai's local population. And as the government of Dubai has admitted, the landing fees and other charges it imposes on airport users are far too low to cover these costs.[163]

Therefore, the resulting subsidy, which amounts to hundreds of millions of dollars per year, would appear to put Emirates in an advantageous position against its foreign competitors. Specifically, the Dubai government is allegedly spending:

> USD7.8 billion to boost capacity at DXB to 90 million passengers by 2018 to accommodate the anticipated traffic growth driven by the rapid expansion of Emirates airline and Flydubai.
>
> USD3.3 billion for the construction of Concourse A of Terminal 3 (Emirates' new A380 hub at DXB), which opened in 2013, and it is for the exclusive use of Emirates.
>
> USD32 billion on the first phase of the expansion of the new Al Mak - toum International Airport at Dubai World Central (DWC), which is

161 Ibid., 7.

162 Dubai Airports, 'Strategic Plan 2020', available at: www.dubaiairports.ae/docs/default-source/Publications/dubai-airports--strategic-plan-2020.pdf?sfvrsn=2

163 Partnership for Open and Fair Skies, 'Restoring Open Skies' 8.

> only 40 miles south of DXB. The ultimate goal of the DWC project is to increase the airport's capacity to 240 million passengers per year and to make it possible for 100 A380s to operate at any given time. The airport's CEO has explained that they are structuring the expansion to add capacity in 20 million passenger increments to mirror Emirates' growth.[164]

The White Paper provides that in combination with government funding the following factors significantly reduce Emirates' operating costs and therefore place it in a more advantageously competitive position against other airlines. The first is artificially low labour costs, which are a result of the government's ban on unions, and other well-documented labour practices. Emirates freely admit that its low labour costs give it advantages over its U.S. and European competitors, which it describes as 'an undeniable fact of life'.[165] These bans on labour rights are partially responsible for the Gulf carriers' extremely low labour costs, the White Paper suggests, as they amount to about half that of their U.S. competitors measured as a proportion of total costs excluding fuel, and provide them with a substantial, government-conferred advantage.

A published empirical analysis by Jarrell and Stanley demonstrates that

> the midpoint of the gap between union and non-union wages was 11 percent. Therefore, if one conservatively assumes that the Gulf carriers' annual labour costs are 11 percent lower than they would have been if their workforces were permitted to unionize, this indicates that the bans on unions have saved them approximately $3.1 billion over the past ten years.[166]

Second, there is an alleged 'freedom from taxation' for corporations in Dubai:

> Under Dubai's corporate tax regime, tax rates are calculated on a sliding scale up to a maximum of 55%. Based on Emirates' pre-tax earnings, the Government's decision not to enforce the law with respect to Emirates saved the airline as much as $523 million in Fiscal Year 2013–2014 alone, and $4.6 billion over the past 10 years.[167]

And finally, there are exemptions for the aviation sector under UAE competition laws, as we have seen above.

164 Ibid., 9.
165 Ibid., 37.
166 Ibid., 38; See Stephen B. Jarrell and T. D. Stanley, 'A Meta-Analysis of the Union-Nonunion Wage Gap' (1990) 44(1) *Industrial and Labor Relations Review* 54.
167 Partnership for Open and Fair Skies, 'Restoring Open Skies' 39.

According to the White Paper, it seems that over the years the other major carrier in the UAE, Etihad, has also received substantial subsidies from the government of Abu Dhabi. In the period from its inception until the end of 2013, the White Paper claims that:

> Etihad received over $13.5 billion in subsidies in the form of interest-free government loans, equity infusions, airport fee exemptions, and other types of government funding that have enabled the airline to continue in operation despite its $4 billion in accumulated losses. The financials also show that the Government of Abu Dhabi has already committed an additional $4.2 billion in subsidies to Etihad – including $3.5 billion in 2014 – which means the total subsidy amount will exceed $17 billion. It is alleged that Etihad's financials evidence that Etihad uses the cash infusions to cover its substantial, ongoing operating losses.[168]

The composition of the alleged subsidies is discussed in detail in the White Paper. It is adequate for the present study to say that the overall tone and message regarding Etihad and Abu Dhabi in the White Paper are similar.

Finally, the White Paper's analysis of Qatar Airways' financial reports also suggests that it received a number of subsidies from the Qatar government; namely an initial loan of $19.2 million, a $19 million loan in 2000, a $36 million loan in 2001, a $39 million loan in 2002, a $10 million loan in 2003 and a $55 million loan in 2004.[169] 'In 2007, the amount of the loans dramatically increased, reaching $596 million in 2007 and $742 million in 2008'.[170] In 2009 repayment was made optional, which the White Paper suggests effectively means the loans were forgiven.[171] The airline allegedly received $7.76 billion up to 2014, notwithstanding interest that would have accrued had the loans been 'commercial'.[172]

White Paper response

Following the public dissemination of the White Paper, all three Gulf carriers issued public responses. Emirates published a 200-page rebuttal in June 2015,[173] Etihad published a press release and created a dedicated website

168 Ibid., 16.
169 Ibid., 21.
170 Ibid., 21.
171 Ibid., 22.
172 Ibid., 22.
173 Emirates, 'Emirates' Response to Claims Raised about State-Owned Airlines in Qatar and the United Arab Emirates' (29 June 2015), online at: http://content.emirates.com/downloads/ek/pdfs/openskies_rebuttal/EK_Response_Main.pdf

'Keep The Skies Open' with a video,[174] and Qatar Airways submitted an 84-page official response to the U.S. Departments of Transportation, Commerce and State in June 2015.[175] All three Gulf carriers refute the claims made in the White Paper. To varying degrees, the Gulf carrier responses point to benefits enjoyed by the 'Big Three' U.S. carriers such as Chapter 11 bankruptcy reorganization (USD70 billion),[176] that equity and loans to airlines are not subsidies and that, crucially, the U.S. carriers have not demonstrated they have suffered harm. The Gulf carriers add that their air services to and from U.S. cities actually *support* U.S. jobs, tourism and trade.

Some doubt has also been raised over the accuracy and intent of the White Paper. For example, Frankie O'Connell from Cranfield University, whose academic journal article was quoted in the White Paper several times subsequently published a commentary to express how 'views were inaccurately interpreted and skewed to serve objectives [of the White Paper] unrelated to [his own] paper'.[177]

It should also be said that in Europe not all airlines speak with one voice on the matter. International Airlines Group (British Airways, Iberia and Aer Lingus) pulled out of the traditional legal carrier lobbying group Association of European Airlines in 2015 to join the European Low Fare Airlines Association (ELFAA) instead. It has been publicized that IAG did not agree with the protectionist stance within the AEA group with respect to the Gulf carriers. It follows that IAG supports global liberalization rather than

174 Etihad Airways, 'Keep The Skies Open' (Media Release, 1 June 2015), online at: www.etihadmediacentre.com/file_transfer.php?f_ID=6094; www.etihad.com/en-us/about-us/keep-the-skies-open

175 Qatar Airways, 'Comments of Qatar Airways Q.C.S.C. Re: Information on Claims Raised about State-Owned Airlines in Qatar and the UAE', online at: www.qatarairways.com/images/Internet/qr_commercial/ecommerce/relaunch-2011/5-column/promotions/americas/us/QatarAirways-openskies-white-paper.pdf.

176 Etihad Airways, 'Keep The Skies Open' 1; see also Karen Walker, 'Etihad Report Alleges 3 Major U.S. Carriers have Received $71.5 Billion in Benefits' *Air Transport World*, 14 May 2015, available online at: http://atwonline.com/open-skies/etihad-report-alleges-3-major-us-carriers-have-received-715-billion-benefits

177 Frankie O'Connell, 'Commentary: US White Paper on Gulf Carriers Distorts my Academic Report' *Air Transport World*, 26 April 2015, available online at: http://atwonline.com/open-skies/commentary-us-white-paper-gulf-carriers-distorts-my-academic-report

protectionism advocated at AEA, most strongly by its largest members Air France–KLM and Lufthansa.[178]

Case study: People's Republic of China

The People's Republic of China's aviation sector has grown exponentially since 1978. Following gradual market reform between 1978 and 2008, which culminated with the government's announcement in 2005 that it would begin to 'permit private capital as well as foreign investment to enter the airline sector as much needed equity investment'.[179] This happened within the Chinese emerging economic environment that promoted a more 'open' China that was simultaneously preparing to meet admissions criteria for membership of the WTO. Thus, swift liberalization of the domestic market as well as China's bilateral agreements with other States – including trade in air services – was given high-level government priority.[180]

As Williams observes: 'The serious attempts by the CAAC [Civil Aviation Administration of China] to bring about airline reform and consolidation have seen Air China, China Southern and China Eastern emerge as the leading-edge carriers, now intent on taking China's civil aviation industry forward in a growing international market'.[181] Under strict regulatory control by the CAAC in preceding years, Air China was the 'international arm of the original CAAC'.[182] We observe that of the three formerly State-owned and controlled major airlines, China Southern and China Eastern are members of the SkyTeam Alliance[183] and Air China is a member of the Star Alliance.[184] Membership of a global airline alliance entails cooperation between the group of airline members as regards quality standards, blocked space and codeshare agreements, joint marketing and sales and even common alliance branding on aircraft livery.[185] Chinese membership in the

178 Anne Paylor, 'British Airways, Iberia Switch Allegiance to ELFAA' *Air Transport World*, 27 April 2015, available online at: http://atwonline.com/associations/british-airways-iberia-switch-allegiance-elfaa; Jens Flottau and Madhu Unnikrishnan, 'Iberia and BA leave AEA in Clash over Gulf Carriers' *Aviation Week*, 15 April 2015, available online at: http://aviationweek.com/commercial-aviation/iberia-and-ba-leave-aea-clash-over-gulf-carriers; CAPA, 'ACI Europe Promotes Open Skies: A Resounding Precedent for Airlines and Other Airports to Follow' (26 June 2015), online at: http://centreforaviation.com/analysis/aci-europe-promotes-open-skies-a-resounding-precedent-for-airlines-and-other-airports-to-follow-232185

179 Alan Williams, *Contemporary Issues Shaping China's Civil Aviation Policy: Balancing International with Domestic Priorities* (Ashgate 2009) 23.

180 Ibid., Ch. 1.

181 Ibid., 93.

182 Ibid., 101.

183 Skyteam, 'Skyteam Airline Alliance' (2016), online at: www.skyteam.com/en/about

184 Star Alliance, 'Member Airlines: Star Alliance' (2016), online at: www.staralliance.com/en/member-airlines

185 See Truxal, *Competition and Regulation in the Airline Industry.*

global alliances certainly demonstrates the important position of Chinese aviation on the global market as well as a liberalized Chinese sector.

The relevant Chinese legislation on competition is the Anti-monopoly Law, which came into effect in 2008.[186] Article 3 of the Anti-monopoly Law sets out the types of 'monopolistic conducts' that are prohibited by the legislation, including:

- monopolistic agreements among business operators;
- abuse of dominant market positions by business operators; and
- concentration of business operators that eliminates or restricts competition or might be eliminating or restricting competition.

The provisions of this legislation relating to anti-monopoly competitive agreements and abuse of a dominant position are very similar to Articles 101 and 102 TFEU, respectively. And, as with Article 101(3) TFEU, an exemption is also permitted by Article 5 of the Chinese Law. Indeed, it provides: 'Business operators may, through fair competition, voluntary alliance, concentrate themselves according to law, expand the scope of business operations, and enhance competitiveness'. The Anti-monopoly Bureau within the Ministry of Commerce investigates cases on concentrations and anti-competitive activity, as established and authorized by the State Council of the People's Republic of China.[187]

With respect to State aid and subsidies for industries that are not 'controlled by the State-owned economy', the Anti-monopoly Law provides in Article 8: 'No administrative organ or organization empowered by a law or administrative regulation to administer public affairs may abuse its administrative powers to eliminate or restrict competition'.[188] The three major Chinese airlines are majority State-owned.[189]

It is prudent for us to note that these Chinese carriers, along with other global players, experienced a downturn in demand in the wave of the global credit crisis of 2008 and 2009. Williams wrote in 2009 that all three major Chinese carriers were 'deeply in the red'.[190] Aviation suffered substantial

186 Anti-monopoly Law of the People's Republic of China, online at: www.china.org.cn/government/laws/2009-02/10/content_17254169.htm

187 The Anti-monopoly Committee of the State Council oversees the work of the Anti-monopoly Bureau. See Ministry of Commerce website: http://english.mofcom.gov.cn/departments/fldj2

188 Article 7 applies to industries controlled by the State-owned economy, which are deemed as protected. However, Article 7 attaches the proviso that business operators in these industries 'shall lawfully operate, be honest and faithful, be strictly self-disciplined, accept social supervision, shall not damage the interests of consumers by virtue of their dominant or exclusive positions'.

189 ICAO, 'List of Government-owned and Privatized Airlines (unofficial preliminary compilation)', online at: www.icao.int/sustainability/documents/privatizedairlines.pdf

190 Williams, *Contemporary Issues Shaping China's Civil Aviation Policy* 204.

losses though it was 'not a sector that [had] been identified in the industrial restructuring programme under the stimulus package'.[191] Nonetheless, the major Chinese airlines as well as some smaller ones have, often vis-à-vis their respective holding companies, lobbied Beijing and regional governments for capital injections.[192] China announced a stimulus package in November 2008 worth four trillion yuan (USD586 billion at the time), which represented about 16 per cent of its GDP; unsurprisingly this sparked controversy.[193] The shares in a number of Chinese airlines rose on the announcement.[194] Then, in 2009, 'Air China submitted a request for a government cash injection of at least CNY3 billion (USD439 million) (the same level as requested in December 2008 by China Southern). The carrier also stated it could be profitable in 2009, with early results showing signs of improvement'.[195]

A report prepared by the Economist Intelligence Unit in 2009 on China's stimulus package has a feature on aviation. It states that 'the central government has injected large amounts of capital in both airline operations and aviation manufacturing ... [including] Rmb176bn in pledged financing for ... aircraft and helicopter manufacturing projects'.[196] Additionally, 'The Ministry of Finance exempted airlines from paying fuel surcharges (retroactively from January 2008), and government assistance to specific airline operations has taken the form of loans (such as Rmb7bn in new funding for China Eastern Airlines, which suffered a Rmb6.2bn loss on fuel-hedging contracts) as well as capital injections'.[197] The report also observes that:

> Chinese aviation has seen the demise of privately held airlines, whereas China Eastern Airlines and China Southern Airlines have benefited from state support. China Eastern secured bank facilities totalling Rmb46bn in the last 12 months from four major banks, among them a loan facility of Rmb11bn from the Bank of Communications, covering areas such as project finance, securitisation of assets, international settlement and internet banking. State support has not been without many strings attached. In return for government funding, enterprises are being pressured into complying with consolidation plans, despite the less-than-

191 Economist Intelligence Unit, 'China's Stimulus Package: A Six-Month Report Card' *The Economist*, July 2009, available online at: http://ftp01.economist.com.hk/090723/Stimulus_new_main_July20.pdf

192 Williams, *Contemporary Issues Shaping China's Civil Aviation Policy*, 204–211.

193 *The Economist*, 'The World in 2009: China's Stimulus Package' *The Economist*, 12 November 2008, available online at: www.economist.com/blogs/theworldin2009/2008/11/chinas_stimulus_package

194 CAPA, 'Chinese Airlines Rise as Beijing Prepares for Fresh Stimulus Package: Share Wrap' (5 March 2009), online at: http://centreforaviation.com/analysis/chinese-airlines-shares-rise-as-beijing-prepares-for-fresh-stimulus-package--share-wrap-5790

195 Ibid.

196 Ibid., 20.

197 Ibid., 20.

> bucolic record of arranged corporate marriages, and the failure of past efforts to push consolidation. In early July, China Eastern and Shanghai Airlines announced their merger. In the case of the logistics sector, Rmb100bn in government funding will support the construction of modern multimodal transport and trans-shipment facilities, but the consolidation that is planned to accompany this will, if implemented, streamline the number of players in the sector from 2.7m trucking firms to a handful of large trucking fleets.[198]

More recently, the Centre for Aviation (CAPA) reported:

> It is no secret some of the Chinese carriers' long-haul growth is underwritten by local Chinese governments. This amounts to more than route launch incentives, which are globally common. Without the subsidies some Chinese carriers' trans-pacific routes would simply not be offered. The US airlines tout their two years' worth of 'forensic investigations'; that they claim found USD42 billion in subsidies to Gulf carriers over the years. Far less effort is needed to investigate the four Chinese airlines serving the US: their 2014 annual reports openly state they collectively received over USD1.1 billion of subsidies and grants in 2014. This includes USD162 million at Air China, USD589 at China Eastern, USD276 million at China Southern and USD82 million at Hainan. Notably, most of the subsidies – USD865 million – were to China Eastern and China Southern, partners with Delta, which is leading the US crusade against Gulf airlines.[199]

What we can conclude from these sources is that Chinese airlines appear to be in receipt of substantial State support; this is no secret. This is perhaps unsurprising given that the three major players in question are also majority State-owned. Nonetheless, the reaction of airlines in other States where such subsidies are much less or altogether non-existent is understandable, especially if the respective airlines compete on the same international routes. As Chinese airlines 'overtake' U.S. carriers on the lucrative trans-Pacific market, which the CAPA traffic data above suggests, it is needful to call into question whether the playing field is level. And if not, *can* it be levelled? So far, rather surprisingly, European carriers have not voiced as loudly their objections to the increased capacities from EU airports on Chinese airlines on routes to Asia and beyond, such as Australia and New Zealand.

198 Ibid., 23.

199 CAPA, 'Chinese Airlines Overtake US Carriers across the Pacific: The Big Dilemma – US-China Open Skies?' (4 May 2015), online at: http://centreforaviation.com/analysis/chinese-airlines-overtake-us-carriers-across-the-pacific-time-for-us-china-open-skies-222454

Global ways forward?

Fair competition

The EU's External Aviation Policy 2012 includes an important normative caveat that EU carriers *should* be able to compete on the global market on an 'open, fair and undistorted basis'.[200] Noting that aviation 'competes as a service industry in a global market ... sustainable competitiveness [therefore] depends upon fair conditions of competition', the European Commission opened a public consultation on proposals for improved protection against subsidization and unfair pricing practices causing injury to EU air carriers in the supply of air services from non-EU countries in 2014.[201]

Looking towards the Gulf, the European Commission noted in 2012 that 'aviation systems against which EU airlines and hubs compete in the Gulf are the result of clear decisions taken to develop aviation as a strategic economic sector generating benefits for the overall economy'; however, 'Gulf carriers insist that they do not enjoy unfair competitive advantages from these systems'.[202]

In an attempt to safeguard fair conditions of competition, the EU intends to incorporate 'standard "fair competition clauses" ... in the respective bilateral air services agreements with EU Member States'.[203] Examples include the current open skies agreements between the EU and key trade partners such as the U.S. and Canada.

Many such 'fair competition clauses' already appear in EU and U.S. ASAs. Take for instance the U.S.–Qatar Open Skies Agreement of 2001, which contains the following provision:

> Each Party shall allow a fair and equal opportunity for the designated airlines of both Parties to compete in providing the international air transportation governed by this Agreement.[204]

The clause above is modelled after the standard terms of open skies agreements. What does the clause mean? It can be said that, '[s]ince there is no intention to have an exactly equivalent exchange of rights under open skies agreements, what the parties exchange under the agreement is essentially the *opportunity to compete* among carriers while using the same agreement'.[205]

200 COM(2012) 556 final.

201 The policy context is available at: http://ec.europa.eu/transport/modes/air/consultations/doc/2014-01-20-protection-against-subsidisation/policy-context.pdf

202 COM(2012) 556 final 8.

203 Ibid.

204 Article 11(1) of the U.S.–Qatar Air Transport Agreement of 3 October 2001, available online at: www.state.gov/e/eb/rls/othr/ata/q/qa/114294.htm

205 For a full discussion of fair competition clauses in air services agreements, see Sean McGonigle, 'Fair Competition, Subsidy, and State Aid Clauses in International Air Services Agreements' (2012) 57 *Annals of Air and Space Law* 199–222.

McGonigle points to Wassenbergh, who contrasted the open skies agreement with previous, restrictive bilateral ASAs, and noted that 'fair and equal opportunity to compete' should be interpreted as: a *level playing field*.[206] McGonigle concludes that 'in an open skies arrangement which contains a "fair and equal opportunity to compete" clause coupled with national competition legislation in place, designated airlines, although free to operate based on "commercial considerations in the marketplace", are nevertheless restrained by competition law'.[207] For a truly fair and equal opportunity to compete on the market to exist would require that transparent systems of regulation and enforcement are in place in all relevant jurisdictions; an undertaking that is easier said than done.

The European Commission identifies that within this 'new commercial context, it is both important and legitimate that the EU is able to act effectively internationally to safeguard the competitiveness of EU airlines against unfair competition and/or practices wherever they may come from'.[208] For this reason, Regulation 868/2004[209] was adopted, which provides a framework for prohibiting subsidies to, or unfair pricing by, third country air carriers insofar as those activities cause or threaten to cause a material injury to the Community air transport industry by allowing the investigation of actual or potential injury following a complaint issued on behalf of the EU air transport industry or on the Commission's own initiative.[210]

However, the major problem for EU firms operating in a service industry such as aviation is that the tools presently available are modelled not on services but on *trade in goods*. They provide relief in the form of anti-dumping and countervailing duties measures to counteract foreign subsidies. The current tools appear to be ineffective as there is no industry specificity to boot.

Thus, the European Commission concludes that the

> considerable difficulties for EU stakeholders to use Regulation 868 are mostly due to its approach based on trade defence notions and practices (e.g. 'like air service' based on the notion of 'like product' used in trade

206 Ibid., 207.

207 Ibid., 208.

208 COM(2012) 556 final 9.

209 Regulation (EC) No 868/2004 of the European Parliament and of the Council of 21 April 2004 concerning protection against subsidisation and unfair pricing practices causing injury to Community air carriers in the supply of air services from countries not members of the European Community, [2004] OJ L162/1, 30 April 2004.

210 European Commission, 'Explanatory Memorandum concerning Amended Proposal for a Regulation of the European Parliament and of the Council concerning protection against subsidisation and unfair pricing practices in the supply of airline services from countries not members of the European Community' (Brussels: Commission of the European Communities, 2003) 2; European Commission, 'Amended proposal for a Regulation of the European Parliament and of the Council concerning protection against subsidisation and unfair pricing practices causing injury to Community air carriers in the supply of airline services from countries not members of the European Community (presented by the Commission pursuant to Article 250(2) of the EC Treaty)' [2003] COM 0228 final; McGonigle, 'Fair Competition, Subsidy, and State Aid Clauses' 210.

> defence instruments, is defined in Article 3(d) of the Regulation as 'air services which are supplied on the same route or routes as the air services under consideration or such air services that are supplied on a route or routes closely resembling the route or routes on which the air service under consideration is supplied'.) which are difficult if not impossible to apply in air transport unless better adapted to the special features of the sector which is regulated by bilateral air services agreements between sovereign states.[211]

Needless to say, this is an area to monitor for future EU legislative developments.

Global competition law

Extraterritoriality in environmental and economic regulation of civil aviation is, in conflict of laws scholarship, 'not exclusively territorial' but the long arm of the regulation. The reach of U.S. Environmental Protection Agency (EPA) standards and the EU ETS on the one hand, and U.S. antitrust and EU competition rules on the other hand, can be felt well beyond the territorial borders of the U.S. and EU Member States. Indeed, the reach of EU competition law appears to be broader than that of U.S. antitrust. We recognize that this gives rise to potential conflicts of jurisdiction – in a conflict of laws context – particularly in an inherently global sector such as aviation. On this, Malanczuk observes:

> Delicate issues in this respect have arisen particularly in international economic relations, in view of the negative response by a number of states (by enacting so-called blocking statutes) to the attempt by the United States to apply its antitrust and securities laws to foreign subsidiaries of American companies with 'extraterritorial effect'. Similar problems have emerged with the more recent application of regulations of the European Community to nationals outside of the Community.[212]

Academic scholarship is flourishing in the area of transnational competition law, especially in the areas of mergers and acquisitions.[213] An emerging global

211 European Commission, 'Roadmap: Protection against subsidisation and unfair pricing practices causing injury to Community air carriers in the supply of air services from countries not members of the European Community' (July 2013) 1, available online at: http://ec.europa.eu/smart-regulation/impact/planned_ia/docs/2014_move_009_unfair_pricing_practices_en.pdf

212 Malanczuk, *Akehurst's Modern Introduction to International Law* 116.

213 See William M. Hannay, 'Transnational Competition Law Aspects of Mergers and Acquisitions' (2000) 20(2) *Northwestern Journal of International Law & Business* 287; Imelda Maher, 'Competition Law and Transnational Private Regulatory Regimes: Marking the Cartel Boundary' (2011) 38(1) *Journal of Law and Society* 119–137.

competition law is also advocated by Gerber, Geradin and Lianos, and others.[214] But global competition law is not pioneering law *per se*. In his work, Gerber discusses patterns in the evolution of global competition law dating back to the 1920s as influenced by politics and economics: 'Events that have come to appear as failures of the transnational competition law idea turn out on closer examination to have been shaped by world wars, depression and the Cold War'.[215] He calls 'deep globalization' the 'increasing intensity of economic, political, intellectual and social relations' since the Second World War. Also, our conceptions have changed, he argues: 'Law is increasingly understood not only in domestic, but also in *transnational* terms. There is far greater awareness of the *transnational implications* of national laws and of the potential value of *transnational cooperation* in law'.[216]

Gerber identifies three patterns as regards global competition on the international level: (1) greater cooperation between competition regulators, particularly EU and U.S.; (2) an increasing role of transnational institutions, such as OECD, UNCTAD and the ICN;[217] and (3) a permeating, transnational influence of U.S. antitrust law.[218] He concludes that the 'patterns and trajectories are central to competition law development in the twenty-first century. They will shape political, institutional and economic forces and supply the elements of collective memory that will interpret them'.[219]

It is exciting to consider the prospect of transnational and global competition law as applied to global aviation in future. For now, we can safely say that there certainly is space for scholarship on fair competition and global competition law for international civil aviation – and the space will fill up quickly.

Environment

In the globalized economy, the nature of the law is layered and at times overlapping in terms of environmental regulation. At the same time pressure is mounting on the international community to reduce greenhouse gas emissions, limit increases to global temperatures, and generally to mitigate the effects of climate change. However, there is no real global consensus on

214 See for example David Gerber, *Global Competition: Law, Markets, and Globalization* (Oxford University Press 2010); Einer Elhague and Damien Geradin, *Global Competition Law and Economics* (Oxford: Bloomsbury 2011); Ioannis Lianos and D. Daniel Sokol, *The Global Limits of Competition Law* (Stanford University Press 2012).

215 Gerber, *Global Competition* 332.

216 Ibid., 332–333 (emphasis added).

217 The OECD, UNCTAD and ICN are presented as examples of transnational institutions working together to provide resources, support and knowledge at the transnational level (Gerber, *Global Competition* 334–336).

218 Ibid., 332–336.

219 Ibid., 334; see also Armin von Bogdandy *et al.* (eds), *The Exercise of Public Authority by International Institutions: Advancing International Institutional Law* (Springer 2010).

how to solve these problems. Instead, there is an uncomfortable divide between developed and developing States, island nations, industrializing States, and other amalgamations, which produces a reinforced sense of State (self) interest and leads to objections by States to proposals on how to move forward. At times it appears that States do not necessarily seek to voice any *substantive objection*, but rather appear to want to *halt the process* altogether, albeit through the usual diplomatic channels.

International aviation contributes to climate change. Normatively speaking, the problem of climate change should not – and cannot – be addressed without the involvement of stakeholders in international aviation. Following the inclusion of 'aviation activities' in the EU ETS,[220] and the subsequent legal challenge to the EU legislation's validity at international law,[221] global aviation has come into the spotlight of environmental scholarship. It is also top of the agenda at ICAO, as its appearance on the agendas of the past four triennial meetings of the General Assembly also evidences. 'In addition, a number of international institutions have singled out international aviation as a potential source of funds for mitigation and adaptation activities in the wider climate change context'.[222]

Air transport has experienced rapid and sustained growth over the past 50 or so years; this 'is projected to continue on a decadal timescale'.[223] According to IATA, global aviation is projected to continue to grow in demand by an annual average of 4.1 per cent between 2014 and 2034.[224] Airbus puts the figure at 4.6 per cent through 2034.[225] In response, aircraft manufacturers are designing planes to carry more traffic: 'Boeing suggests that aeroplanes will carry about 40 percent more traffic in 2027 (measured RPK) than the average aircraft today'.[226] All things being equal, it can be expected that environmental impact from aviation will increase comparatively.

In his work, Daley engages with important questions around the interaction of aircraft with the environment as a starting point for discussing the impacts of aviation on the environment. In this area, his focus is on two

220 Directive 2008/101/EC of the European Parliament and of the Council of 19 November 2008 amending Directive 2003/87/EC so as to include aviation activities in the scheme for greenhouse gas emission allowance trading within the Community [2008] OJ L8/3.

221 Case C-366/10, *Air Transport Association of America, American, Continental and United Airlines and Others* v. *Secretary of State for Energy and Climate Change* [2011] OJ C49/7, [2011] I-13755.

222 Alejandro Piera Valdes, *Greenhouse Gas Emissions from International Aviation: Legal and Policy Challenges* (Eleven Publishing 2015).

223 Daley, *Air Transport and the Environment* 35 referring to Royal Academy of Engineering, 'House of Commons Transport Select Committee: Inquiry into Aviation, Memorandum submitted by the Royal Academy of Engineering' (London, April 2003).

224 IATA, 'IATA 20 Year Passenger Forecast'.

225 Airbus, 'Global Market Forecast 2015–2034: Flying by Numbers'.

226 Stefan Gössling and Paul Upham, 'Introduction: Aviation and Climate Change in Context' in Stefan Gössling and Paul Upham (eds), *Climate Change and Aviation: Issues, Challenges and Solutions* (London: Earthscan, 2009) 3.

specific areas: (1) the emissions from aircraft[227] and airport infrastructure; and (2) the growth in demand for air transport. He also acknowledges the importance of other impacts in the areas of manufacturing, infrastructure development and surface transport;[228] noting, however, that 'the impact of aircraft emissions far outweighs any other aviation environmental effect in its magnitude and significance'.[229] He concludes that the two main challenges are aviation growth and climate change. At the same time the industry, as Gössling and Upham put it,

> presents itself frequently as an environmental champion (e.g. Airbus, Boeing, IATA, ICAO), but much of this may be rhetoric ... Overall, the argument could be made that aircraft manufacturers and airlines create and maintain an elaborate discourse on pro-environmental action, usually forgetting to point out that absolute emissions from the sector are constantly increasing.[230]

The International Air Transport Association (IATA) as industry representative for airlines has developed a 'zero carbon future' proposal, but does not appear to clarify how this will be achieved.[231]

Daley tells us that

> the growth of air transport is transforming the industry from being a relatively minor polluter into being a highly significant source of emissions, especially carbon-dioxide (CO_2). Even using a conservative estimate of the growth of aviation-related emissions, the quantity of CO_2 emitted by air transport is expected to quadruple over the period 1990–

227 'Carbon dioxide (CO_2) is emitted by aircraft in direct proportion to the quantity of fuel burned' (Daley, *Air Transport and the Environment* 24); for more on understanding aircraft emissions, which this book does not set out to provide, see Daley, *Air Transport and the Environment*, and Bows *et al.*, *Aviation and Climate Change: Lessons for European Policy* (Routledge 2009).

228 Daley, *Air Transport and the Environment* 19.

229 Ibid., 19 referring to Bows *et al.*, *Aviation and Climate Change*; P. Upham, 'Intro - duction: Perspectives on Sustainability and Aviation' in P. Upham *et al.* (eds), *Towards Sustainable Aviation* (London: Earthscan 2003).

230 Stefan Gössling and Paul Upham (eds), *Climate Change and Aviation: Issues, Challenges and Solutions* (London: Earthscan 2009) 8; the study considers aviation and climate change in the context of recent trends of network consolidation and more widespread introduction of low-cost strategies.

231 Gössling and Upham, 'Introduction' 8 referring to IATA publication, *Building a Greener Future* (2nd edn, 2008), available online at: www.iata.org/NR/rdonlyres/22669B08-918C-4AB7-8D8F-8F9743BA8FE6/61062/BuildingaGreenerFutureApril2008.pdf; IATA, 'The "Zero Carbon Future" Proposal', online at: www.iata.org/pressroom/pr/Pages/2007-06-04-02.aspx

> 2050, and some forecasts suggest that CO_2 emissions from air transport could increase ten-fold over that period.[232]

Linking this point to climate change, Houghton says that 'controlling the growing influence of aviation on the climate is probably the largest challenge to be solved in the overall mitigation of climate change'.[233] Other challenges in the environment arena are air quality, sustainable development and, of course, noise pollution.

As regards GHG emissions from civil aviation, the international aviation sector contributes between 2 and 2.5 per cent to global GHG emissions.[234] In the EU, aviation emissions account for about 3 per cent of the EU's total GHG emissions, of which a majority are understood to come from international flights.[235] Numerous projections on how this figure will change have been tabled by different bodies; some are more reliable than others. The European Commission projects that global international aviation emissions will be around 70 per cent higher in 2020 than they were in 2005 notwithstanding an improvement in fuel efficiency of 2 per cent per year.[236] ICAO also forecasts that by 2050 emissions could grow by a further 300–700 per cent.[237] Whilst there is no universal consensus on the figure, there is convergence on the belief that there will be a significant increase in future global aviation emissions as demand for flying grows; and it will. 'Air transport is currently a small but nonetheless significant contributor to climate change, mainly as a result of the various, interrelated effects of aircraft emissions'.[238]

The global nature of the problem has called for a global response; and it is well underway. Nearly a decade on since a joint United Nations Environment Programme and World Meteorological Organization Intergovernmental Panel on Climate Change (IPCC) report was first published,[239] one has been able to witness the considerable amount of work the aviation

232 Daley, *Air Transport and the Environment* 206 referring to S. Cairns and C. Newson, *Predict and Decide: Aviation, Climate Change and UK Policy* (Oxford: Environmental Change Institute 2006), online at: www.eci.ox.ac.uk/research/energy/downloads/predictanddecide.pdf

233 J. Houghton, *Global Warming: The Complete Briefing* (4th edn, Cambridge University Press 2009) 346; see Daley, *Air Transport and the Environment* 207

234 David S. Lee *et al.*, 'Aviation and Global Climate Change in the 21st Century' (2009) 43 *Atmospheric Environment* 3520–3537; see also Air Transport Action Group, 'Facts and Figures', online at: www.atag.org/facts-and-figures.html

235 European Commission, 'Reducing Emissions from Aviation', online at: http://ec.europa.eu/clima/policies/transport/aviation/index_en.htm

236 Ibid.

237 Ibid.

238 Daley, *Air Transport and the Environment* 49.

239 United Nations Environment Programme, Intergovernmental Panel on Climate Change, 'Aviation and the Global Atmosphere' (2009), online at: www.ipcc.ch/ipccreports/sres/aviation/index.php?idp=3

industry has undertaken to limit and reduce aviation emissions. In 2009, for example, the industry agreed three essential targets: (1) to improve annual fuel efficiency by 1.5 per cent (to 2020); (2) to cap net emissions through carbon neutral growth (from 2020); and (3) to cut net emissions by 50 per cent (by 2050 as compared to 2005 levels).[240] To achieve this, airlines and aircraft manufacturers have taken crucial, though often costly, steps to improve technologies, for example using biofuels and designing and producing engines that burn fuel more efficiently, adding wingtip devices, using lighter paints and putting lighter seats and trolleys on board.[241] As revenue passenger-kilometres and freight tonne-kilometres have increased, they have done so 'more rapidly than the rate at which emissions have decreased due to improvements in aviation technology and in operational procedures. Consequently, specific emissions have generally declined. On the other hand, absolute emissions have increased due to the vastly increased demand for air transport'.[242]

Gössling and Upham suggest that the 'drivers of aviation growth' must be understood before 'contemporary aviation and its climate impacts can be ... properly understood' owing to the 'interrelationship of climate change and aviation [being] a complex one'.[243] Therefore there is a need for an integrated perspective on growth in demand for air services. 'Rapid growth in air travel is a product of specific and powerful social, economic, cultural, technological and commercial trends as well as a special, often preferential treatment, in politics'.[244] For instance, in Denmark the maritime sector is regulated by the Ministry of Business and Growth whereas aviation is covered by the Ministry of Transport and Building.[245] While the aviation business has become more and more global in the years since 1944, some States continue to view aviation as an important political tool in global affairs, for others it is mostly an economic tool, or for some a combination of the two.[246]

240 IATA, 'New IATA Passenger Forecast Reveals Fast-Growing Markets of the Future' (16 October 2014), online at: www.iata.org/pressroom/pr/pages/2014-10-16-01.aspx.

241 IATA, 'Climate Change', online at: www.iata.org/policy/environment/pages/climate-change.aspx; see also L. Rye *et al.*, 'Sustainability of Supply or the Planet: A Review of Potential Drop-in Alternative Aviation Fuels' (2010) 3 *Energy Environ. Sci.* 17–27; George Marsh, 'Biofuels: Aviation Alternative?' (2008) 9(4) *Renewable Energy Focus* 48–51.

242 Daley, *Air Transport and the Environment* 35 referring to Royal Academy of Engineering, 'House of Commons Transport Select Committee: Inquiry into Aviation, Memorandum submitted by the Royal Academy of Engineering' (London, April 2003).

243 Gössling and Upham, 'Introduction' 13.

244 Ibid.

245 On the face of it, this seems to suggest that Denmark views shipping as a commercial activity and aviation as a different sort of sector alongside railways and road transport. Given Denmark's long history as a seafaring nation, this is perhaps more deep-rooted than taken at first glance.

246 Examples include developing States that may not have a national aviation sector but are very active in ICAO, or relatively 'new' States that take a strategic view of aviation as a means of boosting national economies.

In any case, the perceived impact of global aviation on the environment has prompted regulatory responses at multiple levels.[247] Daley provides an overview of *possible* policy options for aviation and climate change:

> A wide range of regulatory, market-based and voluntary measures designed to reduce the impacts of air transport on climate can be grouped together within the category of policy options. It is clear that improvements in aircraft and engine technology, fuel technology and operational systems and procedures – including the increased efficiency of ATM systems and procedures – could mitigate some of the impacts of aviation on climate, but that those advances will not fully offset the emissions resulting from the projected growth in aviation.[248]

In actuality, policy decisions taken at the national level have manifested vis-à-vis the introduction by some governments of environmental taxes on travel by air, which have been successful at raising tax revenue yet appear to have had no appreciable effect on passenger numbers.[249] At the 'regional' level, the EU introduced an Emissions Trading System[250] in 2005, and extended it to

247 See Andreas Føllesdal *et al.* (eds), *Multilevel Regulation and the EU: The Interplay between Global, European and National Normative Processes* (Martinus Nijhoff Publishers 2008).

248 Daley, *Air Transport and the Environment* 73–74 referring to S. Bishop and T. Grayling, *The Sky's the Limit: Policies for Sustainable Aviation,* (London: Institute for Public Policy Research 2003); Cairns and Newson, *Predict and Decide*; B. Daley and H. Preston, 'Aviation and Climate Change: Assessment of Policy Options' in S. Gössling and P. Upham (eds), *Climate Change and Aviation* 347–372; C. Hewett and J. Foley, *Plane Trading: Policies for Reducing the Climate Change Effects of International Aviation* (London: Institute for Public Policy Research 2000); J. Roberts, *Environmental Policy* (Routledge 2004); and J. E. Penner *et al.* (eds), *Aviation and the Global Atmosphere* (Prepared in collaboration with the Scientific Assessment Panel to the Montreal Protocol on Substances that Deplete the Ozone Layer) (Cambridge University Press 1999), available online at: www.ipcc.ch/ipccreports/sres/aviation

249 Examples include the United Kingdom's Air Passenger Duty (Finance Act 1994, ss. 28–44 and schs 5A and 6, as amended), France's *Taxe de l'aviation civile* (codifiée à l'article 302 bis K du Code Général des Impôts) and Germany's *Luftverkehrsteuergesetz* (LuftVStG §11). For a critical discussion, see Steven Truxal and Rupert Dunbar, 'Evaluating Three Levels of Environmental Taxation in Aviation: Global Limitation, EU Determination and UK Self-interest' in Ana Yabar Sterling *et al.* (eds), *Market Instruments and Sustainable Economy* (Instituto de Estudios Fiscales, Madrid 2012) 275.

250 Directive 2003/87/EC establishing a scheme for greenhouse gas emission allowance trading within the Community and amending Council Directive 96/61/EC [2003] OJ L275/32.

include aviation activities from 2012.[251] Depending on one's persuasion it may be argued that the EU ETS is somewhat of an aviation success story; this is discussed below.

Again it can be said that there is increasing pressure on the international community to work together to tackle complex, global problems that affect humankind such as the threat of climate change. According to Gössling and Upham, 'the latest scientific evidence tells us that within about 10 years the greenhouse gas emissions trends of industrialized nations will need to contract year on year by at least some 4 per cent per annum (on a compound basis) until 2050. However, this is not likely to happen if an economic sector receives special treatment, or is even allowed to grow'.[252]

The international community is also responding, with the most recent tangible outcome being the Paris Agreement 2015.[253] Unlike the Kyoto Protocol, which was the first key agreement to strengthen the UN Framework Convention on Climate Change (UNFCCC) treaty, the Paris Agreement makes no reference to emissions from international maritime shipping or international aviation.[254] Emissions from international aviation are also excluded from the Kyoto Protocol, which provides in Article 2(2): 'The Parties included in Annex I shall pursue limitation or reduction of emissions of greenhouse gases not controlled by the Montreal Protocol from

251 Directive 2008/101/EC of 19 November 2008; The EU ETS requirements were suspended in 2012 for flights to and from non-EU countries. 'The amended law provides for the Commission to report to the European Parliament and Council on the outcome of the 2016 ICAO Assembly and propose measures as appropriate to take international developments into account with effect from 2017' (European Commission, 'Reducing Emissions from Aviation', online at: http://ec.europa.eu/clima/policies/transport/aviation/index_en.htm)

252 Gössling and Upham, 'Introduction' 13 referring to A. Bows *et al.*, 'Technology, Scenarios and Uncertainties' (Tyndall Centre Manchester, The University of Manchester 2007), online at: www.cstt.nl/userdata/documents/bows_anderson_peeters_eclat_2007.pdf; P. Upham *et al.*, 'Aviation Policy Options for Not Exceeding the EU +2 C Threshold' in D. de Jong *et al.* (eds), *Blue Skies or Storm Clouds? Essays on Public Policy and Air Transport* (Scienceguide–Aerlines, NOL 2008) 72–78, available online at: https://aerlinesmagazine.wordpress.com/2009/03/01/aviation-policy-options-for-not-exceeding-the-eu-2-%E2%97%A6c-threshold/

253 Art 2(a) of the Paris Agreement sets out the upper limit of increase in global average temperature 'to well below 2°C above pre-industrial levels and pursuing efforts to limit the temperature increase to 1.5°C above pre-industrial levels, recognizing that this would significantly reduce the risks and impacts of climate change'. According to Art 21(1), the Agreement 'shall enter into force on the thirtieth day after the date on which at least 55 Parties to the Convention accounting in total for at least an estimated 55 per cent of the total global greenhouse gas emissions have deposited their instruments of ratification, acceptance, approval or accession' See UNFCCC, 'Paris Agreement', online at: http://unfccc.int/files/home/application/pdf/paris_agreement.pdf

254 Kyoto Protocol, Art 2(2); United Nations Framework Convention on Climate Change (UNFCCC), 'Kyoto Protocol and the UN Climate Change Secretariat: A Global Framework to Tackle Climate Change' (2007) 37 ILM 32.

aviation and marine bunker fuels, working through the International Civil Aviation Organization and the International Maritime Organization, respectively'. Thus ICAO is mandated to provide a forum for Kyoto Annex I countries to pursue limitation or reduction activities for international aviation.

Global public good

If we frame the environment as a global public good, which is uncontentious, protection of the environment is therefore in the common (global) interest of the global neighbourhood – the global interest. This is evidenced by the prominence of the climate change discourse in global policy work. Relatedly, the problem of international aviation emissions and climate change is of global importance and thus includes oversight and regulation of it within the universal global regulatory framework. It is accepted that the UNFCCC is 'the appropriate legal forum to tackle the problem of climate change'.[255]

The UNFCCC process establishes *national* goals and reduction and limitation commitments that guide the respective *national* strategies of the Parties to the UNFCCC vis-à-vis the Kyoto Protocol; *international* aviation emissions are excluded. This translates for instance to indirect environmental regulation of domestic flights by international law.[256] The Kyoto Protocol's first commitment period ended in 2012. The Doha Amendment to the Kyoto Protocol, adopted in December 2012, created a second commitment period from January 2013 to December 2020.[257] The Kyoto Protocol provides that participating countries will endeavour to address climate change by reducing emissions to 18 per cent below 1990 levels during the second commitment period. Once it enters into force, the Paris Agreement 2015 will require States to limit temperature increases globally to below 2°C above pre-industrial levels with an ambitious caveat that States should pursue efforts to limit the temperature increase to 1.5°C at maximum.

With that said, the consensus view is that to date the UNFCCC process has generally delivered 'inadequate results', owing to what many consider to be an overly ambitious approach. Indeed, the UNFCCC aims 'to articulate a comprehensive framework for climate change regulation that encompasses a wide variety of different sectors, and its commitment to a multilateral approach based upon procedures of consensus-based decision-making'.[258] Nonetheless, the UNFCCC process has been beneficial in many ways. 'An

255 Ibid.

256 In practice, a State makes a commitment to reduce greenhouse gas emissions within its territory, which translates into the imposition of standards or restrictions through *national* rules vis-à-vis its *international* law obligations.

257 Ibid.

258 Jaqueline Peel *et al.*, 'Climate Change Law in an Era of Multi-Level Governance' (2012) 1(2) *Transnational Environmental Law* 250.

important contribution made by the UNFCCC to climate law and governance is providing a principled basis for climate policy and a source of international legitimacy for efforts undertaken at multiple levels that seek to implement its broad objectives'.[259] Whilst it is not the aim of this project to explain or critique the UNFCCC process, it is accepted that it has delivered some slow progress in the area of universal policy on climate change. In 2015, Paris delivered an agreement that is quickly being ratified by States. Once the Paris Agreement comes into force, we are likely to regain the early Kyoto momentum, but this time backed by the commitment of the biggest global economic players.

Globalization

The focus of this book is on international (civil) aviation, now *global* aviation. It is a good, if not the best, example of a sector that drives greater interconnectedness in an increasingly globalized world: 'Air transport plays a vital role in supporting economies and societies that are increasingly interconnected by globalization'.[260] Globalization 'reflects a widespread perception that the world is rapidly being moulded into a shared social space'.[261] This 'worldwide interconnectedness' delivers a need for 'acknowledgement of a real or perceived *intensification* of global interconnectedness'.[262]

Whilst there is no single, agreed definition of globalization, there are three main schools of thought accepted in scholarship.[263] First, the so-called 'hyperglobalizers' are of the view that 'contemporary globalization defines a new era in which peoples everywhere are increasingly subject to the disciplines of the global marketplace'.[264] It follows that this brings about a '[n]ew epoch in human history in which "traditional nation-states have become unnatural, even impossible business units in a global economy"'.[265] According to Held *et al.*, the hyperglobalizers focus on the global market and global competition, which in turn give way to 'denationalization' of economic and political power of States.[266] 'In this "borderless" economy, national governments are relegated to little more than transmission belts for global capital

259 Ibid., 280.
260 Daley, *Air Transport and the Environment* 16.
261 Held *et al.*, *Global Transformations* 1.
262 Ibid., 2 (emphasis added).
263 Jens-Uwe Wunderlich and Meera Warrier, *A Dictionary of Globalization* (Routledge 2007); Anthony Giddens, 'Globalization in the Changing World' in *Sociology* (5th edn, Polity Press 2006).
264 Held *et al.*, *Global Transformations* 2 referring to Kenichi Ohmae, *The Borderless World* (London: William Collins 1990) and Kenichi Ohmae, *The End of the Nation State: The Rise of Regional Economics* (London: Harper Collins 1995).
265 Held *et al.*, *Global Transformations* 3 citing Ohmae, *The Borderless World*.
266 Held *et al.*, *Global Transformations*; see also Susan Strange, *The Retreat of the State* (Cambridge University Press 1999).

or, ultimately, simple intermediate institutions sandwiched between increasingly powerful local, regional and global mechanisms of governance'.[267]

Thus, for hyperglobalizers, globalization is an economic phenomenon. In turn, 'the needs of global capital impose a neoliberal economic discipline on all governments such that politics is no longer the "art of the possible" but rather the practice of "sound economic management"'.[268] This means that 'governments have to "manage" the social consequences of globalization', with a view to ensuring that no country is left behind,[269] while in fact one can link globalization to a 'growing polarization of winners and losers in global economy'.[270] In keeping with the work of Held *et al.*, one can witness an

> emergence of institutions of global governance ... interpreted as evidence of a radically new world order, an order which prefigures the demise of the nation-state.[271] Since the national economy is increasingly a site of transnational and global flows ... the authority and legitimacy of the nation-state are challenged: national governments become increasingly unable either to control what transpires within their own borders or to fulfil by themselves the demands of their own citizens.[272]

Thus, a 'global civil society' emerges, in which States and non-State actors, including private actors, are able to unite around important causes that affect society as a whole, encouraging the use of public–private partnerships to achieve goals for the global society, together.

Second, there are the sceptics. They 'argue that globalization is essentially a myth which conceals the reality of an international economy increasingly segmented into three major regional blocs in which national governments remain very powerful': Asia–Pacific, Europe and North America.[273] The origin of this view is in the work of Gilpin, who argues the 'internationalization [is] largely a by-product of the US-initiated multilateral economic order, which in the aftermath of the Second World War, created the impetus for the liberalization of national economies'.[274]

267 Held *et al.*, *Global Transformations* 3.

268 Ibid., 4.

269 Ibid.; link to ICAO 'NCLB Campaign', online at: http://icao.int/about-icao/NCLB/Pages/default.aspx

270 Held *et al.*, *Global Transformations* 4.

271 E. Luard, *The Globalization of Politics: The Changed Focus of Political Action in the Modern* World (New York University Press 1990); Ohmae, *The Borderless World*; Martin Albrow, *The Global Age* (Stanford University Press 1996) (note in original).

272 Held *et al.*, *Global Transformations* 4–5.

273 Held *et al.*, *Global Transformations* 2 referring to P. Q. Hirst and G. F. Thompson, *Globalization in Question: The International Economy and the Possibilities of Governance* (1st edn, Polity Press 1996).

274 Held *et al.*, *Global Transformations* 5–6 referring to Robert Gilpin, *The Political Economy of International Relations* (Princeton University Press 1987).

Third and finally, there are the 'transformationalists'. They are led by Rosenau and Giddens, who observe globalization as evidence of a changing global order. Fundamentally, they hold that the nation-state is no longer the only or main form of governance.[275] Transformationalists posit that 'contemporary patterns of globalization are conceived as historically unprecedented such that states and societies across the globe are experiencing a process of profound change as they try to adapt to a more interconnected but highly uncertain world'.[276] Thus, 'North and South, First World and Third World, are no longer "out there" but nestled together within all the world's major cities'.[277] The gaps are closing; distant problems are now felt closer to home.

Transformationalists argue that 'national economies are being reorganized by processes of economic globalization such that national economic space no longer coincides with national territorial borders'.[278] Held *et al.* clarify:

> At the core of the transformationalist case is a belief that contemporary globalization is reconstituting or 're-engineering' the power, functions and authority of national governments. While not disputing that states still retain the ultimate legal claim to 'effective supremacy over what occurs within their own territories', the transformationalists argue that this is juxtaposed, to varying degrees, with the expanding jurisdiction of institutions of international governance and the constraints of, as well as the obligations derived from, international law.[279]

Thus the 'modern institution of territorially circumscribed sovereign state rule appears somewhat anomalous juxtaposed with the transnational organization of many aspects of contemporary economic and social life'.[280] Globalization then is a *transformation* or, to use Ruggie's term, an 'unbundling' of the relationships between sovereignty, territoriality and power.[281] Transformationalists

275 Held *et al.*, *Global Transformations* 9 referring to James Rosenau, *Along the Domestic–Foreign Frontier: Exploring Governance in a Turbulent World* (Cambridge University Press 1997).

276 Held *et al.*, *Global Transformations* 2 referring to Anthony Giddens, *The Consequences of Modernity* (Stanford University Press 1990) and Rosenau, *Along the Domestic–Foreign Frontier*.

277 Held *et al.*, *Global Transformations* 8.

278 Ibid., 8 referring to M. Castells, *The Information Age: Economy, Society and Culture, Vol. I, the Rise of the Network Society* (Blackwell 1996).

279 Held *et al.*, *Global Transformations* 8.

280 Held *et al.*, *Global Transformations* 8 referring to M. Sandel, *Democracy's Discontent* (Harvard University Press 1996).

281 Held *et al.*, *Global Transformations* 8 referring to Ruggie, 'Territoriality and Beyond'; Sassen, *Losing Control?*

> assert that a new 'sovereignty regime' is displacing traditional conceptions of statehood as an absolute, indivisible, territoriality exclusive and zero-sum form of public power.[282] Accordingly, sovereignty today is, they suggest, best understood 'less as a territorially defined barrier than a bargaining resource for a politics characterized by complex transnational networks'.[283]

So, as Held *et al.* put it, 'Sovereignty, state power and territoriality thus stand today in a more complex relationship than in the epoch during which the modern nation-state was being forged'.[284]

Transformationalists not only argue that this brings about a new 'sovereignty regime'; but also yields the 'emergence of powerful new non-territorial forms of economic and political organization in the global domain, such as multinational corporations, transnational social movements, international regulatory agencies, etc'.[285] Let us pause then and consider global airlines: there are more airlines owned by multinationals today than ever before. It is argued that cosmopolitan airlines now resemble multinational corporations in many respects, beginning with the composition of owners. With that said the limits to foreign ownership of air carriers tend to remain strict in many parts of the world. But this cannot last forever. In this changing global order, 'governments seek coherent strategies of engaging with a globalizing world'.[286] As a means of attracting much needed foreign investment in failing national airlines, governments begin to appear more amicable to the investment. This is presented as a possible 'push factor' for States – a business opportunity involving financial support for national airlines for some States, and a business or values opportunity for other States as leaders.

According to the transformationalists, 'governments have become increasingly outward looking as they seek to pursue cooperative strategies and to construct international regulatory regimes to manage more effectively the growing array of cross-border issues which regularly surface on national agendas'.[287] What we begin to observe then are seemingly more activist States. Held *et al.* say that 'the power of national governments is not necessarily being diminished by globalization but on the contrary is being reconstituted and restructured in response to the growing complexity of

282 Held *et al.*, *Global Transformations* 9 referring to David Held, *Political Theory Today* (Stanford University Press 1991) (note in original).

283 Held *et al.*, *Global Transformations* 9 citing R. O. Keohane, 'Hobbes Dilemma and Institutional Change in World Politics: Sovereignty in International Society' in H. Holm and G. Sorensen (eds), *Whose World Order?* (Boulder: Westview Press 1995).

284 Held *et al.*, *Global Transformations* 9.

285 Ibid.

286 Ibid. (emphasis added).

287 Ibid. (emphasis added).

processes of governance in a more interconnected world'.[288] Indeed we have witnessed greater State-to-State cooperation in these areas, yet they are still fraught with issues around sovereignty and the resistance to 'outside' interference with the international regulation of a State (within its own territory).

By no means does this book seek to theorize or offer new conceptualizations of globalization. Instead we accept that the most appropriate 'approach' for this project is the transformationalist school of thought. As we have seen in Chapter 2, sovereignty is transforming. Globalization contributes to this transformation and calls for a re-examination of 'the global' and 'the local'.

Globalization is 'located on a continuum with the local, national and regional', as Held *et al.* advocate, where '[a]t the one end of the continuum lie social and economic relations and networks which are organized on a local and/or national basis; at the other end lie social and economic relations and networks which crystallize on the wider scale of regional and global interactions'.[289] Globalization, then, implies 'a *stretching* of social, poetical and economic activities across frontiers such that events, decisions and activities in one region of the world can come to have significance for individuals and communities in distant regions of the globe'.[290] It is also suggested that this also implies 'a *speeding up* of global interactions and processes as the development of worldwide systems of transport and communications increase the potential velocity of the global diffusion of ideas, goods, information, capital and people'.[291] We have witnessed this in recent years insofar as the '*impact* of distant events is magnified while even the most local developments may come to have enormous global consequences. In this sense, the boundaries between domestic matters and global affairs may be blurred'.[292]

In the context of civil aviation, the dissolving separation between global and local[293] is perhaps most evident in noise pollution (as nuisance) from aircraft engines,[294] which also adversely impacts on the environment: 'Aircraft noise is acknowledged to be one of the most significant local

288 Ibid. referring to Rosenau, *Along the Domestic–Foreign Frontier*.

289 Held *et al.*, *Global Transformations* 15.

290 Ibid.

291 Ibid.

292 Ibid.

293 See Saskia Sassen, 'Denationalised State Agendas and Privatized Norm-Making' in Saskia Sassen (ed.), *Territory, Authority, Rights: From Medieval to Global Assemblages* (Princeton University Press 2006).

294 Schulz notes there are physical, physiological, psychological and sociological aspects of aircraft engine noise (Daley, *Air Transport and the Environment* 123 referring to T. J. Schultz, 'Synthesis of Social Surveys on Noise Annoyance' (1978) 64(2) *Journal of the Acoustical Society of America* 377–405).

environmental impacts associated with the operation of airports'.[295] The pollution is mostly 'received' at and in the vicinity of congested airports – of which there are many, particularly in Europe and the U.S. where proposals on airport expansion tend to be politically toxic. Aircraft engine manufacture is subject to ICAO standards and recommended practices (SARPs). In the words of Daley,

> The ICAO aircraft engine certification standards are applied at the point of engine manufacture, but those standards represent the only regulatory control of aviation air pollution and aviation emissions are not directly regulated at most airports. In the short to medium term, policy approaches are likely to focus on encouraging greater use of the most fuel-efficient (and least-polluting) aircraft, especially at major airports where compliance with air quality objectives is already marginal. In the longer term, a combination of policy approaches may be adopted: the use of voluntary agreements within the industry to reduce emissions; the imposition of more stringent emissions standards, especially for NO_X and particles; the removal of existing privileges and subsidies of the industry; the wider use of emissions charges, fuel taxes and other levies; the development of emissions trading schemes for key air pollutants; and, ultimately, the use of demand restraint measures and the restriction of airport infrastructure development.[296]

It is interesting to note the political and legal backdrop of aircraft engine noise pollution vis-à-vis the *Hushkits* dispute between the EU and U.S. In this debacle, the USA argued that the EU's enactment of legislation[297] that effectively prohibited the use of so-called 'hushkits' to reduce aircraft engine noise at EU airports was a 'unilateral measure discriminating against third countries, including operators based in those countries, and is illegal in the light of agreed and applicable global standards, including those of the

295 Daley, *Air Transport and the Environment* 123 referring to reports by UK Department for Transport, U.S. Federal Aviation Administration and academics, e.g. K. I. Hume and A. Watson, 'The Human Health Impacts of Aviation' in P. Upham *et al.* (eds), *Towards Sustainable Aviation* (London: Earthscan, 2003) 48–76; M. May and S. B. Hill, 'Questioning Airport Expansion: a Case Study of Canberra International Airport' (2006) 14(6) *Journal of Transport Geography* 437–450.

296 Daley, *Air Transport and the Environment* 121–122.

297 Council Regulation (EC) No 925/1999 of 29 April 1999 on the registration and operation within the Community of certain types of civil subsonic jet aeroplanes which have been modified and recertificated as meeting the standards of Volume I, Part II, Chapter 3 of Annex 16 to the Convention on International Civil Aviation, third edition (July 1993), OJ L115/1.

Chicago Convention and its Annex 16[298] on the Environment'.[299] The case was settled in 2002 when the legislation was repealed and replaced by new legislation[300] on operational restrictions at airports, whereby shifting from a territorial basis to an 'access to infrastructure' basis.[301] This prompts us to consider another form of environmental law in action devised by the EU in the next section of this chapter.

Case study: EU Emissions Trading System

Protection of the environment is one of the core values of the European Union. This is also reflected in the Treaty on the Functioning of the European Union (TFEU). First and foremost, Article 11 TFEU provides that 'environmental protection requirements must be integrated into the definition and implementation of the Union policies and activities, in particular with a view to promoting sustainable development'. Second, Article 191 TFEU refers to EU policies. They should 'contribute to the pursuit of … preserving, protecting and improving the quality of the environment … [and] promoting measures at international level to deal with regional or worldwide environmental problems, and in particular combating climate change'.[302] It is against this backdrop that the EU may be viewed as exercising 'environmental leadership' globally vis-à-vis its ETS.[303] The ETS,

298 Annex 16 on the environment was included in 1971 to deal with noise (in Volume I). In 1981, its scope was expanded to address aircraft engine emissions (locally, in Volume II). See Dempsey *Public International Air Law* 451.

299 Mendes de Leon 'The Dynamics of Sovereignty and Jurisdiction in International Aviation Law' 493–494; see also Benedicte A. Claes, 'Aircraft Noise Regulation in the European Union: The Hushkit Problem' (2000) 65 *Air L. & Com.* 329; Irina Ionescu, 'Aircraft Noise Regulation' (Thesis, Institute of Air and Space Law, McGill University 2004).

300 Directive 2002/30/EC of the European Parliament and of the Council of 26 March 2002 on the establishment of rules and procedures with regard to the introduction of noise-related operating restrictions at Community airports, [2002] OJ L85/40.

301 Mendes de Leon 'The Dynamics of Sovereignty and Jurisdiction in International Aviation Law' 494; Mendes de Leon also reminds us that EU Member States are subject of international law but not necessarily *independent* subjects of international law; they are required to take a common position vis-à-vis so-called third countries in aviation. The European Parliament repealed the regulation and replaced it with a directive. This shifts responsibility to individual Member States to implement the aims of the legislation in national law.

302 See e.g. the EU's 2030 Climate & Energy Framework http://ec.europa.eu/clima/policies/strategies/2030/index_en.htm; and 2050 Low-Carbon Economy http://ec.europa.eu/clima/policies/strategies/2050/index_en.htm

303 Joanne Scott and Lavanya Rajamani, 'Contingent Unilateralism: International Aviation in the European Emissions Trading Scheme' in Bart Van Vooren *et al.* (eds), *The EU's Role in Global Governance: The Legal Dimension* (Oxford University Press 2013) 209–223; Sanja Bogojević, 'Legalising Environmental Leadership: A Comment on the CJEU's Ruling in C-366/10 on the Inclusion of Aviation in the EU Emissions Trading Scheme' (2012) 24(2) *Journal of Environmental Law* 345.

Piera argues, 'stands as a policy response to the unwillingness of the international aviation community to regulate GHG emissions from international aviation. Europe decided to include foreign aircraft operators into its ETS only after it became abundantly clear that States gathered at ICAO were unwilling to do so'.[304]

The EU established the ETS under Directive 2003/87/EC, which created the world's first international market-based, 'cap-and-trade' system of nationally allocated rights, across the EU based on the proportion of industry in each EU Member State; they are bought and sold.[305] The ETS is heralded as the 'cornerstone' of the EU's climate change policy. It is an open trading scheme in which so-called 'carbon credits' are allocated as marketable rights, quasi licences to pollute, which are subsequently traded freely on the market irrespective of sector and in accordance with National Allocation Plans.[306]

The NAPs prescribe to each aircraft operator an emissions quota; thus, each entity is encouraged to choose the least costly option to meet their respective quota. The allowances allocated to the aviation sector were originally due to be offset in the final two planned phases against the aviation greenhouse gas emissions as set out in Directive 2008/101/EC, which amends Directive 2003/87/EC to include 'aviation activities' in the EU ETS, including those operated by non-EU carriers, from so-called 'third countries'.[307] The agreement to include aviation in the EU ETS was adopted by the European Parliament in its resolution on climate change and is estimated to lead to a reduction of 194 million tonnes of carbon dioxide (CO_2) across the EU by 2020.[308] Through the ETS, the EU aims to achieve its Kyoto commitments while balancing which sectors and installations to include in it, and when.

However, the decision to include aviation activities in the EU ETS has been consistently met with objection owing to the seemingly extraterritorial reach of the legislation, which has as its original object to capture aviation

304 Piera Valdes, *Greenhouse Gas Emissions from International Aviation* 9.

305 Directive 2003/87/EC (n 250); the ETS is now known as the Emissions Trading System.

306 Directive 2008/101/EC of 19 November 2008.

307 Directive 2009/29/EC of the European Parliament and of the Council of 23 Apr. 2009 amending Directive 2003/87/EC so as to improve and extend the greenhouse gas emission allowance trading scheme of the Community [2009] OJ L140/63.

308 European Parliament, *Resolution on Climate Change* [2007] OJ C287 E/344.

emissions for flights beyond EU airspace.[309] The major legal challenge was brought in the UK in the *Air Transport Association* case.[310] In this application for judicial review, the claimants argued that the EU ETS Directive, as an exercise of extraterritoriality by the EU to 'capture the cost' of the total emissions on a flight from, say, Dallas to London, breaches certain principles of customary international law on sovereignty and jurisdiction,[311] and provisions of international laws, namely the Chicago Convention, Kyoto Protocol and the U.S.–EU Air Transport Agreement.[312]

As this book has identified in Chapters 1 and 2, in the context of aviation, sovereignty over 'airspace' is enshrined in Article 1 of the 1944 Chicago Convention, which states: 'The contracting States recognize that every State has complete and exclusive sovereignty over the airspace above its territory'. For international aviation, the Chicago Convention goes on to build imaginary walls along the limits of a State's *terra firma* and 'up to the sky', boxing in the 'territory',[313] insofar as Article 6 allows for operation of international air services 'over or into the territory of a contracting State' only with 'special permission or other authorization of that State, and in accordance with the terms of such permission or authorization'. To register an aircraft, States will require substantial ownership or control by the State or nationals of the State. The registrations are reported to and then distributed to other States by ICAO. And so on.

What ensues is a kind of nationalism-*cum*-protectionism, which is exercised on a reciprocity–recognition basis.[314] The evolution in this area should also be noted, recalling the time when all States had one or more 'flag carriers', to the current position within the EU, where any airline registered

309 Steven Truxal, 'Competitive Distortions, Carbon Emissions Efficiencies or the Green Ultimatum?' (2008) 14(4) *International Trade Law and Regulation* 77–79; Steven Truxal, 'At the Sidelines of Implementing the EU ETS: Objections to "Validity"' (2010) 16(4) *International Trade Law and Regulation* 28–36; Annela Anger, 'Including Aviation in the European Emissions Trading Scheme: Impacts on the Industry, CO_2 Emissions and Macroeconomic Activity in the EU' (2010) 16(2) *Journal of Air Transport Management* 100–105; Brian F. Havel and John Q. Mulligan, 'The Triumph of Politics: Reflections on the Judgment of the Court of Justice of the European Union Validating the Inclusion of Non-EU Airlines in the Emissions Trading Scheme' (2012) 37(1) *Air & Space Law* 3–33.

310 *Air Transport Association.*

311 Specifically, State sovereignty over its airspace, sovereignty over the international waters of the high seas and freedom to fly over the high seas.

312 Air Transport Agreement between the United States of America and the Member States of the European Union, [2007] OJ L134/4, 25 May 2007.

313 'Territory' as interpreted in the Chicago Convention is defined in Article 2, which reads: 'For the purposes of this Convention the territory of a State shall be deemed to be the land areas and territorial waters adjacent thereto under the sovereignty, suzerainty, protection or mandate of such State'.

314 J. Naveau, 'Droit de l'Air et Nationalisme Historique' (1990) 15 *Annals of Air and Space Law* 183.

in a Member State sheds its, for example 'UK carrier' status and is projected now externally as European 'Union carrier'.[315]

Furthermore, Article 15 of the Chicago Convention requires that 'no fees, dues or other charges shall be imposed by any contracting State in respect of the right of transit over or entry into or exit from its territory of any aircraft of a contracting State or persons or property thereon' and that any public airport shall 'be open under uniform conditions of all the other contracting States'.

In the *Air Transport Association* case the Grand Chamber of the CJEU confirmed that Directive 2008/101 is valid.[316] In delivering reference on the preliminary ruling heard by the High Court of Justice of England and Wales, the CJEU held that application of the EU ETS to aircraft operators 'infringes neither the principle of territoriality nor the sovereignty of third States, since the scheme is applicable to the operators only when their aircraft are physically in the territory of one of the Member States of the EU and are thus subject to the unlimited jurisdiction of the EU', so 'linked' to the territory and therefore relying on the territorial interpretation of sovereignty. The CJEU also held: 'Nor can such application of EU law affect the principle of freedom to fly over the high seas since an aircraft flying over the high seas is not subject, in so far as it does so, to the emissions trading scheme'.[317]

In its judgment, the CJEU clarified that the EU is not bound by the Chicago Convention as it is neither a party to it nor has exclusive powers falling within the Convention.[318] It also explained that the Directive does not infringe the principles of territoriality or sovereignty of third countries to or from which flights are operated, nor the freedom to use airspace over the high seas.

The CJEU found that airlines that choose to operate flights to or from EU airports are subject to the ETS. The rationale of the CJEU was that the EU Parliament may permit transport in the EU on the condition that certain

315 Several ICAO Member States do not recognize the Union designation on the basis that the European Union is not a Member of the Chicago Convention.

316 Directive 2008/101/EC of 19 November 2008. The EU ETS was established vis-à-vis Directive 2003/87/EC of 13 October 2003.

317 'The directive including aviation activities in the EU's emissions trading scheme is valid: Application of the emissions trading scheme to aviation infringes neither the principles of customary international law at issue nor the Open Skies Agreement' (CJEU, 'The directive including aviation activities in the EU's emissions trading scheme is valid: Application of the emissions trading scheme to aviation infringes neither the principles of customary international law at issue nor the Open Skies Agreement' (21 December 2011), Press Release No 139/11 available online: www.curia.europa.eu); referring to argument that the emissions are calculated on the basis of fuel consumption/burn over a distance rather than the emissions resulting from flying that distance.

318 The CJEU also found that the Kyoto obligations were 'not unconditional and sufficiently precise' to be relied upon by the claimants (http://ec.europa.eu/dgs/legal_service/arrets/10c366_en.pdf).

criteria are met by the airline and it is irrelevant that part of the activity is performed outside of the EU.[319] Finally, the CJEU held that the ETS Directive does not infringe the U.S.–EU Air Transport Agreement insofar as it is a market-based measure (MBM) and not a tax, duty, fee or charge, and the ETS does not limit frequencies of services to and from the EU or impose any limit on emissions.[320] In the end, the claimants dropped the challenge.

In the light of international pressures[321] and so as to allow space for development of a global market-based measure via ICAO, the EU decided to 'stop the clock' with respect to international flights operating outside the European Economic Area (EEA).[322] The 39th General Assembly of ICAO met between September–October 2016, where a proposal for a GMBM for aviation was presented with a view to implementing it from 2020. What is understood is that until 2017, the ETS will appply only to flights within the EU and EEA, irrespective of the carrier's flag.[323] This will be discussed in detail in Chapter 4.

The *Air Transport Association* case raises interesting questions about the ETS and international agreements. As international agreements are not binding on sovereign states without consent, and because that consent to cooperation has 'failed to materialize',[324] Hertogen argues that the legality of the EU ETS cannot be determined with reference to an international consensus. It is argued that post-Kyoto coupled with the fact that aviation was excluded from the UNFCCC negotiation process at Paris in December 2015, the only likely path to muster the requisite consent appears to be at ICAO.

In fact, Hertogen suggests we approach State sovereignty as 'decisional sovereignty', which she argues 'creates space for a state to regulate unilaterally when multi-territorial activities affect its domestic affairs, even if the

319 A parallel may be drawn here to safety criteria which must be met to fly to, from or over the EU, pursuant to Regulation (EC) 2111/2005 of the European Parliament and Council on the establishment of a Community list of air carriers subject to an operating ban within the Community and on informing air transport passengers of the identity of the operating carrier, the so-called 'EU Safety List' ([2005] OJ L344/15). The current list is available here: http://ec.europa.eu/transport/modes/air/safety/air-ban/index_en.htm

320 Jon Truby, 'Extraterritoriality or an Illegal Tax? A Challenge to the Inclusion of Aviation in the EU Emissions Trading Scheme' (2012) 14 *Environmental Law Review* 301, 305.

321 This includes fears that a trade war would ensue, in particular between the USA and China on one side and the EU on the other. See U.S. Federal Law, the EU ETS Prohibition Act of 2011, S.1956; see also Pilita Clark, 'Airbus Warns of Emissions Trade War' *The Financial Times* 5 June 2012, available online at: www.ft.com/cms/s/0/92dc6fd4-8fa3-11e0-954d-00144feab49a.html#axzz4EqOV58PO

322 The European Economic Area (EEA) includes the 28 Member States of the EU plus Lichtenstein, Norway and Iceland.

323 European Union (EU), 'Reducing Emissions from Aviation', online at: http://ec.europa.eu/clima/policies/transport/aviation/index_en.htm

324 A. Hertogen, 'Sovereignty as Decisional Independence over Domestic Affairs: The Dispute over Aviation in the EU Emissions Trading System' (2012) 1(2) *Transnational Environmental Law* 281–301.

regulation applies to economic actors from other states that are active within the regulating state's territory'.[325] She first cites the U.S. exercise of jurisdiction over actors/activities that have only a nexus with regulating State's territory vis-à-vis taxation of resident aliens on worldwide income as example of extraterritoriality.[326]

> Given that international aviation is a multi-territorial activity, both the EU Member States and their opponents could claim jurisdiction ... [Hertogen] disagrees with the position that the inclusion of international aviation in the EU ETS is extra-territorial because allowances have to be submitted for the portion of a flight that takes place outside the airspace of the EU Member State. Such an interpretation of the territoriality principle limits the valid exercise of territorial jurisdiction to events that fall entirely within a single state's territory.[327]

Hertogen concludes, 'The principles that allocate jurisdiction under customary international law thus do not place international aviation outside the domestic affairs of one of the two sides involved. Instead, they can lead to *double regulation*'.[328]

This suggestion might be useful to explore further given the likelihood of increasing interdependence giving rise to greater numbers of jurisdictional disputes – though, as the point made above, still 'tethered' to a State's territory and therefore territorial sovereignty. This is particularly relevant in the area of climate change owing to its transnational character – and as a case in point, international aviation emissions, which in effect know no boundaries but where a link can be established to a State, for example EU ETS and EU airport, decisional sovereignty might be a good place to start. Furthermore, as Erling argues, the amount of emissions from aviation in emissions trading is only a 'calculation parameter' anyway and therefore 'foreign airspace' is untouched.[329]

325 Ibid., 301.

326 26 U.S.C. 862(b), 911 'Income from sources without the United States'; See Hertogen, 'Sovereignty as Decisional Independence over Domestic Affairs' 294.

327 Hertogen, 'Sovereignty as Decisional Independence over Domestic Affairs' 293.

328 Ibid. (emphasis added).

329 'Hiergegen wird indes eingewandt, dass die Menge der vom Luftverkehr verursachten Emissionen im Emissionshandel nur ein Berechnungsparameter ist und daher fremder Luftraum nicht berührt sei' (U. M. Erling, 'Der EU-Emissionshandel im Luftverkehr' (2009) 58(3) *ZLW* 351, citing Ron Wit *et al.*, 'Giving Wings to Emissions Trading: Inclusion of Aviation under the European Emissions Trading System (ETS) – Design and Impacts', (CE Delft 2004) http://ec.europa.eu/clima/policies/transport/aviation/docs/aviation_et_study_en.pdf).

Throughout, there has been doubt as to whether ICAO has the *political* determination to introduce a GMBM.[330] Milde reminds us that the ICAO Council 'does not act as a Court of law subject to impartial application of law but it is in fact a political arbitration expressing the political will of the Council Member States and not limited to strictly legal considerations'.[331]

The global disagreement on the validity of the EU ETS in the context of international law has troubled the international community since around 2004. States that oppose the EU ETS, including the USA, China, Russia, India and Brazil, have made their position known inside and outside ICAO.[332] First came the New Delhi Joint Declaration in September 2011, transposed as a Working Paper presented to ICAO Council in October 2011 entitled 'Inclusion of International Civil Aviation in the European Union Emissions Trading Scheme (EU ETS) and its Impact',[333] which urges EU Member States to refrain from including flights by non-EU carriers to/from airports in the EU in the EU ETS, and adopted it as Council Declaration in November 2011.[334]

Next was the Moscow Joint Declaration in February 2012, with 24 States in total. The final version of the declaration contained considerably softer language than the New Delhi declaration, for example no agreement on retaliatory measures, particularly relating to trade and 'parties *asked to consider taking* certain measures'. In response to the Moscow Declaration, EU Commissioner for Climate Action, Connie Hedegaard, asked via Twitter: 'Unfortunately, our question for Moscow meeting participants remains unanswered: what's your concrete, constructive alternative?' The EU entered a reservation to Council Decision on Joint Declaration.

Any future legal challenges to the EU ETS under the auspices of ICAO would have to come either under the International Air Services Transit

330 E. Alberola and B. Solier, 'Including International Aviation in the European Union Emission Trading Scheme: A First Step Towards a Global Scheme?' Institute for Climate Economics, *Industry, Energy & Climate: Climate Report No. 34* 24, available online at: www.i4ce.org/download/including-international-aviation-in-the-european-union-emission-trading-scheme-a-first-step-towards-a-global-scheme/

331 M. Milde, 'The EU Emissions Trading Scheme: Confrontation of Compromise?' (2012) 61(2) *ZLW* 186.

332 Interestingly, China and India have reportedly now agreed to participate in the ETS (GreenAir Communications, 'Chinese and Indian Airlines come into Compliance with EU ETS as Swiss Case Moves to EU's Highest Court' (GreenAir Online, 19 May 2015) at: www.greenaironline.com/news.php?viewStory=2084).

333 ICAO, 'Working Paper on the ETS Scheme' C-WP/13790 (17 October 2011).

334 ICAO, Council Decision C-DEC 194/2.

Agreement 1944[335] or Article 84 of the Chicago Convention.[336] The outcome of the latter course could be appealed to the International Court of Justice (ICJ).[337] Murphy notes the troubled, tense relationship between the USA and ICJ to argue that antinomies pull the USA towards court but push it away when 'Court fails to accommodate the special role of the United States on matters such as the maintenance of international peace and security'.[338]

The last time the Article 84 challenge was brought in the area of environmental protection as chance would have it was by the USA on the grounds that Council Regulation 925/1999, the so-called 'Hushkits Regulation' mentioned above, banning aircraft fitted with hushkits from flying into/from the EU, was in breach of the Chicago Convention.[339] Whilst the ICAO Council's decision found *inter alia* that the parties had 'failed to exhaust the remedies that are available in the legal systems of the [other]',[340] and invited them to continue direct negotiations with President of Council, with consent of parties, offering to serve as Conciliator during negotiations, the EU 'appeased' the USA in the end, withdrawing the Regulation in 2001. The EU response in 2002 was to set up a new Directive (allegedly) along the lines of ICAO's 'balanced approach' to noise management established in 2001.

335 Article 2, Section 1 reads: 'A contracting State which deems that action by another contracting State under this Agreement is causing injustice or hardship to it, may request the Council to examine the situation. The Council shall thereupon inquire into the matter, and shall call the States concerned into consultation. Should such consultation fail to resolve the difficulty, the Council may make appropriate findings and recommendations to the contracting States concerned. If thereafter a contracting State concerned shall in the opinion of the Council unreasonably fail to take suitable corrective action, the Council may recommend to the Assembly of the above-mentioned Organization that such contracting State be suspended from its rights and privileges under this Agreement until such action has been taken. The Assembly by a two-thirds vote may so suspend such contracting State for such period of time as it may deem proper or until the Council shall find that corrective action has been taken by such State'.

336 Article 84 reads: 'If any disagreement between two or more contracting States relating to the interpretation or application of this Convention and its Annexes cannot be settled by negotiation, it shall, on the application of any State concerned in the disagreement, be decided by the Council. No member of the Council shall vote in the consideration by the Council of any dispute to which it is a party. Any contracting State may, subject to Article 85, appeal from the decision of the Council to an *ad hoc* arbitral tribunal agreed upon with the other parties to the dispute or to the Permanent Court of International Justice. Any such appeal shall be notified to the Council within sixty days of receipt of notification of the decision of the Council'.

337 Chicago Convention 1944, Art 85.

338 Sean D. Murphy, 'The United States and the International Court of Justice: Coping with Antinomies' in Cesare Romano (ed.), *The United States and International Courts and Tribunals* (Cambridge University Press 2009) 46–111, available online at: http://ssrn.com/abstract=1000391

339 A so-called 'hushkit' is an apparatus attached to aeroplane engines to reduce noise.

340 Decision of the ICAO Council on the preliminary objections in the matter 'United States and 15 European States (2000)'.

> A new, more stringent noise certification standard, defined in Volume 1, Part II, Chapter 4 of Annex 16 to the Convention on International Civil Aviation, has been established within the framework of the International Civil Aviation Organisation (ICAO) and will contribute to an improvement in the noise climate around airports in the longer term.[341]

This evidences one 'success' vis-à-vis annexing consensus at ICAO – on noise management aspect of the environment – to the Chicago Convention.

The plaintiffs in the *Air Transport Association* case ultimately withdrew the UK judicial review application and urged the U.S. government instead to pursue an Article 84 challenge.[342] It should also be noted that EU airlines are lobbying their own ministers on the basis of competitive disadvantage – however artificial that disadvantage might be – as they fear in relation to airlines (e.g. U.S. airlines) in the 'non-regulating states'[343] (e.g. USA) whereby putting the general competitiveness of the EU Member States as 'regulating States' at risk. Hertogen, again, suggests that 'decisional sovereignty' might be a way around this, through what Scott and Rajamani call 'contingent unilateralism',[344] insofar as an incentive is made for the non-regulating States either to engage in multilateral regulation or adopt equivalent regulation.[345]

Opposing States could therefore have proceeded by bringing an Article 84 challenge before ICAO Council at any stage before or subsequent to this, or denied ICAO jurisdiction to deal with this matter, or gone directly to the ICJ, or referred the topic of international aviation emissions to UNFCCC or WTO. The evident consequence of all this is the disrespect for international law and a shift from the earlier premise of *political* towards *legal* determination.

To support this point, we should note that both the U.S. House of Representatives and U.S. Senate passed the European Union Emissions Trading Scheme Prohibition Act 2011,[346] which forbids U.S. airlines from participating in the EU ETS and offering to provide financial assistance to

341 Directive 2002/30/EC of the European Parliament and of the Council of 26 March 2002 on the establishment of rules and procedures with regard to the introduction of noise-related operating restrictions at Community airports, OJ L85/40, 28 March 2002.

342 Doug Cameron 'U.S. Airlines Seek Action on EU Carbon Tax' *Wall Street Journal*, 27 March 2012, available online: http://online.wsj.com/article/SB100014240527023041771045773079808385979 06.html?mod=dist_smartbrief

343 Hertogen, 'Sovereignty as Decisional Independence over Domestic Affairs' 299–300.

344 Joanne Scott and Lavanya Rajamani, 'EU Climate Change Unilateralism' (2012) 23(2) *EJIL* 469–474.

345 Hertogen, 'Sovereignty as Decisional Independence over Domestic Affairs' 300.

346 H.R. 2494 was passed on October 24, 2011. The EU has previously adopted 'blocking statutes' to guard against the extraterritorial effects of U.S. legislation, most notably the Helms-Burton Act. See Huber, 'The Helms-Burton Blocking Statute of the European Union' (1996) 6 *Fordham Int'l LJ* 699.

airlines facing penalties for non-compliance.[347] President Obama signed the bill into law in November 2012.[348]

On the argument that the EU ETS is merely a tax, it is of interest to note that a tax on aviation was once proposed but later vetoed in the EU. Choosing the ETS rather than a tax evidences the EU's drive for 'global leadership'[349] in climate change. Scott argues the EU 'contributes to multi-level climate governance' by showing the world that an ETS can work vis-à-vis a 'federalism dimension of governance as between the EU and its Member States'.[350] Generally speaking, environmental leadership appears to have been 'legalized', from global State-to-State negotiations to regional, multi-level judicial disputes.[351]

Future linking of the EU ETS and/or the GMBM for aviation with other schemes is highly dependent on compatibility. The success of global governance will require harmonization. Here again, an ETS-style system is favoured over tax regimes. According to Peel *et al.*,

> the prospects for a harmonized system remain stronger than where carbon taxation measures are adopted. In contrast to ETS, carbon taxation regimes are difficult to harmonize across States …[352] [T]he case for ETS over carbon taxes has been furthered by their adoption in key jurisdictions as the primary climate change mitigation instrument.[353]

In the meantime, there is mounting concern amongst European airlines about the application of the EU ETS to intra-EEA flights only. The ELFAA, which again now counts IAG in its membership, has been increasing its

347 The Act reads: 'To prohibit operators of civil aircraft of the United States from participating in the European Union's emissions trading scheme, and for other purposes … The Secretary of Transportation shall prohibit an operator of a civil aircraft of the United States from participating in the emissions trading scheme unilaterally established by the European Union in EU Directive 2003/87/EC of October 13, 2003, as amended, in any case in which the Secretary determines the prohibition to be, and in a manner that is, in the public interest, taking into account – (1) the impacts on U.S. consumers, U.S. carriers, and U.S. operators; (2) the impacts on the economic, energy, and environmental security of the United States; and (3) the impacts on U.S. foreign relations, including existing international commitments'.

348 S.1956 (112th) European Union Emissions Trading Scheme Prohibition Act of 2011.

349 Peel *et al.* 'Climate Change Law in an Era of Multi-Level Governance' 254.

350 Joanne Scott, 'The Multi-Level Governance of Climate Change' (2011) 5(1) *Carbon and Climate Law Review* 25.

351 Sanja Bogojević, 'Legalising Environmental Leadership: A Comment on the CJEU's Ruling in C-366/10 on the Inclusion of Aviation in the EU Emissions Trading Scheme' (2012) 24(2) *Journal of Environmental Law* 345.

352 Peel *et al.*, 'Climate Change Law in an Era of Multi-Level Governance' 254 citing L. A. Stein, 'The Legal and Economic Bases for an Emissions Trading Scheme' (2010) 36(1) *Monash University Law Review* 204.

353 Peel *et al.*, 'Climate Change Law in an Era of Multi-Level Governance' 254.

pressure on the European Commission to 'start the clock' again.[354] Clearly, low-cost carriers stand to lose the most from the temporary suspension beyond the EEA as a large majority of their flights are short-haul, within the EEA.

This calls into question the effects of the EU ETS on the sector and issues with its competitiveness. To draw a parallel to developments in the EU maritime sector, the EU maritime emissions tax proposal

> seeks a solution which does not hinder the competitiveness of the maritime sector, but which promotes its development in a sustainable fashion. With the shipping industry struggling financially and host countries unwilling to lose the business of registered vessels which may be re-registered in a State with lighter regulations, there are stark dangers of introducing a measure without clear objectives.[355]

There is no doubt that the value-backed objective of the EU ETS is clear; however, risks to the aviation sector's competitiveness on the global market, in the form of a competitive disadvantage, must also be considered and balanced so far as practicable. It appears that despite that fact that 'unilateral regulatory action on the part of national or sub-national government entities might lead to carbon leakage and competitive disadvantage, and may be ineffective to address the *global* problem of excessive GHG emissions, it is clear that such regulatory action is taking place in many States and across a range of sectors'.[356] What could ensue is an artificial competitive advantage of firms in any non-regulating State; this will put competitiveness of regulating States at risk. Truby suggests that another yet unexplored option is border tax adjustments as a means 'to support tax measures, to support any reduction of competitiveness caused by the EU ETS'.[357] Applying Hertogen's theory of 'decisional sovereignty' to the problem may be a way around this.[358] She, along with Scott and Rajamani, argue the line that through 'contingent unilateralism', non-regulating States will be incentivized either

354 See European Low Fare Airlines Association, 'ELFAA Condemns Proposed Extension of Intra-EU Only Scope for EU ETS' (5 May 2014), online at: www.elfaa.com/press releases.htm; ELFAA, 'EU Commission compromises environmental effectiveness of EU ETS'; EurActiv, 'Low-fare airlines to sue EU for "stopping the clock" on ETS' (22 March 2013), online at: www.euractiv.com/transport/low-fares-airlines-sue-eu-stoppi-news-518657.

355 Truby, 'Extraterritoriality or an Illegal Tax?' 315.

356 Peel *et al.*, 'Climate Change Law in an Era of Multi-Level Governance' 249.

357 Truby, 'Extraterritoriality or an Illegal Tax?' 323; see also Ronald Ismer and Karsten Neuhoff, 'Border Tax Adjustment: A Feasible Way to Support Stringent Emission Trading' (2007) 24 *European Journal of Law and Economics* 137; Javier de Cendra, 'Can Emissions Trading Schemes be Coupled with Border Tax Adjustments? An Analysis vis-à-vis WTO Law' (2006) 15 *Rev Eur Cmty & Int'l Envtl L* 131.

358 Hertogen, 'Sovereignty as Decisional Independence over Domestic Affairs' 300.

to engage in multilateral regulation or adopt equivalent regulation.[359] And, coming back to the EU ETS, Article 25a of the ETS Directive provides an exemption for such equivalent regulation:

> Where a third country adopts measures for reducing the climate change impact of flights departing from that country which land in the Community, the Commission, after consulting with that third country, and with Member States within the Committee referred to in Article 23(1), shall consider options available in order to provide for optimal interaction between the Community scheme and that country's measures.[360]

Thus, there is a strong argument, on the back of this unilateral (or plurilateral) move by the EU, for third countries to engage in multilateral regulation at the international level through ICAO or devise national regulation that aims to achieve similar aims in the case of international aviation emissions. As highlighted above, the reaction thus far from other countries has been mixed but largely unsupportive, which perhaps demonstrates the at times rather divergent political will and political realities.

Guiding principles

Agreed in 2013, ICAO Assembly Resolution A38-18 sets out:

> States, when designing new and implementing existing MBMs for international aviation should: (a) engage in constructive bilateral and/or multilateral consultations and negotiations with other States to reach an agreement, and (b) grant exemptions for application of MBMs on routes to and from developing States whose share of international aviation activities is [de minimis].[361]

As an aside, it is submitted that this provision can be directly linked to the European Commission's 'stop the clock' measure mentioned in the discussion above.

Resolution A38-17 also provides 16 guiding principles for the design and implementation of MBMs for international aviation. Most controversial is the final principle, which reads: '(p) MBMs should take into account the principle of *common but differentiated responsibilities* and respective capabilities, the special circumstances and respective capabilities, and the principle of *non-discrimination and equal and fair opportunities*'.[362]

359 Ibid.; see also Scott and Rajamani, 'EU Climate Change Unilateralism'.

360 EU ETS Directive para 1.

361 The *de minimis* threshold is 1 per cent. ICAO, 'Assembly Resolution A38-18', online at: www.icao.int/Meetings/a38/Documents/Resolutions/a38_res_prov_en.pdf paras 16 (a) and (b).

362 Ibid., Annex, at (p) (emphasis added).

For the first time, ICAO thus has called for application of the UNFCCC core principle, common but differentiated responsibilities,[363] and at the same time its own core principle, non-discrimination and equal treatment, which is significant.[364] According to Piera, 'In international civil aviation, by invok - ing CBDR, developing countries argue that their aircraft operators should not be subject to emission reduction obligations. Developed States contend that CBDR cannot be applied in civil aviation, because it contravenes ICAO's non-discrimination principle and leads to market distortions'.[365]

Over time at ICAO, developing countries have been seen to withdraw objections to a universal market mechanism whereas emerging markets seem to challenge it due to impact on trade and therefore growth and subsidies.[366] Though, in response to this, Lamotte argues,

> that a tariff structure for carbon in the airline sector through a tax on emissions or auctioning emission allowances, rather than allocating them free of charge, would enable the generation of financial resources that could be used to finance: research and development activities in the aircraft industry; offsetting the economic impact of the introduction of these instruments in developing countries; financing the domestic climate policies of developing countries, like the NAMAs [Nationally Appropriate Mitigation Actions] defined in accordance with the Cancun Agreements in 2010.[367]

363 As raised initially by China in 2007. See ICAO Working paper presented by China, 'Addressing aviation emissions based on the principle "common but differentiated responsibilities"' (18 September 2007) A36–WP/235; ICAO, *Resolution 17/2: Consolidated statement of continuing ICAO policies and practices related to environmental protection — Climate change* (7 October 2010) A37–WP/402; perhaps likening with the experience of the International Maritime Organization (IMO). See IMO Submission by China and India, 'Application of the principle of "common but differentiated responsibilities"' to the reduction of greenhouse gas emissions from international shipping' (15 August 2008) MEPC 58/4/32; This, *inter alia*, has resulted in a reference, albeit guarded, to CBDR in a recent Maritime Environment Protection Committee Resolution MO, Annex 4, Resolution MEPC.229 (65) 'Promotion of Technical Co-operation and Transfer of Technology relating to the Improvement of Energy Efficiency of Ships', in *Report of the Marine Environment Protection Committee on its sixty-fifth session (13–17 May 2013)* (24 May 2013) MEPC 65/22.

364 Beatriz Martinez Romera and Harro van Asselt, 'The International Regulation of Aviation Emissions: Putting Differential Treatment into Practice' (2015) 27(2) *Journal of Environmental Law* 1–25.

365 Piera Valdes, *Greenhouse Gas Emissions from International Aviation* 2.

366 The World Bank now classifies Singapore, Qatar and the United Arab Emirates as 'high income' non-OECD countries and China as an 'upper middle income' country (The World Bank, 'Data, Countries and Economies', online at: http://data.worldbank.org/country). See also Alberola and Solier, 'Including International Aviation in the European Union Emission Trading Scheme'.

367 Alberola and Solier, 'Including International Aviation in the European Union Emission Trading Scheme' 25 citing H. Lamotte, 'La tarification du carbone dans le transport aérien et maritime international' [2011] CGEFI, Ministère de l'Economie, des Finances et de l'Industrie, France.

Following the 2013 ICAO agreement to work towards a GMBM, there has been some suggestion that aviation in national and regional regimes with developing-State status will benefit from CBDR *economic* treatment, and through this differentiation a risk to competition and market distortions will ensue. Other States that subject airlines to national or regional regimes with high thresholds for environmental regulation may also be disadvantaged. One suggestion has been to implement the GMBM incrementally and on market basis, i.e. route-by-route.

Without a doubt, establishing a GMBM for GHG emissions is highly political. ICAO has been criticized in the past for failing to deliver a concrete plan. In 2014, Piera proposed a potential path to achieving an incremental, route-based GMBM by proposing a set of criteria that should be applied when determining which routes to include in the GMBM, and when.[368] He suggested a route-based, phased-in approach for ICAO's GMBM. He called it 'phasing in with UNFCCC flavour', over three phases from 2020 to 2030, proposing that 'aircraft operators flying on the same route – whether they are from developed or developing States – will be subjected to the same rules. The scheme would only apply where the points of origin and destination of both routes are subject to the same phase. If not, the scheme would not apply to the route'.[369]

This, Piera argued, would require 'phasing in routes to and from States on the basis of their market share of international aviation traffic [which] follows a UNFCCC-type differentiation between developed and developing States'.[370] He recognized that there would be problems with this. For instance, 'Latin America and Africa have almost insignificant traffic market shares, [however] they are home to some of the world's most prosperous and fastest-growing airlines'.[371]

A criticism offered by Piera is 'that by first phasing in routes to and from developed States, the system incorporates, albeit temporarily, a camouflaged version of the CBDR principle'.[372] However, 'unlike in the UNFCCC context, the differentiation would not be perpetual. It would only be intended to provide temporary headroom. Six years after its adoption, the scheme will cover almost all the relevant routes to and from developed and developing countries alike'.[373]

368 Alejandro Piera Valdes, 'Reconciling CBDR with Non-Discrimination: A Fundamental Requirement for ICAO's Global MBM Success' (23 September 2014) GreenAir Online, online at: www.greenaironline.com/news.php?viewStory=1983; see also Piera Valdes, *Greenhouse Gas Emissions from International Aviation*.

369 Ibid.

370 Ibid.

371 Ibid.

372 Ibid.

373 Ibid.

Bearing in mind the requirement for CBDR and respective capabilities, it is the view of many that developed States *should* take the lead in tackling climate change, but to what extent? Might developed States accept the proposal of a GMBM for aviation with such, even temporary, differentiation? Whilst there appears to be an organic movement towards symmetry and away from the traditional north–south dichotomy, as French and Rajamani put it, 'some developed countries have become disenchanted with differentiation over time, particularly with the way it is articulated in the climate regime, and have attempted to alter it'.[374] They continue:

> This has had a profound impact on their receptivity to differential treatment, even the less contested strains of it such as differentiation in relation to provision of assistance. Indeed, the efforts of some developing countries (notably China and India) to extend the application of the principle of common but differentiated responsibility to the regulation of aviation and maritime emissions, has been met with resistance by some developed countries. It has alerted these countries, arguably, to the extent of their folly, as they perceive it, in agreeing to the breadth and depth of differential treatment in the climate regime, and the precedential value it appears to have generated. These developments have, we argue, led developed states to swing the pendulum in the other direction in more recently negotiated areas of international environmental law.[375]

Given the highly political nature of the debate, until October 2016 it had not been clear whether the political will of States would meet political realities, notwithstanding ICAO's political *determination* to introduce a GMBM.[376]

Towards a global solution?

This book considers aspects of the legal attempts to mitigate the environmental impact of aviation emissions vis-à-vis international and transnational law, and multi-level governance. As necessary, we consider the intersection of globalization, climate change and global aviation. According to Etty *et al.*,

> On the one hand, climate change is a global phenomenon with globally distributed causes, thus requiring a global response. On the other hand, emissions always take place from specific locations within particular

374 Duncan French and Lavanya Rajamani, 'Climate Change and International Environmental Law: Musings on a Journey to Somewhere' (2013) 25(3) *Journal of Environmental Law* 441.

375 Ibid.

376 See Alberola and Solier, 'Including International Aviation in the European Union Emission Trading Scheme'.

> jurisdictions, and the impacts of climate change will vary from place to place, requiring diverse adaptation measures. Thus, it is inherent in the nature of climate change that responses will be multi-scalar and multi-jurisdictional, raising profound issues of governance.[377]

This author is mindful of the difficulty in setting the appropriate scale of regulation of climate change. After all, climate change is, as Osofsky puts it, a 'multi-scalar' regulatory problem as it spans and may involve multiple levels of governance (local, State, national, regional, international, transnational, supranational, global)[378] and requires approaches 'which simultaneously engage more than one level of governance'.[379] Thus one must be mindful of the importance of 'climate governance "beyond" the international climate change regime – climate change law in era of multi-level governance'.[380]

The term 'multi-level governance'[381] as it is used here refers to decision making 'taking place at a range of territorial levels or scales (including sub-national levels) and [the] recognition of the role played by non-State actors in governance, alongside governments'.[382] Peel *et al.* add a third dimension that sees 'climate change, as requiring a multi-faceted regulatory response, rather than a single approach (e.g. emissions reduction targets implemented via ETS)'.[383]

We must consider ways in which best to approach multi-level climate change governance: top–down, bottom–up. A top–down approach would see international standards set and translated into domestic regulatory measures, such as the EU ETS, and it has had its problems beyond the EU.[384] Conversely, a bottom–up approach, 'based on an aggregation of voluntary national commitments, has proven less than satisfactory'.[385] Yet there is still hope for voluntary *private* commitments.

As Osofsky suggests, 'antiregulatory parties attempt to scale up the problem with variations on arguments that climate change is an international problem happening over too long a time period, while those wanting greater regulation try to scale the problem of climate change back down to state or local levels

377 Thijs FM Etty *et al.*, 'Transnational Dimensions of Climate Governance' (2012) 1(2) *Transnational Environmental Law* 235.

378 Peel *et al.*, 'Climate Change Law in an Era of Multi-Level Governance' 271, citing Hari Osofsky 'Is Climate Change "International"?: Litigation's Diagonal Regulatory Role' (2009) 49 *Virginia Journal of International Law* 585.

379 Osofsky, 'Is Climate Change "International"?' 587.

380 Peel *et al.*, 'Climate Change Law in an Era of Multi-Level Governance'.

381 See Henrik Enderlein *et al.*, *Handbook on Multi-Level Governance* (Edward Elgar 2010).

382 Ibid., 251 citing I. Bache and M. Flinders, 'Themes and Issues in Multi-Level Governance' in I. Bache and M. Flinders (eds), *Multi-Level Governance* (Oxford University Press 2004) 4.

383 Peel *et al.*, 'Climate Change Law in an Era of Multi-Level Governance' 251.

384 Ibid., 247.

385 Ibid., 248.

and the present time'.[386] For the purposes of this project, a simplified ordering is adopted, and it is offered without prejudice: international, regional and cross-sectoral regulation of international aviation emissions.[387]

At the international level, there are two approaches that stand out most. Without a doubt, as GHG emissions are a global problem, any effective solution will require multi-level action. The 'consensus analysis suggests that in order to regulate emissions most efficiently, we must consider strategies at multiple levels, as well as find ways of incorporating cultural questions into economic models'.[388] The challenge here is that '[o]ur demarcation of law into distinct levels of governance and the overlapping sovereignty that accompanies it make engagement of multiple scales simultaneously very challenging',[389] as we have seen above.

In his work, Osofsky analyses climate change as an instance of a 'multiscalar problem that law struggles to address effectively', examining 'the multiscalar nature of emissions and impacts [and] the barriers to an effective regulatory regime'.[390] The challenge, he tells us, is in the existing structure of law:

> The structure of law poses a fundamental difficulty for effective regulation of multiscalar problems like climate change. Namely, law's scales are sticky despite the fluid scalar nature of greenhouse gas emissions and impacts. In other words, we have subdivided law into levels of governance – a sensible idea for creating order and administrability – and formal regulation tends to happen within the fixed frames of those structures. As a result, we generally approach regulation as choosing or coordinating among those levels. The current dilemmas over climate regulation reflect those constraints.[391]

In this book we have also noted the difficulty in balancing 'between maintaining the powers of consent that sovereign States have in the creation of principles and rules of international law – and the need to increase the efficiency of international decision-making, including standard-setting, monitoring compliance, dispute settlement, and enforcement'.[392] Brus questions which role non-state actors play,[393] and reminds us that 'true international governance is not only about the development of a process in which States

386 Osofsky, 'Is Climate Change "International"?' 585.
387 Michael Faure and Marjan Peeters, *Climate Change and European Emissions Trading: Lessons for Theory and Practice* (Edward Elgar 2008).
388 Osofsky, 'Is Climate Change "International"?' 597.
389 Ibid., 589–590.
390 Ibid., 591–592.
391 Ibid.
392 Brus, 'Bridging the Gap' 18.
393 Ibid.

are the only actors. It is about making decisions about international societal problems'.[394] Here we must be also mindful to include non-state actors and private actors as key stakeholders in global aviation, including labour groups, consumer groups, airlines, manufacturers and airports as well.

By way of comparison let us now consider the example of global action to protect the ozone layer, as another multi-scalar problem and therefore comparable in some ways to greenhouse gas emissions and climate change. Brus says, 'This is typically an example of a problem that can be addressed effectively only if participating States are prepared to accept decision-making procedures that allow a greater role for majority decisions'.[395] The relevant international law relating to the ozone layer are the Vienna Convention for the Protection of the Ozone Layer 1985 (the framework convention) and the Montreal Protocol on Substances that Deplete the Ozone Layer 1987 (an extraordinary mechanism of decision-making).[396] The latter provides that a panel of qualified experts is to provide assessments every four years with a view to amending or adjusting, if they deem necessary, the legislation.[397] Lammers argues that this Montreal provision on decision making detracts from sovereignty of the parties to the Vienna Convention, but only for 'scientific, technical, and administrative matters' – are these less controversial in practice? By comparison, as regards adoption of decisions under the framework convention by consensus versus qualified majority, he concludes:

> Again, other decisions – after efforts to reach agreement by consensus have been in vain – may be adopted by a qualified majority vote of the parties present and voting, and may under additional conditions be protecting the interests of various groups of States (in particular developed and developing States parties) and become explicitly legally binding on *all* States parties, even on those who voted against the decisions. In respect of other decisions it has again been explicitly provided that they will only lead to *voluntary* 'obligations'.[398]

394 Ibid., 19.

395 Ibid., 18.

396 UN Treaty Series, http://ozone.unep.org/en/handbook-vienna-convention-protection-ozone-layer; UN Treaty Series, www.ozone.unep.org/en/treaties-and-decisions/montreal-protocol-substances-deplete-ozone-layer

397 For an example, see UNEP, 'Environmental effects of ozone depletion: 1988 Assessment' http://ozone.unep.org/pdfs/Environmental-Effects-Assess98.pdf. A full list is available here: www.ozone.unep.org/en/assessment-panels/environmental-effects-assessment-panel

398 Johan Lammers, 'The Mechanism of Decision-making under the Vienna Convention and the Montreal Protocol for the Protection of the Ozone Layer' in Gerard Kreijen (ed.), *State, Sovereignty, and International Governance* (Oxford University Press 2002) 425 (emphasis added).

As we have seen with the UNFCCC negotiations and the Kyoto Protocol, more non-consensual rule-making requires changes to the decision-making process. To achieve better decisions and ensure greater adherence to them, we must include non-state actors in global governance. By way of example, below is a discussion on the inclusion of non-state actors in decision making in the context of ozone protection. Lammers provides an analysis from the perspective of States:

> While the assumption of international legal obligations by entering into a treaty is itself already both a manifestation of the sovereignty of States parties to the treaty *and* at the same time a process leading to restrictions on the exercise of their sovereign rights, (the States Parties to the Vienna Convention and, in particular, the Montreal Protocol) went much further in accepting restrictions on the exercise of their sovereign rights than is the case in most international agreements, even in the field of international environmental law. They did so by agreeing on a remarkable and exceptional mechanism of adopting decisions.[399]

And in turn, States 'considerably restricted their sovereignty in this field and contributed further to the increasingly relative nature of that concept in international relations'.[400] Thus, States can either take this as a *restriction* on the exercise of their sovereignty or a *strengthening* of their position as sovereigns insofar as they now become subject to a 'supra-national style of decision-making … in order to better use their powers for solving problems in a common interest and therewith ultimately in their individual interest … [which] clearly shows that a transformation of State sovereignty through the development of international governance is more than just theory'.[401]

Conclusion

This chapter has identified some of the most pressing, emerging economic and environmental concerns of the global neighbourhood that also affect global aviation. It has also examined respective economic and environmental regulation that attempts to address these contemporary challenges.

First, fair competition safeguards and consumer protection are areas typically regulated nationally, or in the case of the EU, regionally. Yet, market regulation or lack thereof affects the global marketplace; therefore it is classed as a global public good that requires commensurate protection. This chapter reviews instances of market regulation and consumer protection in the EU, and some of the fastest growing States for global airlines and aviation infrastructure: UAE, Qatar and China. In conclusion, we understand

399 Ibid., 424–425.
400 Ibid., 426.
401 Brus, 'Bridging the Gap' 19.

that the EU achieves a very high level of fair competition safeguards including for State aid through the TFEU and relevant legislation. Certain rules are also in force in the other identified jurisdictions though it is difficult to ascertain the standards of enforcement and transparency with respect to airlines, if the relevant legislation even covers the sector. Amidst allegations of State aid or other favourable treatment by national governments in the UAE, Qatar and China, as supported by what appears to be persuasive evidence, one can glean that the current operating environment for global airlines competing for customers within a global marketplace would appear to be imbalanced by artificial competitive advantages. This gives way to a playing field for global airlines that is not level. The Chicago System effectively promotes these economic issues be exclusively regulated by the 'flag' State, but this is ineffective; they are in fact 'borderless' and transnational and therefore *global* problems.

Second, the environment is undisputedly a global public good that deserves appropriate protection. Global aviation contributes to the contemporary challenges of climate change. This chapter has explored ways in which the sector is involved in limiting and reducing its impact on climate change and other environmental areas such as noise pollution. Whilst the EU has led – albeit controversially – the global climate change initiative for aviation activities vis-à-vis its ETS, the future of aviation's inclusion in the ETS must be reviewed in light of the landmark ICAO agreement in 2016 to implement a GMBM scheme for international aviation from 2020.

It is posited that the Chicago System challenges the ability of States to address problems that are of a transnational nature as it promulgates national regulation of these global areas of concern. In the light of incoherent or lacking international economic and environmental regulation, impetus is provided for the introduction of a more transnational approach to global governance of aviation.

The global economic and environmental problems and current national or regional regulation provide the background for theorizing in the next chapter on the emergence of global governance of global aviation.

4 Towards a global governance regime for global aviation

> Our post-war institutions were built for an inter-national world, but we now live in a global world. Responding effectively to this shift is the core institutional challenge for world leaders today.
>
> Former UN Secretary General Kofi Annan (2000)[1]

Introduction

Taking into account the contemporary, transnational economic and environmental challenges presented in the previous chapter, this chapter calls into question the ability of the post-war, *inter-national* Chicago System to deal with the *global* nature of today's aviation sector. It posits that the ongoing work of the global aviation community of not only States but also including non-state and private actors on a global market-based mechanism for international aviation emissions marks an unprecedented, transformational shift in the style of economic and environmental regulation of international aviation. In turn, this reveals the emergence of a new, *global* approach to governance of aviation in which the range of issues that traditionally have been exclusively in the national remit – health, human rights, environment and even market regulation – are elevated to the global level. Indeed, this chapter also identifies new global competition safeguards and principles on consumer protection. This author suggests that these actions create a new governance space for addressing global issues more effectively through enhanced cooperation, shared responsibility between States, non-state actors and private actors and participants as partners in civil aviation.

This book acknowledges that for historical reasons the Chicago System of international civil aviation regulation understandably is inter-national. As a post-war institution, the specialized UN agency for international civil aviation, the ICAO, serves as the Chicago System's inter-governmental forum.

1 Kofi Annan, *We the Peoples: The Role of the United Nations in the 21st Century* (New York: United Nations, 2000) 11.

Its UN-style thus reaffirms the centrality and ultimate authority of (Member) Nation-States.[2] ICAO Member States devise, implement and enforce minimum standards across an array of areas in national systems once they have been agreed at the international level. ICAO's design of a GMBM scheme, and safeguards for fair competition and consumer protection demonstrate that the organization has transcended its mandate as a technical and policy-based standard setter as it now creates new economic and environmental norms for global aviation.

As we know, the provisions of the Chicago Convention establish the international framework for civil aviation. Aircraft nationality is granted by the State.[3] In a regulatory environment absent of 'freedom of the air', States are left voluntarily to negotiate international air services agreements bilaterally. As private actors, airlines are in turn dependent on their respective governments to negotiate air traffic rights on their behalf. ASAs tend to include so-called 'nationality clauses' or 'airline designation and authorization clauses' which ensure that the granting State retains the power to withhold, revoke or impose conditions on any operating permission granted to foreign air carriers if said carriers are not 'substantially owned and effectively controlled' by nationals of the other State. Nationality clauses have their origins in the 1940s, in an era when the world's airlines were State owned.

Liberalization has facilitated evolution of the global market in the decades since, and by now many formerly State-owned airlines have been partially or fully privatized. In addition, globalization continues to impact on the ownership of airlines; many are owned by 'multinationals'. Airlines of today truly are *global* enterprises. Market liberalization and deregulation have also allowed new airlines to enter markets.[4] The success of low-cost and low-fare carriers is particularly noteworthy. LCCs are not associated with the State; the flag is of ancillary concern.[5] Thus, aside from obvious safety and security oversight objectives of nationality clauses, which can arguably be achieved in other ways, one must question the relevance of nationality clauses in today's global airline business. Such permissions are protectionist; but do private actors, or quasi-private actors in the case of State-owned airlines, want or need this protection? It would seem an 'all or nothing' approach would be more appropriate, noting that the airline industry would actually prefer 'the nothing' in this context.

2 By way of ICAO's two governing bodies: ICAO Council and ICAO Assembly.

3 As Article 77 of the Chicago Convention permits aircraft to be operated jointly by 'international operating agencies', aircraft may be registered under a 'common mark' rather than exclusively on a national basis. See Amendment 3, Annex 7 to the Chicago Convention on 'Aircraft Nationality and Registration Marks'.

4 Reference here is to the EU process of liberalization and U.S. deregulation of airline markets. See Truxal, *Competition and Regulation in the Airline Industry: Puppets in Chaos.*

5 Take for example EasyJet, Ryanair, AirAsia, SpiceJet, JetBlue and TigerAir. Norwegian takes the name but the airline's livery features depictions of significant persons in Norwegian, Danish, Swedish and Finnish history.

In response, ICAO encourages States to liberalize ASAs further vis-à-vis various initiatives and policy guidance updates. For example, ICAO suggests that States utilize common criterion for airline designation: 'principal place of business and effective regulatory control'.[6] Unfortunately, to date standard texts used in ASAs have changed very little in this regard.[7] Whilst views on regulatory approaches to ownership and control remain divided across the international community, there has been some success at regional level. Nonetheless, there is significant room for evolution in this area that is crucial for liberalization of the global airline business.

This book theorizes on the emerging global regulatory environment for international civil aviation by considering recent developments in economic and environmental regulation in light of the wider academic debate on how the concepts of sovereignty and jurisdiction are changing. This author argues that because international civil aviation has been *globalized* the airline industry is impacted respectively. Moreover, in the light of globalization of civil aviation, one is able to describe the transformations underway in global (aviation) law and policy. Likewise, the aviation business is no longer international; it is *global* – thus an inter-national Chicago System *prima facie* would appear no longer fit for the purpose of ensuring sustainable and orderly growth in civil aviation.

The changed, global nature of the aviation business also means that, from the point of view of States, civil aviation has evolved from being mainly a political tool of the past to becoming important economic and socio-political tools today. Indeed, civil aviation should be reframed as an economic tool with ever-improving economic benefits for humankind. Herein lies an opportunity for States to act on common global values to ensure economic and environmental 'fair play'. Future growth of civil aviation should be constrained by notions of 'sustainability'; thus it must be managed appropriately to prevent wrongful exploitation.[8] This raises questions around positive and negative, legitimate and unjustified, exploitation 'in the public interest' where the sole actors and decision makers are States, and they do not agree.[9] Inherent in the structure of the Chicago System is the high risk that State action will reflect the self-interest of States rather than values of the global community. The different ways in which States, non-state actors and private

6 ICAO, 'Liberalization of Air Carrier Ownership and Control' (Worldwide Air Transport Conference, Montreal, March 2013) 4, online at: www.icao.int/Meetings/atconf6/Documents/WorkingPapers/ATConf6-wp012_en.pdf

7 Ibid.

8 Robert E. Goodin, 'Exploiting a Situation and Exploiting a Person' in Andrew Reeve (ed.), *Modern Theories of Exploitation* (Sage 1987).

9 Bryan G. Norton *et al.*, 'The Evolution of Preferences: Why "Sovereign" Preferences May Not Lead to Sustainable Policies and What to Do About It' in Bryan G. Norton (ed.), *Searching for Sustainability: Interdisciplinary Essays in the Philosophy of Conservation Biology* (Cambridge University Press 2010) 249–276.

actors are responding to global problems is evidence for this.[10] Therefore there is a need *ex ante* to include non-state actors and private actors in the development of norms and processes as a matter of policy setting and not *ex post* merely as a means for policy justification.

This chapter will examine external and internal limitations of the Chicago System before considering new initiatives in the areas of safeguards for fair competition, principles for consumer protection, and protection of the environment, as evidence of the emerging global governance regime for civil aviation.

The Chicago System: external

The Chicago System faces *external* limitations. First, it can be said to advocate a system of national protectionism. Ownership and control restrictions prevent airline mergers and acquisitions, which may otherwise make sound business sense, to be legally effected across national borders.[11] Nonetheless, it is widely known that foreign direct investment in airlines is on the rise. Nowadays it is commonplace for an airline registered in one State to be at least part-owned by nationals of foreign States. This represents a major change from the traditional, highly political arrangement in which State-owned airlines designated as flag carriers operate routes as determined by the State, whereby creating (unfair) favourable conditions for national airlines and generally restricting market access and entry.[12]

Also, as discussed in earlier chapters, Article 6 of the Chicago Convention lays the foundation for the negotiation of ASAs between States. The incorporation of ownership and control clauses in those ASAs has indirectly given way to the emergence of international airline alliances as a means to overcome the restrictions on market access.[13] Whilst the EU appears to be prepared in principle to remove ownership and control restrictions in ASAs with third countries, it will not go away from the bargaining table empty handed. Granting rights for foreign nationals to establish operations in the EU and freely invest in EU airlines remains conditional upon other trading partners offering the same or similar rights.[14]

10 Most of the world's major airlines are already taking voluntary action on environmental issues under corporate social responsibility initiatives.

11 EU exception.

12 Williams, *Contemporary Issues Shaping China's Civil Aviation Policy* 96.

13 Dempsey, *Public International Air Law*; one can also argue that airlines are creative, responding to a difficult regulatory environment in innovative ways.

14 The EU allows up to 49 per cent foreign ownership of EU carriers whilst the USA allows up to 25 per cent of American carriers. However, the EU is prepared to make exceptions to the rule in negotiations with key trading partners. See European Commission, 'Memo: EU External Aviation Policy', MEMO 12–714 (27 September 2015), online at: http://europa.eu/rapid/press-release_MEMO-12-714_en.htm

According to the European Commission, for any 'global reform ... to advance, the logical starting point is the trans-Atlantic market. Since between them, the EU and USA account for nearly half of global aviation, they represent a powerful bloc and the emergence of genuinely trans-Atlantic carriers would create important momentum'.[15] The U.S.–EU dialogue peaked in 2007 with the signing of the U.S.–EU Air Transport Agreement, though the agreement fell short of achieving true, fully liberalized 'open skies' status. Further work on this has stalled.[16] However, the Canada–EU Air Transport Agreement signed in 2009 removes ownership and control restrictions altogether to create a fully 'Open Aviation Area'. This has been heralded as 'the most ambitious air transport agreement between the EU and a major partner in the world'.[17] Whilst this achievement has not yet been a catalyst for radical liberalization elsewhere, in June 2016 the European Council adopted mandates for the European Commission to negotiate new, comprehensive air transport agreements with the Association of Southeast Asian Nations, Qatar, the UAE and Turkey.[18] In forthcoming negotiations, the EU will press for market development and growth based on common rules for fair and transparent market conditions and transparency. It is noteworthy that the EU–ASEAN agreement will become the first ever EU bloc-to-bloc agreement. The EU also recognizes that it cannot 'go it alone' in fostering the development of Open Aviation Areas. Instead, the EU underlines the opportunity for ICAO to step up on liberalization of the global aviation market:

> Changes are also needed within the global context of aviation. This is where ICAO can play a leading role in modernising the existing framework governing the global aviation market, as it does in other key areas such as safety and security. ICAO can help to further develop the economic regulatory framework for the global aviation sector, including in liberalising ownership and control of airlines, ensuring a worldwide framework for fair competition and ensuring environmentally sustainable development of the sector.[19]

15 COM(2012) 556 final.

16 The U.S.–EU Air Transport Agreement has liberalized the U.S.–EU transatlantic market insofar as it provides both U.S. and EU carriers with Third, Fourth and Fifth Freedom of the Air rights for passenger services and Seventh Freedom rights for all-cargo services. It also contains a 'fair competition' clause. However, it does not fully liberalize the market as the agreement retains 'substantial ownership and effective control' provisions in Article 4. See U.S. Department of State, 'Air Transport Agreements Between the US and the European Union', online at: www.state.gov/e/eb/rls/othr/ata/e/eu/

17 European Commission, 'International Aviation: Canada', online at: http://ec.europa.eu/transport/modes/air/international_aviation/country_index/canada_en.htm

18 European Council, 'Comprehensive EU air transport agreements: Council adopts mandates' (7 June 2016), online at: www.consilium.europa.eu/en/press/press-releases/2016/06/07-comprehensive-eu-air-transport-agreements/

19 COM(2012) 556 final.

At ICAO, the EU Member States seem continuously to reiterate the need to modernize the global framework for international air transport, including in particular the need for 'development of basic principles for fair competition and instruments to establish and maintain it',[20] which is unsurprising given the current state of affairs for national market regulation and consumer protection that affects global competition, as discussed earlier.

The current structure of bilateral regulation of 'fair competition' is inclusion by some States of 'fair competition' clauses in ASAs in addition to provisions for 'settlement of disputes' and 'fair and equal opportunity'. It is argued that these provisions require a shared understanding of core, objective principles on fairness and a willingness to follow through with enforcement.

ICAO policy and guidance material on fair competition is also developing.[21] The core general principles of the Chicago Convention are our first point of reference. The Preamble of the Convention states:

> the undersigned governments having agreed on certain principles and arrangements in order that international civil aviation may be developed in a safe and orderly manner and that international air transport services may be established on the basis of equality of opportunity and operated soundly and economically.

Also, Article 44 of the Convention states:

> The aims and objectives of the Organization are to develop the principles and techniques of international air navigation and to foster the planning and development of international air transport so as to: …
>
> (f) Insure that the rights of contracting States are fully respected and that every contracting State has a fair opportunity to operate international airlines; and
> (g) Avoid discrimination between contracting States.

The onus to ensure that every State has 'a fair opportunity' to operate is on ICAO. Whilst this phrase is qualified by 'equality of opportunity' and the operation of air transport services that are 'sound and economic', all of the above are subject to interpretation.[22]

20 Ibid.

21 See ICAO, 'Existing ICAO Policy and Guidance Material on Competition', Information Paper (April 2015), online at: www.icao.int/sustainability/Documents/Competition_Existing%20Guidance.pdf

22 This will of course differ from State to State, but the general global interest is converging. Arguably there is no longer room for special treatment of global airlines.

To enhance the Chicago Convention's core principles,[23] ICAO Assembly adopted Resolution A38-14, 'Consolidated statement of ICAO continuing policies in the air transport field', in 2013. It provides *inter alia* that the Assembly:

> Urges Member States to take into consideration that fair competition is an important general principle in the operation of international air services.
>
> ...
>
> Requests the Council to develop tools such as an exchange forum to enhance cooperation, dialogue and exchange of information on fair competition between States with a view to promoting compatible regulatory approaches towards international air transport.
>
> ...
>
> Encourages Member States to incorporate the basic principles of fair and equal opportunity to compete, non-discrimination, transparency, harmonization, compatibility and cooperation set out in the Convention and embodied in ICAO's policies and guidance in national legislation, rules and regulations, and in air services agreements.[24]

From the above we can read that ICAO Assembly Resolution A38-14 is a soft law instrument. As such, it does not impose binding obligations on the Member States and therefore cannot be *legally* enforced. However, it does put pressure on States to address the fair competition issue and deliver this via national legislation.

This is nothing new. ICAO's air transport conferences have been recommending the development of regulatory tools for market access, and State aid and subsidies since 1994. The Fifth Worldwide Air Transport Conference (ATConf/5, 2003) considered *inter alia*

> how to ensure fair competition in an environment of liberalization ... including a proposed model clause on 'Safeguards against anti-competitive practices' for optional use by States ... [and] also addressed the issue of State aids/subsidies and concluded that 'in a situation of the transition to liberalization or even in an already-liberalized market, States may wish to continue providing some form of assistance to their airlines

23 See, on guiding principles for the UN Human Rights Council, John Gerard Ruggie, 'Global Governance and "New Governance Theory": Lessons from Business and Human Rights' 20 (2014) *Global Governance* 5–17; on the core principles and values of the WTO, see Pascal Lamy, 'Global Governance: From Theory to Practice' (2012) 15(3) *Journal of International Economic Law* 721–728.

24 ICAO, Doc. 10022, *Assembly Resolutions in Force* (October 2013), III-6, III-7, III-9 (emphasis added). Available online at: www.icao.int/publications/Documents/10022_en.pdf

> … However, States should bear in mind that provision of State aids/subsidies which confer benefits on national air carriers but are not available to competitors in the same market may distort trade in international air services and may constitute unfair competitive practices.[25]

It further concluded that in special cases 'where State assistance can produce economic and/or social benefits … States should take transparent and effective measures accompanied by clear criteria and methodology to ensure that aids/subsidies do not adversely impact on competition in the marketplace'.[26]

The safeguards model clause reads:

> Safeguards against anti-competitive practices
>
> 1. The Parties agree that the following airline practices may be regarded as possible unfair competitive practices which may merit closer examination:
>   a) charging fares and rates on routes at levels which are, in the aggregate, insufficient to cover the costs of providing the services to which they relate;
>   b) the addition of excessive capacity or frequency of service;
>   c) the practices in question are sustained rather than temporary;
>   d) the practices in question have a serious negative economic effect on, or cause significant damage to, another airline;
>   e) the practices in question reflect an apparent intent or have the probable effect, of crippling, excluding or driving another airline from the market; and
>   f) behaviour indicating an abuse of dominant position on the route.
> 2. If the aeronautical authorities of one Party consider that an operation or operations intended or conducted by the designated airline of the other Party may constitute unfair competitive behaviour in accordance with the indicators listed in paragraph 1, they may request consultation in accordance with Article __ (Consultation) with a view to resolving the problem. Any such request shall be accompanied by notice of the reasons for the request, and the consultation shall begin within 15 days of the request.
> 3. If the Parties fail to reach a resolution of the problem through consultations, either Party may invoke the dispute resolution

25 ICAO, 'Existing ICAO Policy and Guidance Material on Competition' (Information Paper, April 2015) 2, online at: www.icao.int/sustainability/Documents/Competition_Existing%20Guidance.pdf

26 Ibid.

mechanism under Article __ (Settlement of disputes) to resolve the dispute.[27]

This book has not undertaken a comprehensive review of ASAs; thus it is unknown the success with which the safeguards clause has been incorporated into new ASAs. What can be said is that basic law of obligations tells us that to be effective the clause must be included when the agreement is made. If the market behaviour of States and/or airlines[28] is anti-competitive, it is difficult to take action in another trading partner State in the absence of an explicit provision in the ASA to rely upon. The only real course of action short of renegotiating the ASA *ab initio* would be to rely on national or regional legislation with extraterritorial effect. Equality of opportunity and fair competition, surely, should be interpreted objectively as meaning all carriers on a particular market should be treated equally and without discrimination. This aspiration if achieved should translate as the *flag* of the carrier being largely irrelevant for all market participants.[29]

From the perspective of consumers,[30] an aircraft's flag may actually also be of relatively little importance so long as safety and licensing standards for aircraft and crew meet the required international standard.[31] Studies show that price and other factors such as flight timings, trip duration, aircraft/service type and loyalty programmes tend to be more relevant for consumer decision making than flag of the aircraft.[32]

Also as regards consumers, our earlier discussion on the EU economic regulation demonstrates that under EU law air passengers are afforded a high level of consumer rights for disrupted air travel. This also impacts on the airline industry, EU airlines especially. According to the Court of Justice of the European Union (CJEU), the Montreal Convention and EU law operate

27 ICAO, Doc. 9587, *ATConf/5 Conclusions for agenda item 2.3 Part I – Safeguards to Ensure fair Competition* (Appendix 4, 2008) A4–8 to A4–9, online at: www.icao.int/sustainability/documents/doc9587_en.pdf

28 Noting that the line between the two may be blurred.

29 See Brian Vasigh *et al.*, *Introduction to Air Transport Economics: From Theory to Applications* (Ashgate 2008).

30 'Consumers' is employed here as meaning consumers of air services, including air passengers and air cargo shippers.

31 In other words, so long as the State of aircraft registry meets ICAO standards under the International Aviation Safety Assessment programme. See the U.S. Federal Aviation Administration Category 1 List, online at: ww.faa.gov/about/initiatives/iasa/media/IASAWS.xlsx

32 There is significant extra-legal scholarship on air passenger preferences. See Phillipp Boksberger, 'Passenger Behaviour' in Andreas Wittmer *et al.* (eds), *Aviation Systems: Management of the Integrated Aviation Value Chain* (Springer 2011) 157–170; Anthony T. H. Chin, 'Impact of Frequent Flyer Programs on the Demand for Air Travel' (2002) 7(2) *Journal of Air Transportation* 53–86; John F. O'Connell and George Williams, 'Passengers' Perceptions of Low Cost Airlines and Full Service Carriers: A Case Study involving Ryanair, Aer Lingus, Air Asia and Malaysia Airlines' (2005) 11(4) *Journal of Air Transport Management* 259–272.

in tandem. Air passengers may avail themselves of Montreal Convention rights, if necessary, through national courts though potentially costly and problematic in terms of enforcement. Consumer protection for air passengers thus is quite robust in some parts of the world. A recent and dramatic proliferation of more than 55 national and regional air passenger rights regimes in addition to the Montreal Convention raised concerns in the airline industry and called for an international regulatory response. On the one hand, overlapping or conflicting regimes cause a confusing situation for air passengers; on the other hand, the overlapping and complex nature of regimes in different parts of the world makes for an uncertain operating environment for airlines. The impact of consumer protection in international aviation has not yet been fully addressed.[33]

At the 38th General Assembly of ICAO in 2013, the Economic Commission called on the Council to

> develop, in the short term, a set of high-level, non-prescriptive core principles on consumer protection, for use as policy guidance, which strike an appropriate balance between protection of consumer and industry competitiveness and which take into account the needs of States for flexibility, given different State social, political and economic characteristics; with existing instruments, in particular that of the [Montreal Convention].[34]

ICAO Council adopted core principles and a long-term vision for air transport liberalization in July 2015.[35] The core principles include recommendations that passengers receive sufficient and transparent advance information before travel, regular updates on any disruptions and possible re-routing, refund, care and/or compensation during travel, and that airlines and other stakeholders coordinate in event of massive disruptions and recognize the fundamental right of access to disabled passengers. If required, complaint handling procedures should also be handled efficiently. The airline industry vis-à-vis the industry representative, IATA unanimously approved the core principles.[36] Again, as principles these are non-binding on States. It remains to be seen how, if at all, the core principles will weigh on the debates of national (and EU) parliaments.

33 See Steven Truxal, 'Consumer Protections and Limited Liability: Global Order for Air Transport?' (2014) 1(1) *Journal of International and Comparative Law* 111–119.

34 ICAO, 'Report of the Economic Commission on Agenda Item 40' (Working Paper, A38-WP/409, 2013) 40–6.

35 ICAO, 'ICAO Council Adopts Core Principles on Consumer Protection and New Long-Term Vision for Air Transport Liberalization' (Montreal, 9 July 2015), online at: www.icao.int/Newsroom/Pages/ICAO-Council-Adopts-Core-Principles-on-Consumer-Protection-and-New-Long-Term-Vision-for-Air-Transport-Liberalization.aspx

36 IATA, 'Core Principles for Passenger Rights Regulation' (Press Release No. 32, 3 June 2013), online at: www.iata.org/pressroom/pr/Pages/2013-06-03-03.aspx

The Chicago System: internal

The Chicago System faces internal limitations. ICAO, as a UN specialized agency, is characterized as an inter-governmental forum. We consider this as an example of a combination of what Ruggie terms 'embedded liberalism'.[37] The objective of the post-war system is to encourage free trade with open borders but the decision making is in fact firmly rooted in national political systems, and what Zürn later called 'executive multilateralism': 'a decision-making mode in which government representatives (mainly cabinet ministers) from different countries coordinate their policies internationally but with little national parliamentary control and away from public scrutiny'.[38]

The Chicago System is predominantly an inter-State system. ICAO official delegations are made up of government representatives; States vote. Observers from industry and special interest groups are admitted to ICAO Assembly proceedings, subject to prior accreditation by the ICAO Secretariat, and may present working and position papers, and take the floor; observers do not vote.[39] Observers may be prevented from attending technical meetings.[40]

The final decision-making authority in the Chicago System of course rests exclusively with States. This is not to say that non-state actors do not contribute to debates, but States have the ultimate power and responsibility for acts and omissions in the Chicago System and the exclusive power to *enforce* them. Industry and consumer groups, non-state actors and private actors ultimately are dependent on government representatives to progress agendas.

As the ICAO forum is inter-governmental, it is down to representatives of national governments to coordinate on negotiation of standards and recommended practices inter-nationally, which are subsequently implemented nationally, subject to the typical law-making consent and any filing of differences, as raised earlier.[41] ICAO decision making that has given way to legislation and guidance vis-à-vis SARPs has been 'successful' in many areas,

37 John Ruggie, 'International Regimes, Transactions, and Change: Embedded Liberalism in the Postwar Economic Order' in Stephen D. Krasner (ed.), *International Regimes* (Cornell University Press 1983); see also Ruggie, 'Global Governance'.

38 Michael Zürn, 'Global Governance as Multi-Level Governance' in Henrik Enderlein *et al.* (eds), *Handbook on Multi-Level Governance* (Edward Elgar 2010) 82.

39 Ad hoc observers at ICAO include regional representatives, e.g. the European Union. Official observers include industry representative groups, e.g. Airport Council International, the Civil Air Navigation Services Organisation and the International Air Transport Association.

40 For instance, European Commission President Jean-Claude Junker's request for five Members of the European Parliament to join an ICAO Committee on Aviation Environmental Protection (CAEP) meeting in February 2016, was denied; see James Crisp, 'UN Rejects EU Request to Attend Green Aviation Meeting' (*EurActiv.com*, 29 January 2016), online at: www.euractiv.com/section/transport/news/un-rejects-eu-request-to-attend-green-aviation-meeting/

41 There is an opt-out procedure ('tacit consent clause') under Article 38 of the Chicago Convention, which allows Member States 60 days to inform Council of non-intention to comply with a SARP. The measure will not be binding on that particular State.

for example safety, security and navigation. Unsurprisingly, States have achieved broad consensus on these low politics areas; they are also aspects of civil aviation which ICAO is expressly mandated to cover.

However, limited in authority and not a political level in its own right, ICAO can have only limited impact on the regulation of transnational issues – e.g. market regulation, consumer protection and climate change – which are more politically charged and do not benefit from unanimity. Whilst international airlines may not necessarily be based in every ICAO Member State, international air navigation and safety are of universal interest and importance. The Chicago System, after all, does not gather a UN summit of heads of States. Instead, ICAO Council Members and Assemblymen are answerable to their respective 'home' governments; members act on instruction. One anecdote highlights this: during the pre-smartphone 1971 dispute between India and Pakistan that was brought before ICAO Council for arbitration, it is understood that one delegate asked to be excused from the chamber before voting as he needed to check his 'position' with headquarters. As regards climate change, if heads of States cannot agree a common, binding position vis-à-vis UNFCCC, how might we expect transport ministers or ambassadors to agree a common, binding position at ICAO? The answer, this book argues, is for the industry actors and participants to lead the push for change on the aspiration of creating a fair, global operating environment for all: a so-called 'level playing field'.

ICAO continues ambitiously to work in the less explored, transnational and more politically sensitive economic and environmental areas, which demonstrates a break from its usual safety-centred approach to civil aviation regulation. Still, whether it has the competence and capability to achieve effective results is questionable. ICAO was not originally mandated to deal with these sorts of problems.[42] And to make matters more difficult, States are the international negotiators, meaning the decision-making environment will always be political. This endorses one's argument for reconsidering the exclusiveness of the Chicago System in the light of possible inclusion of non-state and private actors in the development of norms and processes in the global governance regime for aviation to achieve better outcomes.[43]

Against this, it can be said that ICAO has explicit competencies, for instance for general safety, and implied or customary competencies, to carry out safety audits.[44] Equally, some of these customary competencies, e.g. the environment, flow from the two other social and economic pillars of sustain-

42 UNFCCC and the Kyoto Protocol changed this.

43 Possible limitations are identified below.

44 For example, ICAO's Universal Safety Oversight Audit Programme (USOAP). See ICAO, 'USOAP Continuous Monitoring Approach', online at: www.icao.int/safety/cmaforum/Pages/default.aspx

ability, which have since been firmly planted in the Chicago Convention's Annexes and have by this means become more 'legitimate' competencies.[45]

Abeyratne is of the view that ICAO leadership is central to its future role:

> The archaic and hopelessly obsolete premise that ICAO's aim should be 'to meet the needs of the peoples of the world for safe, regular, efficient and economical air transport' is diametrically opposed to the new thinking that ICAO has to perform 100 percent in safety and security in helping develop an air transport system that is sustainable and efficient.
> ...
> The exponential growth in air traffic brings to bear the existence of a complex global civil aviation regulatory system that has transcended the stage of formulation and standardization and reached a stage of implementation of technical and commercial measures[46] ... [leading to a] steady evolutionary flow of the *Standards, Recommended Practices and Guidelines of ICAO*.[47]

Complementary to the discussion above on fair competition, safeguards and consumer protection as now viewed from the external perspective, this author considers arguments for how ICAO can achieve change in these areas. It is undisputed that there is a need for greater liberalization of international aviation, though it can also be argued that liberalization is 'rolling back'.[48] One way to further support liberalization would be for ICAO to 'rid itself of the shackles of the Chicago syndrome'.[49] Abeyratne suggests that 'liberalization at regional level is a good way forward in the process, and can contribute to a more flexible approach to market access ... [and that] ICAO should *facilitate interaction between States* and their components that interact in matters of civil aviation'.[50] To that end, ICAO should 'act as *global forum* in the key areas of concern to international civil aviation through cooperation between its member States ... [and] should also extend to *providing guidance*, mainly to States which still look up to ICAO as a global forum of aviation experts'.[51] We note examples above of ICAO guidance on fair competition and core principles on consumer protection, and possible limitations of these in action.

45 E.g. Chicago Convention Appendix 16.

46 Ruwantissa Abeyratne, 'The Role of the International Civil Aviation Organization (ICAO) in the Twenty First Century' (2009) 34 *Annals of Air and Space Law* 529, 534.

47 Ibid., 541.

48 Recent examples include difficulties faced by Norwegian Airlines International in the USA and the reaction of U.S. airlines to alleged State aid received by Middle East airlines. See Barry Humphreys, 'The Gulf Carrier Row: Real Risk of Pantomime?' *Aviation Strategy* (May 2015), online at: www.aviationstrategy.aero

49 Abeyratne, 'The Role of the International Civil Aviation Organization (ICAO) in the Twenty First Century' 541.

50 Ibid., 542 (emphasis added).

51 Ibid., 543 (emphasis added).

ICAO's aims and objectives have progressed: from safety and technical to environmental and economic. Abeyratne claims ICAO has *rediscovered itself* as a results based, performance driven Organization', and that in the process it has 'shed its traditional role of being only a standard setter to embark on a diligent path of implementation and assistance, while retaining its fundamental role as the global forum for international aviation and standard setting body'.[52] According to ICAO, 'With effective implementation of ICAO SARPs comes the critical regulatory framework that builds trust between States and assures global connectivity, through which there can be growth in traffic, trade and tourism, resulting in economic benefits for a State'.[53]

Following introduction of its 'No Country Left Behind' initiative in 2014, ICAO assists States in implementing SARPs, with a view to ensuring that implementation is harmonized globally. 'The NCLB effort also promotes ICAO's efforts to resolve Significant Safety Concerns (SSCs) brought to light through ICAO's safety oversight audits as well as other safety, security and emissions-related objectives'.[54]

The next section unpicks the Chicago System by looking at the Chicago Convention and ICAO governance.

Chicago Convention

Does the Chicago Convention adequately reflect the twenty-first century, global nature of the airline business and the transnational nature of the challenges facing it? Probably not.

Should it be amended to provide a legal framework that is more open and inclusive, and strengthens ICAO governance? In an ideal world, yes.

To that end, it is of use to note the past and ongoing attempts to renew the Convention and review ICAO governance.

Adopted in 1950, Assembly Resolution A4-3 effectively prevents ICAO Council from proposing amendments to the Convention unless they are deemed to be urgent under Paragraph 7, which provides: 'the Council should not itself initiate any proposal for amendment to the Convention for submission to the Assembly unless in the opinion of the Council such amendment is urgent in character'.[55]

In a Working Paper presented to the 36th General Assembly in 2007, under the agenda item 'Increasing the effectiveness of ICAO', a group of

52 Ibid., 529 (emphasis added).

53 ICAO, 'Action on the Environment' (2015) 70(4) *The ICAO Journal* 3, online at: www.icao.int/publications/journalsreports/2015/7004_en.pdf

54 ICAO, 'No Country Left Behind', online at: www.icao.int/about-icao/nclb/Pages/default.aspx

55 ICAO, Doc. 9790, *Assembly Resolutions in Force* (5 October 2001), online at: www.icao.int/publications/documents/9790_en.pdf

States proposed to suspend Paragraph 7 vis-à-vis a draft Assembly Resolution,[56]

> and that the Assembly request Council to invite national experts to study the governance framework of civil aviation without addressing any proposal for specific amendments at this early stage, and to report to the next regular session of the Assembly in 2010 on ways in which it could be improved to ensure more efficient and effective delivery of the critical emerging strategic needs of international civil aviation.[57]

The following was the rationale for this proposal:

> The current governance structures have served international civil aviation well for over sixty years. But the changed conditions of the 21st century have led to the agreement of strategic objectives for ICAO very different from those envisaged over 60 years ago. In order to ensure effective delivery of these objectives by the international community, therefore, these governance structures – which include the annexes, guidance material and potentially the Chicago Convention itself, including its legal and regulatory framework – should be examined to identify those areas which continue to be fit for the purpose for which they were agreed in 1944, and those which may need modernisation.[58]

At the 36th Assembly, the Executive Committee noted the contents of the paper. 'However, most delegations felt it would be premature to change the Chicago Convention that had served the international aviation community so well. Resolution A4-3 was flexible enough to allow a strategic review and it was proposed to refer this matter to the Council for further study'.[59]

In 2009, ICAO's Working Group on Governance (Policy) presented a 'Review of international governance (Chicago Convention)', in which it reflected on the need to update the Chicago Convention, citing the frequency with which ICAO Member States file differences and enter reservations as undermining the effectiveness of ICAO governance:

56 The Working Paper was ultimately presented by Canada on behalf of Antigua and Barbuda, the Bahamas, Barbados, Belize, Canada, Dominica, Grenada, Guyana, Haiti, Hungary, India, Jamaica, Pakistan, the Republic of Korea, Saint Kitts and Nevis, Saint Lucia, Saint Vincent and the Grenadines, South Africa, Suriname, Trinidad and Tobago, the United Arab Emirates and the United Kingdom.

57 ICAO, 'Working Paper: A Proposal for a Study of Policy and Programme with Respect to Examining the International Governance of Civil Aviation' (A36-WP/284, EX/91, 21/9/07, Revision No. 1, 24/9/07) 1, online at: www.icao.int/Meetings/AMC/MA/Assembly%2036th%20Session/wp284rev_en.pdf

58 Ibid.

59 ICAO, 'Assembly – 36th Session, Executive Committee, Draft Text for the Report on Agenda Item 23' (A36-WP/352, EX/115, 26/9/07) para 23.4, online at: www.icao.int/Meetings/AMC/MA/Assembly%2036th%20Session/wp352_en.pdf

> it is sometimes considered that customary law is self-sufficient whereas in other cases it is deemed necessary to enshrine it in the Convention. ICAO's practice has created 'customary' competencies, but entails fragility as a Contracting State could in theory dissociate itself from this consensus by reservation and, for example, refuse security audits or deny ICAO's jurisdiction and action on environmental matters. It may also lead to a conflict of jurisdiction with other organizations holding explicit competencies by treaty in the same fields, such as UNFCCC in the case of environment.[60]

In the end, ICAO Council decided not to initiate any further action on this issue, it being understood that all Member States had the right to present proposals to amend the Chicago Convention pursuant to Assembly Resolution A4-3.

It does not appear that much formal progress has been made on this issue since 2007. It has been made public that, at the 39th Assembly, 'The Council will present a report on initiatives to, inter alia, enhance communications with Member States and improve the working methods, procedures and *governance of the Organization* under Agenda Item 27: *Increasing the efficiency and effectiveness of ICAO*'.[61] This is most likely to be a report on minor administrative improvements rather than an announcement of a strategic review of the organization's governance.

One major change approved by the full Plenary of the 39th General Assembly in 2016 is amendment of Article 50 of the Chicago Convention via the proposed enlargement of ICAO Council from 36 to 40 Member States,[62] and the composition of the Council membership as regards distribution of seats in the exiting Parts I, II and III, as well as election of officers of the Assembly. Whilst the original text of the Chicago Convention provided for only 21 members on ICAO Council, the text was subsequently amended by the 13th (Extraordinary) Session of the Assembly in 1961 (27 seats); the 17th (A) (Extraordinary) Session of the Assembly in 1971 (30 seats); the 21st Session of the Assembly in 1974 (33 seats); the 28th Session (Extra - ordinary) of the Assembly (36 seats).

Whilst a wide consensus on any change to the Convention would be preferable, under Article 94(b) of the Chicago Convention,[63] the ICAO

60 ICAO, 'Review of International Governance (Chicago Convention)' Working Paper C-WP/13416 (22 June 2009); also noted in ICAO, Doc. 9921, *Annual Report of the Council* (2009), online at: www.icao.int/publications/Documents/9921_en.pdf

61 ICAO, 'Assembly – 36th Session, Plenary, Provision Agenda for the 39th Session of the ICAO, Assembly' (A39-WP/1, P/1, Appendix) A-6 (emphasis added), online at: www.icao.int/Meetings/a39/Documents/WP/wp_001_en.pdf

62 Though arguably this does not change 'governance' much in real terms.

63 The UNFCCC amendment procedure is found in Article 15(1), which permits any party to propose amendments to the Convention and provides that amendments should be made by consensus (Article 15(3)). Article 15(4) sets out the process.

Assembly can amend the Convention by a two-thirds majority that the 'present and voting' members consider to be 'of such a nature to justify such a course of action ... [and] that any State which has not ratified within a specified period after the amendment has come into force shall thereupon cease to be a Member of the Organization and a party to the Convention'.[64] Interestingly and perhaps most telling is that although not all Member States have ratified every amendment, none has been expelled from the organization to date.[65]

As is the case with any multilaterally negotiated, international convention, changing the Chicago Convention would not be quickly or easily accomplished. Indeed, the proposal to expand ICAO Council to 40 seats was first presented back in 2010.[66] By comparison let us consider the experience in international law of the sea. The Third UN Conference on the Law of the Sea held between 1973 and 1982, resulted in the UN Convention on the Law of the Sea (UNCLOS), which did not enter into force until 1994; that process took 20 years. UNCLOS replaced four post-Second World War treaties from 1958. With that said, UNCLOS is a more inclusive convention as membership is not restricted only to nation-states; the EU acceded to UNCLOS in 1994.[67]

Whilst traditionally ICAO has functioned as international standard setter, contemporary changes and challenges demand that it now moves beyond standards to exercise greater global governance. As we examine below in relation to the GMBM, a space is provided for the emergence of new forms of decision making that reflects the common interest rather than merely State interest. With that said, ICAO is an international institution with delegated authority, as limited by its Member States. Whilst it is highly

64 Article 94: '(a) Any proposed amendment to this Convention must be approved by a two-thirds vote of the Assembly and shall then come into force in respect of States which have ratified such amendment when ratified by the number of contracting States specified by the Assembly. The number so specified shall not be less than two thirds of the total number of contracting States; (b) If in its opinion the amendment is of such a nature as to justify this course, the Assembly in its resolution recommending adoption may provide that any State which has not ratified within a specified period after the amendment has come into force shall thereupon cease to be a member of the Organization and a party to the Convention'.

65 Ebere Osieke, 'Sanctions in International Law: The Contributions of International Organizations' (1984) 31(2) *Netherlands International Law Review* 185–186; See also D. B. Hollis (ed.), *The Oxford Guide to Treaties* (Oxford University Press 2012) 352–361, on the process of amending treaties.

66 See ICAO, 'Working Paper: Increasing ICAO Council seats to 39' (A37-WP/333, P/28, 1/10/10), online at: www.icao.int/Meetings/AMC/Assembly37/Working%20Papers%20by%20Number/wp333_en.pdf

67 Council Decision of 23 March 1998 concerning the conclusion by the European Community of the United Nations Convention of 10 December 1982 on the Law of the Sea and the Agreement of 28 July 1994 relating to the implementation of Part XI thereof; OJ L179 of 23/06/1998, 3.

political in orientation, ICAO is so far not a political level in its own right.[68] The fact that international aviation emissions were not included in the Paris Agreement in 2015 can be interpreted as giving ICAO 'free hand', or as a vote of confidence in ICAO, or as a failure of ICAO to 'step up'. If we accept that heads of States intentionally omitted mention of aviation, we may in turn interpret this as a signal for ICAO's possible recognition as a more autonomous political level, though well short of becoming supranational-type entity.

International Civil Aviation Organization

This author concurs that ICAO has evolved significantly since it was established on 4 April 1947, following the interim Provisional ICAO (PICAO) that functioned from 6 June 1945. Indeed, this book substantiates in many respects the claim that ICAO has *dynamically* evolved.[69] As we will see, ICAO has created new environmental standards, a course of action that rests within ICAO's usual competence in the Chicago System. Excitingly, it is now on the verge of establishing the world's first global market-based mechanism – an altogether new course of action that sits at the edge of *economic* regulation and thus represents a competence of a different incarnation. ICAO Council's leadership in global governance of the GMBM is noteworthy.

As we explained earlier, although emissions from international aviation are excluded from the Kyoto Protocol to the UN Framework Convention on Climate Change, Article 2(2) provides that ICAO shall be the relevant body through which to seek reductions of GHG emissions in civil aviation.[70] Thus ICAO is mandated to provide a forum for Annex I countries to pursue limitation or reduction activities.

ICAO and UNFCCC each have independent and distinct decision-making processes.[71] Despite this, there are 'synergies' between the two and 'if the major portion of emissions from international aviation occurs in international airspace, reason seems to support that ICAO is the relevant and

68 Miles Kahler, 'Defining Accountability Up: The Global Economic Multilaterals' (2004) 39(2) *Government and Opposition* 132–158 as referred to in Zürn, 'Global Governance as Multi-Level Governance'.

69 As put forward by Mendes de Leon, 'The Dynamics of Sovereignty and Jurisdiction in International Aviation Law'.

70 It reads: 'The Parties included in Annex I shall pursue limitation or reduction of emissions of greenhouse gases not controlled by the Montreal Protocol from aviation and marine bunker fuels, working through the International Civil Aviation Organization and the International Maritime Organization, respectively'. International aviation is also left out of the Paris Agreement 2015.

71 Truxal and Dunbar, 'Evaluating Three Levels of Environmental Taxation in Aviation' 275.

appropriate UN body to oversee the environmental aspects of international civil aviation'.[72]

In light of the projected growth in demand for global aviation, it is essential to note ICAO's mandate laid down in Article 44 of the Chicago Convention, which is *inter alia* 'to foster the planning and development of international air transport so as to insure safe and orderly *growth* of civil aviation throughout the world'.[73] Arguably, this places ICAO in the unique and difficult position of fulfilling its core objectives while also balancing other values and schemes such as a robust environmental protection policy. The focus is on *growth*; there is no mention of 'environment' in the 1944 Convention. 'Acquiring and maintaining a foothold for clear environmental protection policy in the sector has proved challenging – an emerging cycle of practical details defeating broad declarations'.[74]

The Chicago Convention has been 'extended' vis-à-vis SARPs to include regulation of environmental pollution, for example noise[75] and the sector's greenhouse gas emissions.[76] The GMBM comprises only one part of ICAO's comprehensive mitigation strategy. Agreement was also reached on voluntary submission to ICAO of States' Action Plans, which reflects ICAO's environmental policy move as a 'dynamic shift'[77] from its 'Standards and policy setting phase' (service-oriented) to 'implementation mode' (plus assistance). Evidence of 'assistance' is the fact that between May and November 2011, ICAO organized six regional 'hands-on training workshops'[78] to 'assist member States of each ICAO Region in preparing and submitting their action plans, by providing tools and appropriate information (guidance material, interactive website – electronic template)'.[79] ICAO efforts on implementation and assistance regionally have thus been an important driver in the success in the development of environmental SARPs and other policies, and advising on States' Action Plans. ICAO has organized numerous regional meetings and seminars to support ICAO Member States on instituting climate-friendly aviation. Invitees have included ICAO Member States, and representatives from industry, interest groups as well as the

72 Steven Truxal, 'The ICAO Assembly Resolutions on International Aviation and Climate Change: An Historic Agreement, a Breakthrough Deal, and the Cancun Effect' (2011) 36(3) *Air & Space Law* 219.

73 Chicago Convention (emphasis added).

74 Truxal and Dunbar, 'Evaluating Three Levels of Environmental Taxation in Aviation' 277.

75 Chicago Convention Annex 16, vol. I.

76 Ibid., Annex 16, Volume II; noting noise and emissions are only two of the harms.

77 UNFCCC, 'Agenda Item 10(d) Emissions from fuel used for international aviation and maritime transport', The Thirty-sixth Session of the UNFCCC Subsidiary Body for Scientific and Technological Advice (SBSTA36), Bonn (May 2012) 1.

78 Mexico City, Bangkok, Dubai, Nairobi, Paris and Montreal.

79 ICAO, 'Aviation and Climate Change' (Germany, June 2011), online at: www.icao.int/environmental-protection/Documents/Presentations/ICAO%20Secretariat%20-%20Opening.pdf

general public. It is noteworthy that ICAO has also paired up States that did submit States' Action Plans with States that did not, which it is understood has had a positive bearing on subsequent submission rates.

The above, alongside ICAO's provision of access to financial resources for Member States,[80] evidences the power and effectiveness of partnerships for aviation environmental performance. Such partnerships are crucial, according to the UAE representative on ICAO Council: 'Challenges facing the industry today cannot be addressed solely within national boundaries; there has to be cooperation in nations and regions throughout the world. The past, present and future of civil aviation is built through mutual partnerships'.[81] States' Action Plans also provide a strong incentive to build partnerships at the national level *beyond* aviation. Jane Hupe, Chief of ICAO's Environment Unit, tells us: 'Partnerships lead us to set common goals. Partnerships lead us to break the silos. Partnerships not only multiply environmental actions, they also multiply their effects'.[82]

States' Action Plans also contribute to Intended Nationally Determined Contributions under the UNFCCC process. As States have carried out work for States' Action Plans, they have made the link that this robust data collection has also 'enabled them to collect data related to *domestic* aviation and thus see synergies and opportunity to prepare the information to feed into the UNFCCC reporting mechanism as the ICAO States' Action Plan structure already reflects the actions to reduce domestic emissions as co-benefits'.[83] This shows how the parallel, harmonized and complementary reporting systems work together. Furthermore, according to IATA: 'This dual-reporting mechanism significantly contributes to capacity building, as it multiplies the effects of emissions reductions and environmental benefits of these initiatives in aviation and creates synergies with other sectors of the economy, while respecting both organizations' mandates and regulatory frameworks. A clear win-win-win situation'.[84]

In 2007, ICAO passed Assembly Resolution A36-22, in relation to emissions trading in international civil aviation, which established that emissions trading schemes should only be 'on the basis of mutual agreement between those States',[85] which amounted to a stalemate on international aviation emissions and climate change. ICAO's 37th General Assembly 'agreed to an historic agreement on aviation and climate change' in 2010, adopting two key resolutions: A37-18 and 19, which superseded Resolution A36-22. The intended outcomes of these Resolutions were 'essentially non-specific,

80 E.g. ICAO–EU Joint Assistance Plan; see ICAO, 'Action on the Environment'.
81 Ibid., 23.
82 Ibid., 7.
83 Ibid., 9.
84 Ibid., 9–10.
85 ICAO, 'Resolutions Adopted at the 36th Assembly' (A36-22, October 2007), online at: www.icao.int/icao/en/env/A36_Res22_Prov.pdf

meaning it is yet unclear whether an actual reduction will be achieved; [but] they are not necessarily weak in effect. For instance, specific elements of the resolutions include an agreement with two requirements: aircraft emissions must be stabilized and State Action Plans will be introduced. Of course, the most significant, extensive goal is for [carbon neutral growth] by 2020'.[86]

In the interim, ICAO has adopted a strategy to develop a 'basket of measures' for mitigating the effects of international aviation on the environment; they are technological and operational improvements, sustainable alternative fuels and market-based measures. The past and ongoing initiatives to reduce the environmental footprint of aviation in various areas are: aircraft technology and research programmes, recycling of aircraft, next-generation air navigation and green operations, sustainable alternative fuels and renewable energy, financing for aviation environmental activities and carbon markets.[87]

In the area of environmental protection, ICAO performs its work through three groups: the Committee on Aviation Environmental Protection,[88] the Group on International Aviation and Climate Change and since March 2014 the ICAO Council Environment Advisory Group.[89]

The Council's EAG oversees all work related to the GMBM and makes recommendations to Council. EAG regularly makes requests to CAEP, a technical committee which has been working on a range of environmental protection issues since it was formed in 1983. In the context of aircraft carbon dioxide (CO_2) emissions, CAEP has been assisting Council in developing new policies and adopting new SARPs through two main tasks.

The first main undertaking is the development of CO_2 and non-volatile particulate matter (nvPM) certification standards for aircraft, with a view to ensuring that 'the best available technology is on board future aircraft'.[90] At

86 Truxal, *Competition and Regulation in the Airline Industry* 237; it must be noted that ICAO's goal is far less ambitious than the EU's original (unilateral) position to include aviation in its ETS from 2012, which called for a 10 per cent reduction of 2005 baseline levels by 2020 and reducing carbon emissions in the sector by 50 per cent by 2050. Although ICAO is currently working towards this more modest carbon neutral growth, it should be mentioned that agreements at ICAO are multilateral in nature.

87 ICAO, 'Action on the Environment' 14.

88 As of 2016, CAEP membership includes 22 States: Argentina, Australia, Brazil, Canada, China, Egypt, France, Germany, India, Italy, Japan, Netherlands, Poland, Russian Federation, Singapore, South Africa, Spain, Sweden, Switzerland, Ukraine, United Kingdom and United States; and 16 observers: Greece, Norway, Peru, Saudi Arabia, Turkey, Arab Civil Aviation Commission, Airports Council International, Civil Air Navigation Services Organisation (CANSO), EU, IATA, International Business Aviation Council (IBAC), International Coordinating Council of Aerospace Industries Associations (ICCAIA), International Coalition for Sustainable Aviation (ICSA), International Federation of Air Line Pilots' Associations (IFALPA) and UNFCCC.

89 We note that EAG's work programme has effectively finished. It may be reconvened in the future if necessary. The 'new' EAG would reflect relevant changes to ICAO Council membership following the 39th Assembly.

90 ICAO, 'Action on the Environment' 11.

its 38th General Assembly in 2013, ICAO adopted Resolution A38-18, which requests the Council to 'develop a global CO_2 Standard[91] for aircraft aiming to finalize analyses by late 2015 and adoption by the Council in 2016'.[92] It should be noted that reservations to particular paragraphs in Resolution A38-17 were entered by multiple States, including Brazil, China, India, EU, Russian Federation, Singapore, United Arab Emirates and the United States.[93] The CO_2 standard was unanimously recommended by the 170 international experts on CAEP and is understood to have been adopted by Council without challenge in June 2016. Subject to final adoption by the 39th Assembly, these SARPs will be included in an entirely new Volume of Annex 16 (Volume III).[94] CAEP's recommendation for this standard represents 'a significant exercise within CAEP to ensure that the new Standard is environmentally effective and economically reasonable'.[95] According to ICAO, 'the new CO_2 emissions standard would not only be applicable to new aircraft type designs as of 2020, but also to new deliveries of current in-production aircraft types from 2023. A cut-off date of 2028 for production of aircraft that do not comply with the standard was also recommended'.[96]

The second main task is the GMBM itself, which has been 'one of the most challenging technical tasks within the scope of CAEP's work'.[97] The committee has developed the technical design side of the GMBM, 'including a set of recommendations on the means to assess the eligibility of emission units (carbon credits) to be used',[98] how monitoring, reporting and verification (MRV) should be carried out, and possible options for developing international and national registries. 'As per the requests from the Council and EAG, CAEP has been undertaking technical analyses on the assessment of costs and environmental impacts of the GMBM of different approaches for a global MBM scheme being considered by the EAG'.[99] The GMBM proposal was considered and approved by ICAO Assembly at its 39th Session in September–October 2016. The following section sets out the main points of the GMBM scheme for international aviation.

91 ICAO, 'New CO_2 Standard for Aircraft now Being Finalized for 2016 under ICAO's Committee on Aviation Environmental Protection (CAEP)'; see ICAO, 'Action on the Environment' 3.

92 ICAO, Doc. 10022, 'Assembly Resolution A38-18: Consolidated statement of continuing ICAO policies and practices related to environmental protection – Climate change' (2010), para 33(e), online at: www.icao.int/Meetings/a38/Pages/resolutions.aspx

93 Ibid.; see also Alberola and Solier, 'Including International Aviation in the European Union Emission Trading Scheme' 23.

94 ICAO, 'Action on the Environment' 13.

95 Ibid.

96 ICAO, 'New ICAO Aircraft CO_2 Standard One Step Closer to Final Adoption' (Press release, 8 February 2016), online at: www.icao.int/Newsroom/Pages/New-ICAO-Aircraft-CO2-Standard-One-Step-Closer-To-Final-Adoption.aspx

97 ICAO, 'Action on the Environment' 12.

98 Ibid.

99 Ibid.

Resolution 22/2: Consolidated statement of continuing ICAO policies and practices related to environmental protection – Global Market-based Measure (MBM) scheme

Assembly Resolution A38-18 provides the mandate for Council and Member States *inter alia* to:

> finalize the work on technical aspects, environmental impacts and modalities of possible options for a GMBM scheme, including on its feasibility and practicability, taking into account the need for develop - ment of international aviation, the proposal from the aviation industry and other international developments, as appropriate, and without prejudice to the negations under the UNFCCC.
> ...
> Identify the major issues and problems, including for Member States, and make a recommendation on a GMBM scheme that appropriately addresses them and key design elements, including a means to take into account *special circumstances and respective capabilities*, and the mechanisms for the implementation of the scheme from 2020 as part of a basket of measures which also include technologies, operational improvements and sustainable alternative fuels to achieve ICAO's global aspirational goals.[100]

Following the work mentioned above led by the ICAO's EAG and High-Level Group on a Global MBM Scheme (HLG-GMBM) with technical input provided by CAEP, two rounds of Global Aviation Dialogues (GLADs) on MBMs were held in all regions in April 2015 and March–April 2016.[101]

At the 39th General Assembly, ICAO Assembly adopted Resolution A39-22/2.[102] Assembly Resolution A39-22/2 refers to Assembly Resolution A38-18 on developing a GMBM for international aviation. The GMBM is emphasized as playing a 'complementary role ... to the other elements of a basket of measures, as a temporary emissions gap filler to achieve the global aspirational goal, without imposing inappropriate economic burden on international aviation' to achieve carbon neutral growth by 2020 (CNG 2020).[103]

100 ICAO, 'Assembly Resolution A38-18', paras 19(a) and 19(c) (emphasis added).

101 See ICAO, '2016 Global Aviation Dialogues (GLADs)', online at: www.icao.int/meetings/GLADs-2016/Pages/default.aspx

102 ICAO, 'Assembly Resolution A39-22/2' (A39-WP/462, EX/179, 5 October 2016), online at: www.icao.int/Meetings/a39/Documents/WP/wp_462_en.pdf

103 Resolution A39-22/2 para 3; see IATA, 'Historic Agreement on Carbon-Neutral Growth', online at: www.iata.org/pressroom/pr/Pages/2013-06-03-05.aspx; it can be argued that the CNG 2020 is perhaps more achievable for aviation than are the universal targets under the Paris Agreement as the aviation sector is better equipped to achieve CNG 2020 in reality.

Following approval of Resolution A39-22/2 ('the Resolution') a phased implementation of a GMBM scheme will follow in the form of a Carbon Offsetting and Reduction Scheme for International Aviation (CORSIA).[104] The core objective of the CORSIA is 'to address any annual increase in total CO_2 emissions from international civil aviation (i.e. civil aviation flights that depart in one country and arrive in a different country) above the 2020 levels, taking into account *special circumstances and respective capabilities*'.[105]

Paragraph 9 of the Resolution sets out a 'phased implementation' for the CORSIA to account for 'special circumstances and respective capabilities of States, in particular developing States, while minimizing market distortion'.[106] A pilot phase will apply from 2021 through 2023 to States that have volunteered to participate in the scheme. The first phase will apply from 2024 through 2026 to States that voluntarily participate in the pilot phase, as well as any other States that volunteer to participate in the first phase, noting that all States are strongly encouraged volutarily to particpate in the pilot and first stages.[107]

The second implementation phase will apply from 2027 through 2035 to:

> all States that have an individual share of international aviation activities in RTKs in year 2018 above 0.5 per cent of total RTKs or whose cumulative share in the list of States from the highest to the lowest amount of RTKs reaches 90 per cent of total RTKs...[108]

The CORSIA would not apply to States classified as Least Developed Countries, Small Island Developing States or Landlocked Developing Countries, unless they volunteer to participate in the second phase.[109] Nevertheless, voluntary participation is encouraged.[110]

In Paragraph 10 of the Resolution it is provided that the CORSIA would apply to 'all aircraft operators on the same routes between States with a view to minimizing market distortion',[111] as determined by the following three categories of routes:

> a) all international flights on the routes between States, both of which are included in the CORSIA by paragraph 7 above, are covered by the offsetting requirements of the CORSIA;[112]

104 GMBM and CORSIA are referred to interchangeably in this section.
105 Resolution A39-22/2 para 5 (emphasis added).
106 Ibid., para 9.
107 Ibid., para 9(a)–(c).
108 Ibid., para 9(e).
109 Ibid., para 9(3).
110 Ibid., para 9(f).
111 Ibid., para 10.
112 Ibid., para 10(a).

b) all international flights on the routes between a State that is included in the CORSIA and another State that is not included in the CORSIA by paragraph 7 above are exempted from the offsetting requirements of the CORSIA, while retaining simplified reporting requirements;[113] and

c) all international flights on the routes between States, both of which are not included in the CORSIA by paragraph 7 above, are exempted from the offsetting requirements of the CORSIA, while retaining simplified reporting requirements.[114]

Thus Paragraph 10 of the Resolution, which determines the *route* between States, must be read in conjunction with Paragraph 9 to determine the appropriate *implementation phase and State* from which an international flight departs and the State to which an international flight arrives. Paragraph 10(b) above supports differentiation while Paragraph 10(c) minimizes market distortion.

Finally, Paragraph 11 of the Resolution sets out the method of calculation of 'the amount of CO_2 emissions required to be offset by an aircraft operator in a given year from 2021' as follows:

a) an aircraft operator's offset requirement = [% Sectoral × (an aircraft operator's emissions covered by CORSIA in a given year × the sector's growth factor in the given year)] + [% Individual × (an aircraft operator's emissions covered by CORSIA in a given year × that aircraft operator's growth factor in the given year);

b) where the sector's growth factor = (total emissions covered by CORSIA in the given year – average of total emissions covered by CORSIA between 2019 and 2020)/total emissions covered by CORSIA in the given year;

c) where the aircraft operator's growth factor = (the aircraft operator's total emissions covered by CORSIA in the given year – average of the aircraft operator's emissions covered by CORSIA between 2019 and 2020)/the aircraft operator's total emissions covered by CORSIA in the given year.[115]

Paragraphs 12 to 14 are also important for discussion; they provide, respectively, that new entrants would be exempted from the application of the CORSIA for three years or until annual emissions surpass the threshold

113 Ibid., para 10(b).
114 Ibid., para 10(c).
115 Ibid., paras 11(a), 11(b) and 11(c).

of 0.1 per cent of total emissions in 2020;[116] the CORSIA would not apply to low levels of international aviation activity;[117] and there would be no redistribution of exempted emissions.[118] A periodic review of the CORSIA will be undetaken by ICAO Council every three years, beginning in 2022, to contribute to effectiveness of the scheme.[119] In the GMBM, aircraft operators will be required to 'reconcile their offsetting requirements under the scheme, while they report the required data to a single State authority every year' within an ongoing, three-year compliance cycle, the first of which would be from 2021 to 2023.[120]

Crucial to success of the GMBM will of course be successful *implementation*. To that end, there are four major actions that would need to be taken to establish the necessary mechanism for implementation of the CORSIA from 2020. The first action regards implementation of the MRV system. With the Resolution is approved, the Assembly now requests Council, with technical input from CAEP, to develop the MRV rules as SARPs along with related guidance for implementation of the MRV system under the CORSIA, for adoption by June 2017; and for 'Member States whose aircraft operator undertakes international flights to develop necessary arrangements for imple - mentation of the MRV system from 1 January 2018', in essence for rule implementation.[121]

The second action would be for ICAO Council to develop, with technical input from CAEP, necessary guidance material on Emissions Unit Criteria to support the purchase by aircraft operators of appropriate emissions units from eligible programmes under the scheme, for adoption by Council by 2018.[122] This author expects that ultimately the use of emissions units, with respect to quality of the offsets, could create hurdles for implementation. It is commonly understood by experts that aviation-related methodologies for use in offsetting programmes will need further development.[123] Additionally, ICAO Council and Member States will need to identify and reduce risks associated with double-counting of emissions

116 Assembly Resolution A39-22/2 defines a new entrant as 'any aircraft operator that commences an aviation activity falling within the scope of the scheme on or after its entry into force and whose activity is not in whole or in part a continuation of an aviation activity previously performed by another aircraft operator'. Assembly Resolution A39-22/2 para 12.

117 Ibid., para 13; Assembly Resolution A39-22/2 terms these 'technical exemptions': 'aircraft operators emitting less than 10,000 metric tonnes of CO_2 emissions from international aviation per year; aircraft with less than 5,700 kg of Maximum Take Off Mass (MTOM); or humanitarian, medical and firefighting operations'.

118 Ibid., para 13.

119 Ibid., para 18.

120 Ibid., para 14.

121 Ibid., paras 20(a)–(b).

122 Ibid., paras 20(c)–(d). This will also take into account relevant developments in the UNFCCC and under Article 6 of the Paris Agreement 2015.

123 Ibid., para 24.

reduction, which could undermine the GMBM. CAEP has already made recommendations for the quality of carbon credits for use in the GMBM scheme for international aviation. Thus, most expectedly the emphasis will be on a high-quality offsetting programme. An issue of contention is defining 'quality', particularly when carbon offset prices vary widely.[124]

Third, with respect to establishment of registries under the CORSIA, ICAO Council and CAEP would develop registry guidance (by 2018), and Council would establish a consolidated central registry under ICAO (to operate from 1 January 2021).[125] Member States included in the GMBM would develop national registries or group registries, beginning with those in the first implementation phase.[126]

Finally, and most noteworthy for this book are the provisions located towards the end of the Resolution. ICAO Council would oversee the functioning of the CORSIA with support from CAEP, as needed. Thus, the overall, global *governance* of the CORSIA will be within the exclusive remit of ICAO while Member States will devise and implement national regulatory frameworks for aircraft operators, as necessary, to ensure compliance and enforcement of the GMBM.[127]

ICAO will assist Member States on capacity building and assistance as they prepare and execute action plans for implementation of the MRV system and create registries by 1 January 2018.[128] Member States should 'build partnerships among themselves to cooperate on the implementation of the MRV system' and 'on the establishment of their own registries or group registries established by groups of States, and possible pilot implementation'.[129]

The reliance on public–public and public–private partnerships for implementation, particularly at regional level, is noteworthy. It appears to emphasize that ICAO is *just* the global forum. Does ICAO realize it cannot do it (alone)? The NCLB initiative and partnering up of States on States' Action Plans is telling. Implementation is done 'on the ground'; thus, States and non-State/private actors must be on board to implement the GMBM and enforce compliance.[130]

124 See UNFCCC Carbon Offsetting Platform, https://offset.climateneutralnow.org; and the ICAO Carbon Calculator, www.icao.int/environmental-protection/CarbonOffset/Pages/default.aspx.

125 Assembly Resolution A39-22/2, paras 20(e)–(f).

126 Ibid., paras 20(g)–(h).

127 Ibid., paras 20(i)–(j).

128 Ibid., paras 20(a), (c).

129 Ibid., paras 20(b), (d).

130 A connection can be made here to the emphasis on partnerships in ozone layer governance as discussed in Chapter 2.

This call for States to build partnerships signals the apparent goal of network development, moving away from traditional and 'strictly legalist command-and-control' regulation towards a wider notion of law operating in a global space.[131] Networks can be 'important building blocks of global governance … needed to respond to the increased complexity and volatility of many transnational regulatory arenas'.[132] Minas identifies that they vary in strength from the sovereignty-sharing EU to more informal and non-binding ASEAN coordination,[133] amidst recent 'growth in processes of cross-border cooperation on climate change which take place beyond, alongside or in tandem with the UNFCCC'.[134] 'A reconceptualization of the global response to climate change cannot be limited to the networks, but it would do well to engage with the agility and innovative potential of networks, as well as to grapple with the legitimacy, accountability and steering challenges that they may present'.[135] Thus, a global network or networks of ICAO States vis-à-vis the GMBM can give way to, in the climate arena, the innovative design of standards, norms and values. In keeping with Minas, 'Norm/policy entrepreneurs and deal-brokers play important roles in the process of climate networks … resultants of these networks have significant influence on the creation and dissemination of climate norms and regulatory interventions, which range from "hard law" such as legislation to non-binding market standards'.[136] The GMBM and its processes are examples of how transnational climate governance is developing outside the UNFCCC negotiations and, if successfully implemented, can thus serve as a prospect for influencing global climate policy.[137] 'Transnational climate governance thereby contributes to innovation in global climate policy, potentially changing incentives and preference orders within the UN negotiations, where national representatives bargain "in the shadow of globalisation"'.[138] As such, the GMBM scheme for aviation has the ability to

131 Stephen Minas, 'The Rise of Transnational Networks in Climate Change Governance: A Study in Hybridity' (2015) 05 *TLI Think!* 20–21; see also M. Patrick Cottrell and David M. Trubek, 'Law as Problem Solving: Standards, Networks, Experimentation, and Deliberation in Global Space' (2012) 21 *Transnational Law & Contemporary Problems* 359.

132 See Olaf Dilling, Martin Herberg and Gerd Winter, 'Introduction: Exploring Transnational Administrative Rule-Making' in Olaf Dilling, Martin Herberg and Gerd Winter (eds), *Transnational Administrative Rule-Making: Performance, Legal Effects and Legitimacy* (Hart Publishing 2011).

133 Minas, 'The Rise of Transnational Networks in Climate Change Governance' 20.

134 Ibid., 32.

135 Ibid., 32–33.

136 Ibid., 23.

137 Ibid., 22; see also Boaventura de Sousa Santos, 'Law: A Map of Misreading – Toward a Postmodern Conception of Law' (1987) 14 *Journal of Law and Society* 279.

138 Minas, 'The Rise of Transnational Networks in Climate Change Governance' 23 citing Alex Mills, *The Confluence of Public and Private International Law* (Cambridge University Press 2009) 2.

be a 'force multiplier of UNFCCC processes and resultants … to finally make "the link that governments and international organisations seem to find so difficult: translating global obligations into domestic action and implementation"'.[139]

Realizing aviation's potential

Owing to an ongoing lack of consensus on whether or how to regulate economic and environmental aspects of international civil aviation, unilateral and plurilateral action has followed. Krisch also explains that in some areas 'unilateral action and informal structure … appear more useful for problem solving and the effective exercise of power than formal institutions and the increasingly firm and demanding process of multilateral treaty making'.[140] But unilateralism is only useful, really, if the actor has significant political and economic strength. We may expect that, if multilateralism fails to deliver or progresses too slowly, unilateralism vis-à-vis design and dissemination of norms for civil aviation and beyond will continue, led by the EU and other powerful States or groups of States,[141] to drive reactionary change in other parts of the world or create new opportunities for States to utilize aviation more as an economic and social tool – and less as purely a political tool – to grow into regional or global leaders in these value areas.

Dąbrowski tells us that in addition to importing norms from ICAO,[142] 'the EU strives to export its rules to ICAO using various mechanisms, from bold attempts at shaping the *global rules* through the use of its market power, through bargaining and conditionality, to the discreet export of *technical standards* through persuasion'.[143] He continues:

> Even though to date the vertical export of EU aviation norms has been moderate, the EU has used conditionality to shake up the status quo concerning a global approach to tackling aviation emissions and there is some evidence of successful vertical export of the less politically controversial technical aspects of the EU aviation acquis.

139 Minas, 'The Rise of Transnational Networks in Climate Change Governance' 23 citing P. Sands and J. Peel, *Principles of International Environmental Law* (3rd edn, Cambridge University Press 2012) 92.

140 Krisch, 'The Decay of Consent' 2.

141 It can be alternatively argued that EU action on aviation and climate change vis-à-vis the EU ETS is not an example of unilateralism but rather *plurilateralism*, on the basis that the ETS operates in 28 EU countries and three EEA–EFTA countries (Iceland, Lichtenstein and Norway).

142 Marcin Dąbrowski, 'Transport Policy: EU as Taker, Shaper or Shaker of the Global Civil Aviation Regime?' in Gerard Falkner and Patrick Müller (eds), *EU Policies in a Global Perspective: Shaping or Taking International Regimes?* (Routledge 2013) 137.

143 Ibid., 131 (emphasis added).

> Thus, the EU has been successfully exporting its norms to the wider European neighbourhood, taking advantage of its authority and market power while encouraging countries in other parts of the world to adopt EU aviation norms through a combination of conditionalities and 'soft' mechanisms of influence.[144]

But as a supranational entity the EU is also uniquely placed to exert such influence. If the transnational problems facing the world today are left unaddressed, they may fester and threaten world peace. Since legal norms flow over national borders, territorial borders cannot always solve problems. '[T]ransnational issues over which individual states have very limited control have become sources of conflict: global warming, migration and resource scarcity have created profound collective action problems'.[145] Thus, we can view the attempts by the EU and others to deal with contemporary, global problems as a good opportunity to utilize civil aviation as a tool for enhancing solidarity in the international community. In the same vein, Goedhuis wrote in 1955:

> The realization that the chances for peace are furthered by an increase in general prosperity and perception of the important role air transport can play in a balanced growth of world economy will favor the recognition of the necessity for sovereignty limiting rules of law. As the legal conscience tends to further the factors that protect, promote and enhance life, it is the task of the lawyers to help to create in the minds of the public a realization of the social element in aviation. It is this element that Sir Winston Churchill undoubtedly had in mind when he declared Civil Aviation to be 'the greatest instrument for international solidarity'.[146]

Thus it can confidently be stated that civil aviation will continue to be recognized as a potential tool for solidarity in the international community. It should therefore come as no surprise that aviation is in the global spotlight for emissions and to a lesser extent for fair competition. The aviation GMBM is linked to the wider UNFCCC agenda; a sectoral agreement is an ideal stepping stone to progressing global climate change governance.[147]

With the objectives of peace and security in mind, this author thus supports the argument that the transnational law approach can bring about new forms of decision making that are more inclusive and norms-based,

144 Ibid.

145 Caroline Bouchard *et al.*, 'Introduction' in Caroline Bouchard *et al.* (eds), *Multilateralism in the 21st Century: Europe's Quest for Effectiveness* (Routledge 2013) 1.

146 Goedhuis, 'The Air Sovereignty Concept and United States Influence on its Future Development' 221.

147 Steven Truxal, 'The ICAO Assembly Resolutions on International Aviation and Climate Change'.

which can lead to more non-consensual rule-making and better adherence to the norms. The social 'push factors' make this approach more acceptable.

Unilateralism, despite its possible indirect effects on promoting change, is not usually well received by sovereign States either. In its place, multilateralism may be the more appropriate approach. Along these lines, Lazarou *et al.* warn us that:

> In re-establishing the principled basis for multilateralism, actors should take note that globalisation could strengthen threats to peace, and that a combination of instruments might be needed to combat these threats effectively. Hence, cooperation with and support for *ad hoc*/hybrid interstate and institutional arrangements and decision-making forums (regional, bilateral, national and with participation by non-state and private actors) would be necessary to combat transnational threats and problems.[148]

Indeed, multilateralism is often proposed as 'the best means of combating new types of transnational problems and specifically outlines the conditions and rules governing the specific type of cooperation best suited to the particular challenge(s) in view'.[149] In some market areas – e.g. securities, financial markets and trade and investment – there has been slow progress though multilateralism. For instance, there have been calls for international cooperation in the regulation of capital markets following the 2008 financial crisis,[150] for international labour standards, in multilateral agreements on investment,[151] and with respect to EU securities and financial market regulation.[152] One notes these examples are very EU-centric. Interestingly, Peterson and Bouchard tell us:

> The EU's mission to promote multilateralism is frequently discredited by claims that Europe's own experience of cooperation cannot be replicated elsewhere. Moreover, the EU's pursuit of bilateral 'strategic partnerships' with emerging powers – as well as established ones – is often viewed as contrary to any effort to build multilateralism globally.

148 Elena Lazarou *et al.*, 'The Evolving "Doctrine" of Multilateralism in the Twenty-First Century' in Caroline Bouchard *et al.* (eds), *Multilateralism in the 21st Century: Europe's Quest for Effectiveness* (Routledge 2013) 47.

149 Ibid., 42.

150 Kathleen L. Casey 'The Role of International Regulatory Cooperation and Coordination in Promoting Efficient Capital Markets' (Instituto Bruno Leoni, Italy 2010), online at: www.sec.gov/news/speech/2010/spch061210klc.htm

151 E. Nieuwenhys and Marcel Brus, *Multilateral Regulation of Investment* (Wolters Kluwer 2001); Ellís Ferran *et al.*, *The Regulatory Aftermath of the Global Financial Crisis* (Cambridge University Press 2012).

152 Niamh Moloney, *EU Securities and Financial Markets Regulation* (3rd edn, Oxford University Press 2014).

> Still, other regions of the world, including Asia, increasingly appear to look to the EU for lessons that can be learned about how cooperation can solve transnational problems. European policy-makers argue that the EU seeks privileged bilateral relationships with the BRICS countries (Brazil, Russia, India, China and South Africa) because it wants to maximise opportunities to convince them to embrace the goal of building multilateralism.[153]

Lee claims that 'multilateralism still plays a limited role in international air transport irrespective of the alleged benefits claimed by economists, academics and practitioners'.[154] Indeed, multilateral efforts on market regulation and *enforcement* have largely faded, or failed. This has given impetus to unilateralism.[155]

Havel advocates that a plurilateral agreement may be the solution for modernizing the Chicago System.[156] He puts forward a plurilateral air transport treaty that could begin with the U.S. and EU joining airspaces in a 'transcontinental zone of free and fair competition'[157] with the following seven guiding principles:[158]

> Abrogating Managed Trade [non-discrimination – one freedom only]
> ...
> Abrogating Chicago's Artifice of Freedoms [releasing all points into grand network pool]
> ...
> Adopting A New Doctrine of 'Regulatory' Nationality [dismantling the nationality rule ('citizenship purity test')]
> ...
> Abrogating Pricing Controls
> ...
> Adopting A 'Deep Integration' Program of Regulatory Convergence
> ...
> Adopting Mandatory Supranational Appellate Jurisdiction
> ...
> Adopting the EU 'Community Designation Clause' For Third Countries Outside the Plurilateral

153 John Peterson and Caroline Bouchard, 'Making Multilateralism Effective: Modernising Global Governance' in Caroline Bouchard *et al.* (eds), *Multilateralism in the 21st Century: Europe's Quest for Effectiveness* (Routledge 2013) 15.

154 Lee, 'Revisiting Freedom of Overflight in International Air Law' 352.

155 Caroline Bouchard *et al.* (eds), *Multilateralism in the 21st Century: Europe's Quest for Effectiveness* (Routledge 2013).

156 Havel, *Beyond Open Skies* 5. For a treatise on pluralism, see Berman, *Global Legal Pluralism*.

157 Havel, *Beyond Open Skies* 18.

158 Ibid., 18–21.

Havel also admits that this would be an extremely challenging if not impossible undertaking, however, without the U.S. and its aviation trading partners on board.[159] Generally speaking, multi/plurilateral treaty-making is difficult as experience shows. Such agreements are more likely to succeed under the auspices of the WTO, with its supranational features, but there again membership is open only to States. As the experience of the multilateral UNFCCC process demonstrates, even if heads of States lead official delegations, it is extremely difficult to agree, let alone enforce, one universal set of rules at international level owing to many, and often divergent, interests and political realities. With that said, Berman explains that:

> In contrast to a reassertion of sovereigntist territorial prerogative, a *universalist* vision tends to respond to normative conflict by seeking to erase normative difference altogether ... [S]ome have suggested that the nation-state legal regimes of the world are increasingly converging and developing a 'world law'. This supposed new world order variously focuses on the religiously based natural law principles of international human rights or the neoliberal ideology of free trade and its need to harmonize rules that regulate commerce.[160]

At the same time, we witness a layered, overlapping nature of law under globalization, that does not always respect national borders. 'Isolation of legal jurisdictions from each other is a thing of the past ... As lawyers, we must engage with the increasingly transnational nature of law ... We are fated to live in a hybrid, contested, constantly renegotiated legal world that ultimately has limited respect for national boundaries'.[161]

If this is true, we can observe that convergence of national legal regimes into a global regime is *prima facie* problematic in the absence of a supranational to enforce rules and a major modification of State sovereignty; an idea that perhaps it is too utopian anyway. Even so, Held *et al.* argue that there has been a gradual shift in regional and international law 'albeit unevenly – away from the principle that state sovereignty must be safeguarded irrespective of the consequences for individuals, groups and organizations'.[162] Citing the context of the transnational struggle over human rights, they continue:

> Respect for the autonomy of the subject, and for an extensive range of human rights, creates a new set of ordering principles in political affairs which can delimit or curtail the principle of effective state power. These

159 See J. H. H. Weiler, 'The Geology of International Law: Governance, Democracy and Legitimacy' (2004) 64 *ZaöRV* 547–562; see Havel, *Beyond Open Skies*.

160 Berman, *Global Legal Pluralism* 128 (emphasis added).

161 Berman, *Global Legal Pluralism*.

162 Held *et al.*, *Global Transformations* 69.

> developments are indicative of the state system and, on the other hand, to those made on behalf of an alternative organizing principle of world order, in which unqualified state sovereignty no longer reigns supreme.[163]

Even in the case of the supranational EU, treaty rules require effective action:

> The needs of meaningful enforcement of the Treaty antitrust rules require effective enforcement action … The [European] Commission can, whenever a case raises issues of 'Community interest' and has a clear 'transnational dimension', seize jurisdiction over it and thus pre-empt other [antitrust] agencies [in the European Competition Network] from examining its merits or inflict sanctions on the firms found to be responsible for the antitrust infringement in question. However, it has no obligation to take this action.[164]

Conclusion

This book has argued that the inter-governmental Chicago System, as viewed in the context of its historical, post-war underpinnings and modelled on territorial sovereignty, is an inter-national system of regulation that gives way to polycentric, fragmented, multi-layered and overlapping governance, and competition between authorities, which in turn appears to impact on the ability of States to address transnational challenges such as market regulation and environmental protection.

In the light of the antiquated ideals of 'absolute and exclusive' sovereignty, this book has considered the current legal structure of global governance for civil aviation vis-à-vis the Chicago System and identified its limits in light of the 'consensual structure of the international legal order, with its strong emphasis on sovereign equality of states, [which] has always been somewhat precarious'.[165]

Recent developments at ICAO in the areas of *global* safeguards for 'fair competition', core principles for consumer protection and protection of the environment indicate that the Chicago System is capable of a dramatic innovation that will allow it to foster more 'productive interaction' at

163 Ibid.

164 The European Commission and the national competition authorities in all EU Member States cooperate with each other through the ECN; see European Commission, European Competition Network http://ec.europa.eu/competition/ecn/index_en.html. Ioannis Lianos and D. Daniel Sokol, *The Global Limits of Competition Law* (Stanford University Press 2012) 29.

165 Krisch, 'The Decay of Consent' 1; for a discourse on the politics of international law and the post-national legal order, see Krisch, 'Pluralism in Postnational Risk Regulation'.

multiple levels.[166] It appears that the main challenge to this indirect modernization will be to find ways to recognize and manage legal pluralism rather than eliminate it to mediate conflicts and add norms, viewpoints of actors and participants.[167] Despite the apparent lack of political will to confer ICAO membership on non-state actors and private actors formally, movement towards their informal inclusion in the design of norms and decision making is noteworthy.

Zooming out, one sees that the international system is changing and State sovereignty is transforming. States appear 'no longer [to] have the monopoly of the production of international/global law, and consensus operates on key levels of this system'.[168] Rather than construe this as evidence that the State is diminishing or is somehow less relevant, this author agrees that the changes in the international system are down to the emergence of a new but highly contested 'dualistic sovereignty regime ... that is redefining the legal prerogatives of sovereign states thanks partly to the increased salience of cosmopolitan principles and institutional elements and legal transformations within this dualistic system'.[169] Whilst for global legal pluralists 'the sovereignty-based model of international law and of the state is part of the problem, rather than a component of the solution', this author does not advocate a new paradigm of unregulated global governance.[170] Nor should we leave behind the 'outmoded frames for thinking about global political and legal ordering' so as to take a purely post-modern purview, but rather this book attempts to locate impetus in civil aviation within the reality of the global nature of the changes and challenges it faces.[171]

Scholarship in international law, international politics and international relations generally advocate a need to rethink international law, its universality and its function within what is perceived as a global fragmentation. We note and accept that international law 'is primarily concerned with the legal regulation of the international intercourse of states'.[172] It is suggested that we must recognize the proliferation of actors and participants in the reordering of international law. A refocusing from *the territorial* (local, political) to *the global* (economic, more functional) approach to civil aviation governance, we leave behind traditional binary thinking – domestic/international and public/private – and the difficulty of locating law and jurisdiction,[173] to observe how international law *is* changing rather than should change.

166 Berman, *Global Legal Pluralism*.
167 Ibid.
168 Jean L. Cohen, *Globalization and Sovereignty: Rethinking Legality, Legitimacy, and Constitutionalism* (Cambridge University Press 2012) 24.
169 Ibid., 23.
170 Ibid.
171 Ibid.
172 Malanczuk, *Akehurst's Modern Introduction to International Law* 3.
173 Neil Walker, 'Out of Place and Out of Time: Law's Fading Co-ordinates' (2010) 14 *Edinburgh Law Review* 13.

The formal and informal proliferation of actors and participants in the Chicago System and the emerging non-territorial, global governance regime vis-à-vis the GMBM is considered in this analysis. This provides a space for non-state actors and private actors to join States as partners in local and global public policy networks through e.g. public–private partnerships and partnerships between ICAO Member States, working towards more effective, stronger decision-making and better designed norms and procedures, thereby performing government functions internationally: true 'global governance'.[174] This leads to stronger international law and stronger sovereign States in these (functional) policy areas.

Friedman puts forward a functionalist approach that focuses on collective interests as means to reorientate the way we think in international law, distinguishing between international law of coexistence and international law of cooperation.[175] It is 'no miracle solution, but it affords an important means of by-passing the propagandist atmosphere of political international assemblies, and of bringing the nations together in practical tasks of mutual interest and benefit'.[176] Since international legal personality has been conferred on ICAO as a functional international organization, as derived from sovereign States from inter-State agreements,[177] the status of ICAO as a subject of international law, formed as an expression of the sovereignty of States gives way to functional cooperation, even if this can be read as a 'gradual hollowing out of national sovereignties'.[178] In the context of the GMBM, ICAO Council governance is exercised through functional sovereignty insofar as we allow for reframing the concept and scope of sovereignty beyond the purely territorial sort, which in turn substantiates earlier claims of sovereignty's 'dynamic evolution'.[179] Against this it can be argued that the 'pooled sovereignty' between an exclusive group of governments would create a stronger authority, which while 'joint' remains fragmented as it only applies to a particular policy field.[180] As we have seen, the functional approach is already employed in the Chicago System notwithstanding differences of opinion on how 'the collective' is defined.

174 Berman, *Global Legal Pluralism*.

175 J. Nijman, 'Sovereignty and Personality: A Process of Inclusion' in Gerard Kreijen (ed.), *State, Sovereignty, and International Governance* (Oxford University Press 2002) 132 citing W. G. Friedmann, *The Changing Structure of International Law* (Columbia University Press 1964) 7.

176 Nijman, 'Sovereignty and Personality' 132 citing Friedmann as quoted in R. A. Falk, 'New Approaches to the study of International Law' (1967) 61 *AJIL* 492.

177 Nijman, 'Sovereignty and Personality' 135.

178 Ibid., 132 citing Friedmann, *The Changing Structure of International Law* 216.

179 Mendes de Leon, 'The Dynamics of Sovereignty and Jurisdiction in International Aviation Law'.

180 Van Staden and Vollaard, 'The Erosion of State Sovereignty' 180.

This book has attempted to theorize on the emerging complex global governance regime for civil aviation as crucial for the success of the global - ized industry and for dealing with the global challenges it faces. After all, the industry also takes responsibility, not only States. This book has identified the context within which economic and environmental regulation is taking place, and the relevant actors. The assistance of the scholarly work on concepts of sovereignty, jurisdiction and territory, and power and authority has been invaluable to this project, in particular theories of international law, politics and international relations, and transnational law and global governance.

In light of the changed, global nature of the airline business in the twenty-first century in the face of such complex, transnational economic and environmental challenges, this author argues that the emerging global governance regime for international aviation can be used as an opportunity to manage power based on *economic* incentives and greater effectiveness rather through *legal* force.[181] But this also requires a level playing field. There is no room for 'free riders' in global aviation. If (some) States cannot understand the political, maybe they will understand the economic imperatives. The push factor for States is that this *new* governance would 'not only seek solutions to problems through specific arrangements … it also sets up its responses to problems with the least possible expenditure of political resources'.[182]

According to Foucault, 'success or failure, rather than legitimacy or illegitimacy, now become the criteria of governmental action'.[183] So, the focus in global governance is not so much on international law or sovereignty but 'rather to the question in which manner the authority of law can be maintained or improved under the changing circumstances in the world'.[184] National law and international law reinforce each other, and 'sovereign States are an indispensable element in the creation of an authoritative legal system … providing guarantees that States act in accordance with basic obligations of the international community and … effective procedures for addressing community problems'.[185] Brus tells us that building international governance requires more than building institutions, but 'also requires that the participants have to be actively engaged in a process of the development of and working with the basic values that are the foundations on which the

181 See Maria Rosaria Ferrarese, 'Governance: A Soft Revolution with Hard Political and Legal Effects' (2014) 1(1) *Soft Power* 35–58; see also Ernst-Otto Czempiel, 'Governance and Democratization' in James N. Rosenau and Ernst-Otto Czempiel (eds), *Governance without Government: Order and Change in World Politics* (Cambridge University Press 1992).

182 Ferrarese, 'Governance' 49.

183 M. Foucault, *The Birth of Biopolitics: Lectures at the College de France. 1978–79* (Palgrave Macmillan, Basingstoke, 2008) 16.

184 Brus, 'Bridging the Gap between State Sovereignty and International Governance' 22.

185 Ibid.

institutions rest'.[186] The proliferation of actors and participants in the Chicago System is only a starting point; there must also be a greater emphasis on norm building and decision-making processes that reflect wider global community interests and not only the interests of States. But with this innovation comes burden and responsibility sharing between all actors and participants and across all levels, judged ultimately for the successful action or failure of the global neighbourhood.

It is crucial to give credence to the common desires of the global neighbourhood and utilize the global interest 'collectively to find solutions for the collective problems and the acceptance of the outcome of the decision-making process'.[187] In this, 'supranationality' does play a key role, '[n]ot in the literal sense of creating a government or institution that has power over the sovereign States, but in a sense of a supra-national style of decision-making aiming at upgrading the common interest'.[188]

This books accepts that the major limitation to the emerging global governance regime for international aviation is enforcement. States must thus accept the common interest in enforcement and recognize that the industry also wants a level playing field. There is some imbalance in this regard in some parts of the world for now, and the involvement of non-state and private actors will surely expose those who 'do not play along', and thereby 'upgrade the common interest'.[189] Global airlines are big business – they have the economic power and socio-political force potential to pull the strings.

The products of enhanced, global cooperation in the areas of economic and environmental regulation will ultimately rely on territorial enforcement.[190] As we have seen with the GMBM, Assembly Resolution A39-22/2 provides that the ICAO Assembly *requests* ICAO Member States to ensure that their national regulatory frameworks are established ahead of final implementation of the global CORSIA.[191] Without this crucial step, the GMBM will not be successfully implemented. In this respect, can we still view this as an example of international law that is only a normative framework for global governance? If 'governance of world affairs *can no longer be based on purely voluntary* cooperation of sovereign States, but will be based on shared normative concepts and other international actors', how can the Chicago System measure up?[192]

186 Ibid., 23.
187 Ibid., 7; see also Marcel Brus, *Third Party Dispute Settlement in an Interdependent World: Developing a Theoretical Framework* (Springer 1995).
188 Brus, 'Bridging the Gap between State Sovereignty and International Governance' 7.
189 Ibid., 7.
190 Buxbaum calls this the 'reality of territorial enforcement' (Buxbaum, 'Territory, Territoriality, and the Resolution of Jurisdictional Conflict' 673).
191 Assembly Resolution A39-22/2 para 20(j).
192 Brus 'Bridging the Gap between State Sovereignty and International Governance', 4 (emphasis added).

Global governance of civil aviation is necessary to allow the industry to respond to issues arising as a result of the globalization of aviation and international society in general. As we have seen, contemporary transnational issues facing international aviation can no longer be solved by States alone, notably safeguarding fair competition, consumers and the environment. The 'collective management and governance' of public goods and resources is global values-based. This book has identified market regulation and the environment as global public goods. Global governance then is not only about dealing with global problems through international cooperation but should also entail a different structure of decision making from the traditional intergovernmental cooperation that is backed by the sovereignty of States and dictated by State-interest.

There is a need for development of a more effective form of global governance for civil aviation than the inter-national, inter-State Chicago System appears able to provide. Whilst this book has explored numerous theories which suggest that State sovereignty is on the decline, it has also discussed ideas around the *transformation* of State sovereignty on the global plane, which again represents an opportunity for States to act. The proposed solution is for global aviation to *harness* this transformed and changed State sovereignty, so as to make better, collective decisions and take stronger, collective action *with* States giving effect to international law and giving way to *stronger* not weaker sovereign States.

To that end, future work on global governance of aviation must focus on the more technical side of developing processes for effective decision making as well as implementation of and adherence to decisions in areas of global concern that demand international cooperation.

The *inter-national* Chicago System thus can indeed be utilized to create a level playing field for the now *global* aviation industry. This may only be achieved, as this book has shown, through the involvement of States, non-state actors and private actors in the design of norms and decision-making processes that reflect global values. The impetus for new forms of economic and environmental regulation of international aviation is giving way to an emerging global governance regime for civil aviation that in turn makes States and airlines stronger as global community partners.

At last, economic and environmental regulation of international aviation – designed for an inter-national world of yesterday – evolves into global governance of aviation, more suited for today's global world.

Bibliography

Texts

Abbott K, 'Modern International Relations Theory: A Prospectus for International Lawyers' (1989) 14 *Yale J. Int'l L.* 335.
Abeyratne R, *Convention on International Civil Aviation: A Commentary* (Springer 2014).
Abeyratne R, 'The Role of the International Civil Aviation Organization (ICAO) in the Twenty First Century' (2009) 34 *Annals of Air and Space Law* 529, 534.
Alberola E and Solier B, 'Including International Aviation in the European Union Emission Trading Scheme: A First Step Towards a Global Scheme?' (2012) *Climate Report No. 34*, CDC Climate Research 23.
Albrow M, *The Global Age* (Stanford University Press 1996).
Anderson B, *Imagined Communities: Reflections on the Origins and Spread of Nationalism* (Verso 2006).
Anger A, 'Including Aviation in the European Emissions Trading Scheme: Impacts on the Industry, CO_2 Emissions and Macroeconomic Activity in the EU' (2010) 16(2) *Journal of Air Transport Management* 100–105.
Annan K, *We the Peoples: The Role of the United Nations in the 21st Century* (United Nations 2000).
Armitage D, 'Introduction' in Hugo Grotius (ed.), *The Free Sea* (Richard Hakluyt tr, Indianapolis: Liberty Fund, 2004).
Aust A, *Handbook of International Law* (Cambridge University Press 2010).
Bache I and Flinders M, 'Themes and Issues in Multi-Level Governance' in Ian Bache and Matthew Flinders (eds), *Multi-Level Governance* (Oxford University Press 2004).
Baldus, 'on Codex' VI.24.1 in *Iuriusconsulti Omnium,* vol. 7, *fol* 70v (1577).
Banner S, *Who Owns the Sky?* (Harvard University Press 2008).
Bartleson J, *The Genealogy of Sovereignty* (Cambridge University Press 1995).
Beale J, 'The Jurisdiction of a Sovereign State' (1923) 36 *Harv. L. Rev.* 241.
Beckham R, 'The UN Convention on the Law of the Sea and Maritime Disputes in the South China Sea' (2013) 107(1) *American Journal of International Law* 142.
Benveniste E, *Indo-European Language and Society* (Faber and Faber 1973).
Berman P, *Global Legal Pluralism: A Jurisprudence of Law beyond Borders* (Cambridge University Press 2012).
Berman P, 'Towards a Cosmopolitan Vision of Conflict of Laws: Redefining Governmental Interests in a Global Era' (2005) 153 *U. Pa. L. Rev.* 1819, 1880.

Blackstone W, *Commentaries on the Laws of England* (Oxford University Press 1765–1769).
Bobek M and Prassl J (eds), *Air Passenger Rights – Ten Years On* (Bloomsbury 2016).
Böckstiegel K and Berkö M, *Space Law* (Martinus Nijhoff 1990).
Bogojević S, 'Legalising Environmental Leadership: A Comment on the CJEU's Ruling in C-366/10 on the Inclusion of Aviation in the EU Emissions Trading Scheme' (2012) 24(2) *Journal of Environmental Law* 345.
Bokareva O, 'Air Passengers' Rights in the EU: International Uniformity versus Regional Harmonization' (2016) 41(1) *Air & Space Law* 3–24.
Boksberger P, 'Passenger Behaviour' in Andreas Wittmer, Thomas Berger and Rolland Müller (eds), *Aviation Systems: Management of the Integrated Aviation Value Chain* (Springer 2011).
Bonnefoy G, *Le Code de l'air* (Rivière 1909).
Bouchard C, Peterson P and Tocci N, 'Introduction' in Caroline Bouchard, John Peterson, Nathalie Tocci (eds), *Multilateralism in the 21st Century: Europe's Quest for Effectiveness* (Routledge 2013).
Boutros-Ghali B, *An Agenda for Peace*, Report of the Secretary General, United Nations, NY, June 1992; UNDPI publication 1247.
Bows A, Anderson K and Upham P, *Aviation and Climate Change: Lessons for European Policy* (Routledge 2009).
Boyle E and Meyer J, 'Modern Law as a Secularized and Global Model' (1998) 49 *Soziale Welt* 275–294.
Braithwaite J and Drahos P, *Global Business Regulation* (Cambridge University Press 2000).
Brown W, 'At the Edge' in Stephen K White and J Donald Moon (eds), *What is Political Theory?* (Sage Publications 2004).
Brown W, 'Power after Foucault' in JS Dryzek, B Honig and A Phillips (eds), *The Oxford Handbook of Political Theory* (Oxford University Press 2006).
Brus M, 'Bridging the Gap between State Sovereignty and International Governance: The Authority of Law' in Gerard Krijen (ed.), *State, Sovereignty and International Governance* (1st edn, Oxford University Press 2002).
Brus M, *Third Party Dispute Settlement in an Interdependent World: Developing a Theoretical Framework* (Springer 1995).
Bull H, *The Anarchical Society* (Macmillian 1977).
Buxbaum H, 'Territory, Territoriality, and the Resolution of Jurisdictional Conflict' (2009) 57 *The American Journal of Comparative Law* 631–676.
Calliess G and Zumbansen P, *Rough Consensus and Running Code: A Theory of Transnational Private Law* (Hart Publishing 2010).
Caporaso J, 'Changes in the Westphalian Order: Territory, Public Authority, and Sovereignty' (2000) 2(2) *International Studies Review* 1–28.
Cassese A, *Violence and Law in the Modern Age* (Polity Press 1988).
Castelli G, 'Il dominio dell'aria', *Rivista internazionale di scienze sociali e discipline ausiliarie*, vol. 47 (1908).
Castells M, *The Information Age: Economy, Society and Culture, Vol. I, the Rise of the Network Society* (Blackwell 1996).
Chayes A and Chayes A, 'On Compliance' (1993) 4 *Int'l Org.* 174, 172.
Cheng B, 'The Destruction of KAL flight KE007, and Art. 3 *bis* of the Chicago Convention' in JWE Van Gravesande and A Van der Veen Vonk (eds), *Air Worthy* (Kluwer Law and Taxation Publishers 1985).

Cheng B, *General Principles of Law as Applied by International Courts and Tribunals* (Cambridge University Press 2003).

Cheng B, 'The Legal Status of Outer Space' (1983) *J. Space L.* 89.

Cheng B, *Studies in International Space Law* (Oxford University Press 1997).

Chin A, 'Impact of Frequent Flyer Programs on the Demand for Air Travel' (2002) 7(2) *Journal of Air Transportation* 53–86.

Christol C, *The Modern International Law of Outer Space* (Pergamon Press 1982).

Christol C, *Space Law* (Eleven Publishing 2005).

Claes B, 'Aircraft Noise Regulation in the European Union: The Hushkit Problem' (2000) 65 *Air L. & Com.* 329.

Clark I, *Globalization and International Relations Theory* (Oxford University Press 1999).

Clark P, 'Airbus Warns of Emissions Trade War', *The Financial Times* 5 June 2011.

Cohen J, *Globalization and Sovereignty: Rethinking Legality, Legitimacy, and Constitutionalism* (Cambridge University Press 2012).

Cooper JC, 'The International Air Navigation Conference Paris 1910' (1952) 19 *J. Air L. & Com.* 127, 128.

Cooper J, 'Sovereignty in Space' (1959) 64(1) *Flying* 31.

Cormack B, *A Power to Do Justice: Jurisdiction, English Literature, and the Rise of the Common Law, 1509–1625* (University of Chicago Press 2007).

Cottrell M and Trubek D, 'Law as Problem Solving: Standards, Networks, Experimentation, and Deliberation in Global Space' (2012) 21 *Transnational Law & Contemporary Problems* 359.

Cox R, 'Globalization, Multilateralism and Social Choice' (1990) 13(1) *Work in Progress* 1.

Crawford J, *The Creation of Studies in International Law* (2nd edn, Oxford University Press 2007).

Croon J, 'Placing Wallentin-Hermann in Line with Continuing Airworthiness: A Possible Guide for Enforcers of EC Regulation 261/2004' (2011) 36(1) *Air and Space Law* 1–6.

Croxton D, 'The Peace of Westphalia of 1648 and the Origins of Sovereignty' (1999) 21(3) *The International History Review* 1.

Cuadra E, 'Air Defense Identification Zones: Creeping Jurisdiction in the Airspace' (1978) 18 *Virginia Journal of International Law* 485.

Czempiel E-O, 'Governance and Democratization' in James N Rosenau and Ernst-Otto Czempiel (eds), *Governance without Government: Order and Change in World Politics* (Cambridge University Press 1992).

Dąbrowski M, 'Transport Policy: EU as Taker, Shaper or Shaker of the Global Civil Aviation Regime?' in Gerard Falkner and Patrick Müller (eds), *EU Policies in a Global Perspective: Shaping or Taking International Regimes?* (Routledge 2013).

Daley B, *Air Transport and the Environment* (Ashgate 2010).

Daley B and Preston H, 'Aviation and Climate Change: Assessment of Policy Options' in S. Gössling and P. Upham (eds), *Climate Change and Aviation: Issues, Challenges and Solutions* (Earthscan 2009).

De Cendra J, 'Can Emissions Trading Schemes be Coupled with Border Tax Adjustments? An Analysis vis-à-vis WTO Law' (2006) 15 *Rev Eur Cmty & Int'l Envtl L* 131.

De Murias R, *The Economic Regulation of Air Transport* (McFarland 1989).

De Sousa Santos B, 'Law: A Map of Misreading. Toward a Postmodern Conception of Law' (1987) 14 *Journal of Law and Society* 279.

Dempsey P, *Public International Air Law* (McGill University 2008).

Diederiks-Verschoor I, *An Introduction to Air Law* (6th revised edn, Kluwer Law International 1997).

Diederiks-Verschoor I, *An Introduction to Air Law* (8th revised edn, Kluwer Law International 2006).

Diederiks-Verschoor I and Kopal V, *An Introduction to Space Law* (3rd edn, Kluwer Law International 2008).

Dilling O, Herberg M and Winter G, 'Introduction: Exploring Transnational Administrative Rule-Making' in Olaf Dilling, Martin Herberg and Gerd Winter (eds), *Transnational Administrative Rule-Making: Performance, Legal Effects and Legitimacy* (Hart Publishing 2011).

Douzinas C, 'The Metaphysics of Jurisdiction' in Shaun McVeigh (ed.), *Juris-prudence of Jurisdiction* (Routledge 2007).

Duval D, 'Aeropolitics and Economics of Aviation Emissions Mitigation' in Stefan Gössling and Paul Upham (eds), *Climate Change and Aviation: Issues, Challenges and Solutions* (Earthscan 2009).

Elden S, *The Birth of Territory* (University of Chicago Press 2013).

Elden S, 'Territory: Part I' in JA Agnew and JS Duncan (eds), *The Wiley-Blackwell Companion to Human Geography* (Wiley-Blackwell online 2011).

Elhague E and Geradin D, *Global Competition Law and Economics* (Bloomsbury 2011).

Enderlein H, Wälti S and Zürn M, *Handbook on Multi-Level Governance* (Edward Elgar 2010).

Erling U, 'Der EU-Emissionshandel im Luftverkehr' (2009) 58(3) *ZLW* 351.

Erotokritou C, 'Sovereignty Over Airspace: International Law, Current Challenges, and Future Developments for Global Aviation' (2012) 4(5) *Student Pulse* 2–4.

Etty T, Heyvaert V, Piñon Carlarne C, Farber D, Lin J and Scott J. 'Transnational Dimensions of Climate Governance' (2012) 1(2) *Transnational Environmental Law*.

Fahey E and Herlin-Karnell E, 'EU Law qua Global Governance Law? Deciphering Regulatory and Constitutional Competence Between EU Environmental Law and Global Governance' (2012) 13 *German Law Journal* 1149.

Falk R, 'New Approaches to the Study of International Law' (1967) 61 *AJIL* 492.

Faure M and Peeters M, *Climate Change and European Emissions Trading: Lessons for Theory and Practice* (Edward Elgar 2008).

Feintuck M, 'Regulatory Rationales Beyond the Economic: In Search of the Public Interest', in Robert Baldwin, Martin Cave and Martin Lodge (eds), *The Oxford Handbook of Regulation* (Oxford University Press, 2010).

Ferrasrese M, 'Governance: A Soft Revolution with Hard Political and Legal Effects' (2014) 1(1) *Soft Power* 35–58.

Fischer-Lescano A, Teubner G and Everson M, 'Regime-Collisions: The Vain Search for Legal Unity in the Fragmentation of Global Law' (2004) 24 *Mich. J. Int'l L.* 999.

Føllesdal A, Wessel R and Wouters J, *Multilevel Regulation and the EU: The Interplay between Global, European and National Normative Processes* (Martinus Nijhoff 2008).

Ford R, 'Law's Territory (A History of Jurisdiction)' (1999) 98 *Michigan Law Review* 843.

Foucault M, *The Birth of Biopolitics: Lectures at the College de France, 1978–79* (Palgrave Macmillan 2008).

Freestone D, 'International Governance, Responsibility and Management of Areas beyond National Jurisdiction' (2012) 27 *Int'l J. Marine & Coastal L.* 191.

French D and Rajamani L, 'Climate Change and International Environmental Law: Musings on a Journey to Somewhere' (2013) 25(3) *Journal of Environmental Law* 441.

Frey B and Eichenberger R, *The New Democratic Federalism for Europe. Functional, Overlapping, and Competing Jurisdictions* (Cheltenham: Edward Elgar 1999).

Friedmann W, *The Changing Structure of International Law* (Columbia University Press 1964).

Gavouneli M, *Functional Jurisdiction in the Law of the Sea* (Martinus Nijhoff Publishers 2007).

Gerber D, *Global Competition: Law, Markets, and Globalization* (Oxford University Press 2010).

Geseel L and Dempsey P, 'Aircraft and Aviation Technology' in *Air Transportation: Foundations for the 21st Century* (3rd edn, Coast Air Publications 2010).

Giddens A, *The Consequences of Modernity* (Stanford University Press 1990).

Giddens A, 'Globalization in the Changing World' in A Giddens and S Grifiths, *Sociology* (5th edn, Polity Press 2006).

Gillispie C, *The Montgolfier Brothers and the Invention of Aviation 1783–1784* (Princeton University 1983).

Gilpin R, *The Political Economy of International Relations* (Princeton University Press 1987).

Goedhuis D, 'The Air Sovereignty Concept and United States Influence on its Future Development' (1955) 22 *J. Air L. & Com.* 209.

Goldsmith J and Posner E, *The Limits of International Law* (Oxford University Press 2005).

Goodin R, 'Exploiting a Situation and Exploiting a Person' in Andrew Reeve (ed.), *Modern Theories of Exploitation* (Sage Publications 1987).

Gössling S and Upham P, 'Introduction: Aviation and Climate Change in Context' in Stefan Gössling and Paul Upham (eds), *Climate Change and Aviation: Issues, Challenges and Solutions* (Earthscan 2009).

Grant R G, *Flight: The Complete History* (DK Publishing 2007).

Grimme W, 'The Growth of Arabian Airlines from a German Perspective: A Study of the Impacts of New Air Services to Asia' (2011) 17(6) *Journal of Air Transport Management* 333–338.

Grotius H, *Mare liberum, 1609–2009* (Robert Feenstra Brill 2009).

Gunston B (ed.), *Chronicle of Aviation* (JL Publishing 1992).

Gupta A and Ferguson J, 'Culture, Power, Place: Ethnography at the End of an Era' in Akhil Gupta and James Ferguson (eds), *Culture, Power, Place: Explorations in Critical Anthropology* (Duke University Press 1997).

Hailbronner K, 'Freedom of the Air and the Convention on Law of the Sea' (1983) 77 *American Journal of International Law* 490.

Hakimi M, 'Unfriendly Unilateralism' (2014) 55 *Harvard Int'l L. J.* 105, 125.

Hamilton K, *Bertie of Thame: Edwardian Ambassador* (Royal Historical Society studies in History, Woolnough 1990).

Hannay W, 'Transnational Competition Law Aspects of Mergers and Acquisitions' (2000) 20(2) *Northwestern Journal of International Law & Business* 287.

Havel B, *Beyond Open Skies* (Wolters Kluwer 2009).
Havel B and Mulligan J, 'The Triumph of Politics: Reflections on the Judgment of the Court of Justice of the European Union Validating the Inclusion of Non-EU Airlines in the Emissions Trading Scheme' (2012) 37(1) *Air & Space Law* 3–33.
Havel B and Sanchez G, *The Principles and Practice of International Aviation Law* (Cambridge University Press 2014).
Hazeltine H, *The Law of the Air* (University of London Press 1911).
Heere W, 'Problems of Jurisdiction in Air and Outer Space' (1999) 24 *Air & Space Law* 70.
Held D, *Democracy and the Global Order: from the Modern State to Cosmopolitan Governance* (Stanford University Press 1995).
Held D, McGrew A, Goldblatt D and Perraton, J. *Global Transformations: Politics, Economics, and Culture* (Polity Press 1999).
Held D, *Political Theory Today* (Stanford University Press 1991).
Heller P, 'Flying over the Exclusive Economic Zone' (1978) *ZLW* 15–17.
Hertogen A, 'Sovereignty as Decisional Independence over Domestic Affairs: The Dispute over Aviation in the EU Emissions Trading System' (2012) 1(2) *Transnational Environmental Law* 281–301.
Hewett C and Foley J, *Plane Trading: Policies for Reducing the Climate Change Effects of International Aviation* (Institute for Public Policy Research 2000).
Higgott R, Underhill G and Bieler A (eds), *Non-State Actors and Authority in the Global System* (Routledge 2000).
Hinsley F, *Sovereignty* (CA Watts & Co 1966).
Hinsley F, *Sovereignty* (2nd edn, Cambridge University Press 1986).
Hirst PQ and Thompson GF, *Globalization in Question: The International Economy and the Possibilities of Governance* (1st edn, Polity Press 1996).
Hollis D (ed.), *The Oxford Guide to Treaties* (Oxford University Press 2012).
Hooghe L and Marks G, 'Types of Multi-Level Governance' in Henrik Enderlein, Sonja Wälti and Michael Zürn (eds), *Handbook on Multi-level Governance* (Edward Elgar 2010).
Houghton J, *Global Warming: The Complete Briefing* (4th edn, Cambridge University 2009).
Huber J, 'The Helms-Burton Blocking Statute of the European Union' (1996) 6 *Fordham Int'l LJ* 699.
Hume K and Watson A, 'The Human Health Impacts of Aviation' in Paul Upham, Janet Maughan, David Raper and Callum Thomas (eds), *Towards Sustainable Aviation* (Earthscan 2003).
Ionescu I, 'Aircraft Noise Regulation' (Thesis, Institute of Air and Space Law, McGill University 2004).
Ismer R and Neuhoff K, 'Border Tax Adjustment: A Feasible Way to Support Stringent Emission Trading' (2007) 24 *European Journal of Law and Economics* 137.
Jackson R, *Quasi-States: Sovereignty, International Relations and the Third World* (Cambridge University Press 1990).
Jarrell B and Stanley T, 'A Meta-Analysis of the Union-Nonunion Wage Gap' (1990) 44(1) *Industrial and Labor Relations Review* 54.
Jaspers N and Falkner R, 'International Trade, the Environment, and Climate Change' in Robert Falkner (ed.), *The Handbook of Global Climate and Environmental Policy* (John Wiley & Sons 2013).

Jayasuriya K, 'Globalization, Law and the Transformation of Sovereignty: The Emergence of Global Regulatory Governance' (1999) 6(2) *Indiana Journal of Global Legal Studies* 425.

Jennings R, 'Sovereignty and International Law' in Gerard Kreijen (ed.), *State, Sovereignty, and International Governance* (Oxford University Press 2002).

Jessup P, *Transnational Law* (Yale University Press 1956).

Kahler M, 'Defining Accountability Up: The Global Economic Multilaterals' (2004) 39(2) *Government and Opposition* 132–58.

Kaushal A, 'The Politics of Jurisdiction' (2015) 78(5) *The Modern Law Review* 780.

Kelsen H, *General Theory of Law and State*, Anders Wedberg tr. (Harvard University Press 1949).

Kennedy K, 'Competition Law and the World Trade Organisation' (2001) 33 *Geo. Wash. Int'l L. Rev.* 585.

Keohane RO, 'Hobbes Dilemma and Institutional Change in World Politics: Sovereignty in International Society' in H Holm and G Sorensen (eds), *Whose World Order?* (Westview Press 1995).

Kingsbury B, 'The Concept of Law in Global Administrative Law' (2009) 20 *Eur. J. Int'l L.* 3.

Koliba C, Mills R and Zia A, 'Accountability in Governance Networks: An Assessment of Public, Private, and Nonprofit Emergency Management Practices Following Hurricane Katrina' (2011) 71 *Public Administration Review* 210–220.

König D, 'The Enforcement of the International Law of the Sea by Coastal and Port States' (2002) 62 *ZaöRV* (*Zeitschrift für ausländisches öffentliches Recht und Völkerrecht*) 1, 15.

Koskenniemi M, 'Fragmentation of International Law: Difficulties arising from the diversification and expansion of International Law' (Report of the Work of the Study Group of the International Law Commission, U.N. Doc. A/CN.4/L.682 2006).

Koskenniemi M and Leino P, 'Fragmentation of International Law: Postmodern Anxieties?' (2002) 15 *Leiden Journal of International Law* 553–579.

Krasner S, *International Regimes* (Cornell University Press 1983).

Krasner S, *Sovereignty: Organized Hypocrisy* (Princeton University Press 1999).

Kreijen G (ed.), *State, Sovereignty, and International Governance* (Oxford University Press 2002).

Krisch N and Kingsbury B, 'Global Governance and Global Administrative Law in the International Legal Order' (2006) 17 *Eur. J. Int'l L.* 1.

Krisch N, 'Pluralism in Postnational Risk Regulation' in *Beyond Constitutionalism: The Pluralist Structure of Postnational Law* (Oxford University Press 2010).

Krisch N, 'The Decay of Consent: International Law in an Age of Global Public Goods' (2015) *AJIL* 108.

Lamotte H, 'La tarification du carbone dans le transport aérien et maritime international' [2011] CGEFI, Ministère de l'Economie, des Finances et de l'Industrie, France.

Lammers J, 'The Mechanism of Decision-making under the Vienna Convention and the Montreal Protocol for the Protection of the Ozone Layer' in Gerard Kreijen (ed.), *State, Sovereignty, and International Governance* (Oxford University Press 2002) 425.

Lamy P, 'Global Governance: From Theory to Practice' (2012) 15(3) *Journal of International Economic Law* 721–728.

Larsen P, Sweeney J and Gillick J, *Aviation Law: Cases, Laws and Related Sources* (Martinus Nijhoff Publishers 2012).

Lauterpacht E, 'Sovereignty: Myth or Reality' (1997) 73 *Int'l Aff.* 137.

Lazarou E, Edwards G, Hill C and Smith J, 'The Evolving "Doctrine" of Multilateralism in the Twenty-First Century' in Caroline Bouchard, John Peterson and Nathalie Tocci (eds), *Multilateralism in the 21st Century: Europe's Quest for Effectiveness* (Routledge 2013).

Lee D, Fahey D, Forster P, Newton P, Wit R, Lim L, Owen B and Sausen R, 'Aviation and Global Climate Change in the 21st Century' (2009) 43 *Atmospheric Environment* 3520–3537.

Lee J, 'Revisiting Freedom of Overflight in International Air Law: Minimum Multilateralism in International Air Transport' (2013) 38(4/5) *Air & Space Law* 356.

Lelieur I, *Law and Policy of Substantial Ownership and Effective Control of Airlines* (Ashgate 2003).

Lianos I and Sokol D, *The Global Limits of Competition Law* (Stanford University Press 2012).

Lindahl H, 'A-Legality: Postnationalism and the Question of Legal Boundaries' (2010) 73 *Modern L. Rev.* 30.

Lissitzyn O, 'The Treatment of Aerial Intruders in Recent Practice and International Law' (1953) 47 *AJIL* 559, 586.

Lissitzyn O, 'Some Legal Implications of the U-2 and RB-47 Incidents' (1962) 56 *Am. J. Int'l L.* 135.

Lohmann G, Albers S, Koch B and Pavlovich K, 'From Hub to Tourist Destination: An Explorative Study of Singapore and Dubai's Aviation-based Transformation' (2009) 15(5) *Journal of Air Transport Management* 205–211.

Luard E, *The Globalization of Politics: The Changed Focus of Political Action in the Modern World* (New York University Press 1990).

Lyall F and Larsen P, *Space Law: A Treatise*, Chapter 6, "The Air/Space Boundary Question," (Ashgate Publishing Group 2009).

Maher I, 'Competition Law and Transnational Private Regulatory Regimes: Marking the Cartel Boundary' (2011) 38(1) *Journal of Law and Society* 119–137.

Malanczuk P, *Akehurst's Modern Introduction to International Law* (7th edn, Routledge 1997).

Mann F, 'The Doctrine of Jurisdiction in International Law' (1964) 111 *Recueil des Cours* 1–162.

Marsh G, 'Biofuels: Aviation Alternative?' (2008) 9(4) *Renewable Energy Focus* 48–51.

Martinez Romera B and van Asselt H, 'The International Regulation of Aviation Emissions: Putting Differential Treatment into Practice' (2015) 27(2) *Journal of Environmental Law* 1–25.

Matte N, *Aerospace Law* (Sweet & Maxwell 1969).

Matte N, *Treatise on Air-Aeronautical Law* (McGill 1981).

May M and Hill S, 'Questioning Airport Expansion: A Case Study of Canberra International Airport' (2006) 14(6) *Journal of Transport Geography* 437–450.

McGonigle S, 'Fair Competition, Subsidy, and State Aid Clauses in International Air Services Agreements' (2012) 57 *Annals of Air and Space Law* 199–222.

Mendes de Leon P, 'The Dynamics of Sovereignty and Jurisdiction in International Aviation Law' in Gerard Kreijen (ed.), *State, Sovereignty, and International Governance* (Oxford University Press 2002) 483.

Milde M, 'The EU Emissions Trading Scheme: Confrontation of Compromise?' (2012) 61(2) *ZLW* 186.

Milde M, *International Air Law and ICAO* (Eleven Publishing 2008).

Mills A, *The Confluence of Public and Private International Law* (Cambridge University Press 2009).

Mills R and Koliba C, 'The Challenge of Accountability in Complex Regulatory Networks: The Case of the *Deepwater Horizon* Oil Spill' (2015) 9 *Regulation & Governance* 77–91.

Minas S, 'The Rise of Transnational Networks in Climate Change Governance: A Study in Hybridity' (2015) 05 *TLI Think!* 20–21.

Montenot G, 'La Circulation Adrienne envisagée au point de vue juridique' (Thesis Dijon, 1911).

Murel M and O'Connell F, 'Potential for Abu Dhabi, Doha and Dubai Airports to Reach their Traffic Objectives' (2011) 1(1) *Research in Transportation Business & Management* 36–46.

Murphy S, *Humanitarian Intervention: The United Nations in an Evolving World Order* (University of Pennsylvania Press 1996).

Murphy S, 'The United States and the International Court of Justice: Coping with Antinomies' in Cesare Romano (ed.), *The United States and International Courts and Tribunals* (Cambridge University Press 2009).

Nataraja S and Al Aali A, 'The Exceptional Performance Strategies of Emirate Airlines' (2011) 21(5) *Competitiveness Review* 471–486.

Naveau J, 'Droit de l'air et nationalisme historique' (1990) 15 *Annals of Air and Space Law* 183.

Nijman J, 'Sovereignty and Personality: A Process of Inclusion' in Gerard Kreijen (ed.), *State, Sovereignty, and International Governance* (Oxford University Press 2002).

Norton B, Constanza R and Bishop R, 'The Evolution of Preferences: Why "Sovereign" Preferences May Not Lead to Sustainable Policies and What to Do About It' in Bryan G. Norton (ed.), *Searching for Sustainability: Interdisciplinary Essays in the Philosophy of Conservation Biology* (Cambridge University Press 2010).

O'Connell J, 'The Rise of the Arabian Gulf Carriers: An Insight into the Business Model of Emirates Airline' (2011) 17(6) *Journal of Air Transport Management* 339–346.

O'Connell J and Williams G, 'Passengers' Perceptions of Low Cost Airlines and Full Service Carriers: A Case Study Involving Ryanair, Aer Lingus, Air Asia and Malaysia Airlines' (2005) 11(4) *Journal of Air Transport Management* 259–272.

O'Rourke R, 'Maritime Territorial and Exclusive Economic Zone (EEZ) Disputes Involving China: Issues for Congress' (2014) 23(1/2) *Current Politics and Economics of Northern and Western Asia* 1–66.

Oduntan G, *Sovereignty and Jurisdiction in the Airspace and Outer Space: Legal Criteria for Spatial Delimitation* (Routledge 2012).

Ohmae K, *The Borderless World* (William Collins 1990).

Ohmae K, *The End of the Nation State: The Rise of Regional Economics* (Harper Collins 1995).

Oppenheim L and Roxburgh R, *International Law: A Treatise, Volume 1 – Peace* (3rd edn, The Lawbook Exchange 2005).

Osieke E, 'Sanctions in International Law: The Contributions of International Organizations' (1984) 31(2) *Netherlands International Law Review* 185–186.

Osofsky H, 'Is Climate Change "International?": Litigation's Diagonal Regulatory Role' (2009) 49 *Virginia Journal of International Law* 585.

Pariotti E, 'International Soft Law, Human Rights and Non-State Actors: Towards the Accountability of Transnational Corporations?' (2009) 10(2) *Human Rights Review* 139–155.

Peel J, Godden L and Keenan R, 'Climate Change Law in an Era of Multi-Level Governance' (2012) 1(2) *Transnational Environmental Law* 271.

Penner J, Lister D, Griggs D, Dokken D, McFarland M (eds), *Aviation and the Global Atmosphere* (Cambridge University Press 1999).

Peters A, Koechlin L, Förster T and Zinkernager G (eds), *Non-State Actors as Standard Setters* (Cambridge University Press 2009).

Peterson J, 'Qatar and the World: Branding for a Micro-State' (2006) 60(4) *Middle East Journal* 732–748.

Philpott D, *Revolutions in Sovereignty: How Ideas Shaped Modern International Relations* (Princeton Studies in International History and Politics) (Princeton University Press 2008).

Piera Valdes A, *Greenhouse Gas Emissions from International Aviation: Legal and Policy Challenges* (Eleven Publishing 2015).

Piernas López J, *The Concept of State Aid Under EU Law: From Internal Market to Competition and Beyond* (Oxford University Press 2015).

Pollack M and Shaffer G, *When Cooperation Fails* (Oxford University Press 2009).

Ratner S, *The Thin Justice of International Law* (Oxford University Press 2015).

Reinicke W, 'Global Public Policy' (1997) 76 *Foreign Pol'y* 132.

Reinicke W, 'The Other World Wide Web: Global Public Policy Networks' (1999–2000) 117 *Foreign Pol'y* 44–45.

Resnik J, 'Foreign as Domestic Affairs: Rethinking Horizontal Federalism and Foreign Affairs Preemption in Light of Translocal Internationalism' (2007) 57 *Emory L.J.* 31.

Resnik J, 'Globalization(s), Privatization(s), Constitutionalization, and Statization: Icons and Experiences of Sovereignty in the 21st Century' (2013) 11(1) *International Journal of Constitutional Law* 162–199.

Roberts J, *Environmental Policy* (Routledge 2004).

Rosenau J, *Along the Domestic–Foreign Frontier: Exploring Governance in a Turbulent World* (Cambridge University Press 1997).

Royal Academy of Engineering, 'House of Commons Transport Select Committee: Inquiry into Aviation, Memorandum submitted by the Royal Academy of Engineering' (London, April 2003).

Ruggie J, 'International Regimes, Transactions, and Change: Embedded Liberalism in the Postwar Economic Order' in Stephen D. Krasner (ed.), *International Regimes* (Cornell University Press 1983).

Ruggie J, 'Global Governance and "New Governance Theory": Lessons from Business and Human Rights' (2014) 20 *Global Governance* 5–17.

Ruggie J, 'Territoriality and Beyond: Problematizing Modernity in International Relations' (1993) 47 *Int'l Org.* 174.

Rye L, Blakey S and Wilson C, 'Sustainability of Supply or the Planet: A Review of Potential Drop-in Alternative Aviation Fuels' (2010) 3 *Energy Environ. Sci.* 17–27.

Ryngaert C, 'Jurisdiction' (Utrecht University 2014) http://unijuris.sites.uu.nl/wp-content/uploads/sites/9/2014/12/Jurisdiction.pdf accessed 12 May 2016.

Ryngaert C, *Jurisdiction in International Law* (Oxford University Press 2008).

Ryngaert C, 'Subsidiary and the Law of Jurisdiction' (Utrecht University 2014) https://unijuris.sites.uu.nl/wp-content/uploads/sites/9/2014/12/Subsidiarity-and-the-law-of-jurisdiction.pdf accessed 8 May 2016.

Ryngaert C, 'The Concept of Jurisdiction in International Law' in Alexandre Orakhelashvili (ed.), *Research Handbook on Jurisdiction and Immunities in International Law* (Edward Elgar 2015).

Sandel M, *Democracy's Discontent* (Harvard University Press 1996).

Sands P and Peel J, *Principles of International Environmental Law* (3rd edn, Cambridge University Press 2012).

Sassen S, 'Denationalised State Agendas and Privatized Norm-Making' in *Territory, Authority, Rights: From Medieval to Global Assemblages* (Princeton University Press 2006).

Sassen S, *Losing Control? Sovereignty in an Age of Globalization* (Columbia University Press 1996).

Sassen S, *Territory, Authority, Rights: From Medieval to Global Assemblages* (Princeton University Press 2006).

Sassen S, *Territory, Authority, Rights: From Medieval to Global Assemblages* (2nd edn, Princeton University Press 2008).

Schermers H, 'Different Aspects of Sovereignty' in Gerard Kreijen (ed.) *State, Sovereignty, and International Governance* (Oxford University Press 2002).

Scheuerman W, 'Cosmopolitanism and the World State' (2013) 40(3) *Review of International Studies* 419–441.

Scheuerman W, 'From Global Governance to Global Stateness' in P Strik (ed.), *The Concept of the State in International Relations: Philosophy, Sovereignty and Cosmopolitanism* (Edinburgh University Press 2015).

Schultz T, 'Synthesis of Social Surveys on Noise Annoyance' (1978) 64(2) *Journal of the Acoustical Society of America* 377–405.

Scott J, 'The Geographical Scope of the EU's Climate Responsibilities' (2015) 17(1) *Cambridge Yearbook of European Legal Studies* 92–120.

Scott J, 'The Multi-Level Governance of Climate Change' (2011) 5(1) *Carbon and Climate Law Review* 25.

Scott J and Rajamani L, 'Contingent Unilateralism: International Aviation in the European Emissions Trading Scheme' in Bart Van Vooren, Steven Blockmans and Jan Wouters (eds), *The EU's Role in Global Governance: The Legal Dimension* (Oxford University Press 2013).

Scott J and Rajamani L, 'EU Climate Change Unilateralism' (2012) 23(2) *EJIL* 469–474.

Shaffer G, 'Transnational Legal Ordering and State Change' in Gregory Shaffer (ed.), *Transnational Legal Ordering and State Change* (Cambridge University Press 2010).

Shaw M, *International Law* (5th edn, Cambridge University Press 2003).

Slaughter A-M, 'Governing the Global Economy through Government Networks' in M Byers (ed.), *The Role of Law in International Politics* (Oxford University Press 2000).

Slaughter Burley A-M, 'International Law and International Relations Theory: A Dual Agenda' (1993) 87 *American Journal of International Law* 205.

Somek A, 'Accidental Cosmopolitanism' (2012) 3(4) *Transnational Legal Theory* 371–392.

Somek A, 'Any Further Bids on Popular Sovereignty?' (King's College London, 2016).

Somek A, 'The Individualisation of Liberty: Europe's Move from Emancipation to Empowerment' (2013) 4(2) *Transnational Legal Theory* 258–282.

Stein L, 'The Legal and Economic Bases for an Emissions Trading Scheme' (2010) 36(1) *Monash University Law Review* 204.

Storey I, 'Japan's Maritime Security Interests in Southeast Asia and the South China Sea Dispute' (2013) 65(2) *Political Science* 135.

Strange S, *The Retreat of the State* (Cambridge University Press 1999).

Straub E, *Pax et Imperium: Spaniens Kampf um seine Friedensordnung in Europa zwischen 1617 und 1635* (Schoningh 1980).

Teubner G, 'Societal Constitutionalism: Alternatives to State-Centered Constitutional Theory' in Christian Joerges, Inger-Johanne Sand and Gunther Teubner (eds), *Transnational Governance and Constitutionalism* (Hartford Publishing 2004).

Thomson J, 'State Sovereignty in International Relations: Bridging the Gap between Theory and Empirical Research' (1995) 39(2) *International Studies Quarterly* 213–233.

Truby J, 'Extraterritoriality or an Illegal Tax? A Challenge to the Inclusion of Aviation in the EU Emissions Trading Scheme' (2012) 14 *Environmental Law Review* 301, 305.

Truxal S, 'At the Sidelines of Implementing the EU ETS: Objections to "Validity"' (2010) 16(4) *International Trade Law and Regulation* 28–36.

Truxal S, *Competition and Regulation in the Airline Industry: Puppets in Chaos* (Routledge 2012).

Truxal S, 'Competitive Distortions, Carbon Emissions Efficiencies or the Green Ultimatum?' (2008) 14(4) *International Trade Law and Regulation* 77–79.

Truxal S, 'Consumer Protections and Limited Liability: Global Order for Air Transport?' (2014) 1(1) *Journal of International and Comparative Law* 111–119.

Truxal S, 'The ICAO Assembly Resolutions on International Aviation and Climate Change: An Historic Agreement, a Breakthrough Deal, and the Cancun Effect' (2011) 36(3) *Air & Space Law* 219.

Truxal S and Dunbar R, 'Evaluating Three Levels of Environmental Taxation in Aviation: Global Limitation, EU Determination and UK Self-interest' in Ana Yabar Sterling *et al.* (eds), *Market Instruments and Sustainable Economy* (Instituto de Estudios Fiscales, Madrid 2012).

Truxal S and Harris S, 'Airfreight: Regulatory Environment Encourages or Imposes Price Co-ordination?' (2013) 78(3) *Journal of Air Law & Commerce* 541–584.

Upham P, 'Introduction: Perspectives on Sustainability and Aviation' in Paul Upham, Janet Maughan, David Raper and Callum Thomas (eds), *Towards Sustainable Aviation* (Earthscan 2003).

Van Dam C, 'Air Passenger Rights after *Sturgeon*' (2011) 36(4/5) *Air and Space Law* 259–274.

Van Staden, 'Same Bed, Same Dreams? Europe's Search for Autonomy in Inter - national Security' (2000) 3 *Bologna Center J. Int'l Aff.* 17.

Van Staden A and Vollaard H, 'The Erosion of State Sovereignty: Towards a Post-Territorial World?' in Gerard Kreijen (ed.), *State, Sovereignty, and International Governance* (Oxford University Press 2002).

Vasigh B, Fleming K and Tacker T, *Introduction to Air Transport Economics: From Theory to Applications* (Ashgate 2008).

Vogel K, 'Intervention' in Walter Rudolf and Walter S Habscheid (eds), *Territoriale Grenzen der Staatlichen Rechtsetzung* (C F Muller 1973) 83.

Von Bogdandy M *et al.*, (eds), *The Exercise of Public Authority by International Institutions: Advancing International Institutional Law* (Springer 2010).

Walker N, *Intimations of Global Law* (Cambridge University Press 2015).

Walker N, 'Out of Place and Out of Time: Law's Fading Co-ordinates' (2010) 14 *Edinburgh Law Review* 13.

Weiler J, 'The Geology of International Law: Governance, Democracy and Legitimacy' (2004) 64 *ZaöRV* 547–562.

Wessel R and Wouters J, 'The Phenomenon of Multilevel Regulation: Interactions between Global, EU and National Regulatory Spheres' (2007) *International Organizations Law Review* 282–283.

Williams A, *Contemporary Issues Shaping China's Civil Aviation Policy: Balancing International with Domestic Priorities* (Ashgate 2009).

Wunderlich J-U and Warrier M, *A Dictionary of Globalization* (Routledge 2007).

Zaring D, 'International Law by Other Means: The Twilight Existence of International Financial Regulatory Organizations' (1998) 33 *Tex. Int'l L.J.* 281, 285.

Zürn M, 'Global Governance as Multi-Level Governance' in Henrik Enderlein, Sonja Wälti and Michael Zürn (eds), *Handbook on Multi-Level Governance* (Edward Elgar 2010).

Internet resources

Air Transport Action Group, 'Facts & Figures' www.atag.org/facts-and-figures.html accessed 19 May 2016.

Airbus, 'Global Market Forecast; Flying by Numbers 2015–2034' www.airbus.com/company/market/forecast/ accessed 19 May 2016.

America By Air, 'The early years of Air Transportation, 1914–1927' https://airandspace.si.edu/exhibitions/america-by-air/online/early_years/early_years01.cfm accessed 13 May 2013.

Andoh D, 'Airspace dispute resolved', B&FT Online (17 February 2016) http://thebftonline.com/business/aviation/17388/airspace-dispute-resolved-.html.

Archives Municipales de Nantes, 'L'aérostat Nantais, de 1783 à nos jours' (Archives.nantes.fr, 2016) www.archives.nantes.fr/PAGES/DOSSIERS_DOCS/aerostats_nantais/pages/accueil.html accessed 13 May 2016.

Bartels L, 'The Inclusion of aviation in the EU's ETS: WTO law considerations' (2012) ICTSD online, www.ictsd.org/bridges-news/biores/news/the-inclusion-of-aviation-in-the-eu%E2%80%99s-ets-wto-law-considerations accessed 1 June 2016.

Bishop S and Grayling T, 'The Sky's the Limit: Policies for Sustainable Aviation' (Institute for Public Policy Research 2003) www.ippr.org/files/.../the_skys_the_limit_1280.pdf accessed 19 May 2016.

Bows A, Anderson K and Peeters P, 'Technology, Scenarios and Uncertainties' (Tyndall Centre Manchester, The University of Manchester 2007) www.cstt.nl/userdata/documents/bows_anderson_peeters_eclat_2007.pdf accessed 29 February 2016.

Cairns S and Newson C, *Predict and Decide: Aviation, Climate Change and UK*

Policy (Environmental Change Institute 2006) www.eci.ox.ac.uk/research/energy/downloads/predictanddecide.pdf accessed 2 March 2016.

Cameron D, 'US Airlines Seek Action on EU Carbon Tax' *Wall Street Journal* (27 March 2012) http://online.wsj.com/article/SB10001424052702304177104577307980838597906.html?mod=dist_smartbrief accessed 11 May 2015.

CAPA, 'ACI Europe Promotes Open Skies: A Resounding Precedent for Airlines and Other Airports to Follow' (26 June 2015) http://centreforaviation.com/analysis/aci-europe-promotes-open-skies-a-resounding-precedent-for-airlines-and-other-airports-to-follow-232185 accessed 19 May 2016.

CAPA, 'Chinese Airlines Overtake US Carriers across the Pacific: The Big Dilemma: US-China Open Skies?' (4 May 2015) http://centreforaviation.com/analysis/chinese-airlines-overtake-us-carriers-across-the-pacific-time-for-us-china-open-skies-222454 accessed 19 May 2016.

CAPA, 'Chinese Airlines Rise as Beijing Prepares for Fresh Stimulus Package – Share Wrap' (5 March 2009) http://centreforaviation.com/analysis/chinese-airlines-shares-rise-as-beijing-prepares-for-fresh-stimulus-package--share-wrap-5790 accessed 19 May 2016.

Casey KL, 'The Role of International Regulatory Cooperation and Coordination in Promoting Efficient Capital Markets' (Instituto Bruno Leoni, Italy 2010) www.sec.gov/news/speech/2010/spch061210klc.htm

Civil Aviation Authority of Singapore, 'ENR 2.1 Air Traffic Services Airspace' (18 November 2010) www.caas.gov.sg/caasWeb2010/export/sites/caas/en/Regulations/Aeronautical_Information/AIP/enroute/enr2/ENR2.1.pdf accessed 23 February 2016.

CJEU, 'Judgment in Joined Cases C-581/10 Nelson and Others v. Deutsche Lufthansa AG and C-629/10 TUI Travel and Others v. Civil Aviation Authority' 23 October 2012) Press release No 135/12 http://curia.europa.eu/jcms/upload/docs/application/pdf/2012-10/cp120135en.pdf accessed 12 December 2015.

CJEU, 'The directive including aviation activities in the EU's emissions trading scheme is valid: Application of the emissions trading scheme to aviation infringes neither the principles of customary international law at issue nor the Open Skies Agreement' (21 December 2011), Press Release No 139/11 http://europa.eu/rapid/press-release_CJE-11-139_en.htm?locale=en www.curia.europa.eu accessed 19 May 2016.

Conférence Internationale de Navigation Aérienne, 'Procès-Verbaux Des Séances Et Annexes' (Paris, 18 Mai–29 Juin, 1910) https://archive.org/stream/procsverbauxde00conf/procsverbauxde00conf_djvu.txt accessed 13 May 2016.

Crisp J, 'UN Rejects EU Request to Attend Green Aviation Meeting' (29 January 2016) www.euractiv.com/section/transport/news/un-rejects-eu-request-to-attend-green-aviation-meeting/ accessed 6 June 2016.

Dubai Airports, 'Strategic Plan 2020' www.dubaiairports.ae/docs/default-source/Publications/dubai-airports--strategic-plan-2020.pdf?sfvrsn=2 accessed 19 May 2016.

Economist Intelligence Unit, 'China's Stimulus Package: A Six-month Report Card', *The Economist* (20 July 2009) http://ftp01.economist.com.hk/090723/Stimulus_new_main_July20.pdf accessed 19 May 2016.

Emirates, 'Emirates' Response to Claims Raised about State-owned Airlines in Qatar and the United Arab Emirates', (29 June 2015) http://content.emirates.com/downloads/ek/pdfs/openskies_rebuttal/EK_Response_Main.pdf accessed 19 May 2016.

Etihad Airways, 'Keep the Skies Open' www.etihad.com/en-us/about-us/keep-the-skies-open/ accessed 28 April 2016.

Etihad Airways, 'Keep the Skies Open' Media Release (1 June 2015) www.etihad-mediacentre.com/file_transfer.php?f_ID=6094 accessed 19 May 2016.

EurActiv, 'Low-fare Airlines to sue EU for "Stopping the Clock" on ETS' (22 March 2013) www.euractiv.com/transport/low-fares-airlines-sue-eu-stoppi-news-518657 accessed 1 May 2015.

EUROCONTROL, 'ATM Lexicon' www.eurocontrol.int/lexicon/lexicon/en/index.php/Non-scheduled_air_service accessed 19 May 2016.

Europa, 'Passenger Rights' http://europa.eu/youreurope/citizens/travel/passenger-rights/index_en.htm accessed 19 May 2016.

European Cockpit Association, 'The Case for Fair Competition in Europe's Aviation: Why Action is Needed to Safeguard our Aviation's Future' www.eurocockpit.be/sites/default/files/the_case_for_fair_competition_in_eus_aviation_14_1125_online_f.pdf accessed 19 May 2016.

European Commission, 'Amended proposal for a Regulation of the European Parliament and of the Council concerning protection against subsidisation and unfair pricing practices causing injury to Community air carriers in the supply of airline services from countries not members of the European Community (presented by the Commission pursuant to Article 250(2) of the EC Treaty)' [2003] COM 0228 final http://eur-lex.europa.eu/legal-content/EN/TXT/?uri=celex%3A52003PC0228 accessed 2 December 2015.

European Commission, 'Aviation: EU to Launch Negotiations with China and Japan for New Safety Agreements (8 March 2016) http://ec.europa.eu/transport/modes/air/news/2016-03-08-china-japan-safety-agreements_en.htm

European Commission, 'Aviation Security' http://ec.europa.eu/transport/modes/air/security/index_en.htm accessed 8 June 2016.

European Commission, 'C-366/10 Air Transport Association of America, judgment of 21 December 2011 http://ec.europa.eu/dgs/legal_service/arrets/10c366_en.pdf accessed 12 May 2015.

European Commission, 'Commission presents a new Aviation Strategy for Europe', Press Release IP/15/6144 (7 December 2015) http://europa.eu/rapid/press-release_IP-15-6144_en.htm accessed 19 May 2016.

European Commission, 'Competition: Commission ends block exemption for IATA passenger tariff conferences for routes between the EU and non-EU countries', Press Release IP/07/973 (29 June 2007) http://europa.eu/rapid/press-release_IP-07-973_en.htm accessed 19 May 2015.

European Commission, Communication from the Commission to the European Parliament, The Council, The European Economic and Social Committee and the Committee of the Regions, 'The EU's External Aviation Policy – Addressing Future Challenges', COM (2012) 556 final http://ec.europa.eu/transport/modes/air/international_aviation/doc/com_2012_556_fr.pdf accessed 8 June 2016.

European Commission, 'Environment' http://ec.europa.eu/transport/modes/air/environment/index_en.htm accessed 8 June 2016.

European Commission, 'European Competition Network' http://ec.europa.eu/competition/ecn/index_en.html accessed 6 June 2016.

European Commission, 'External Aviation Policy' http://ec.europa.eu/transport/modes/air/international_aviation/external_aviation_policy/global_partners_en.htm accessed 8 June 2016.

European Commission, 'International Aviation: Canada' http://ec.europa.eu/transport/modes/air/international_aviation/country_index/canada_en.htm accessed 6 June 2016.

European Commission, 'Reducing Emissions from Aviation' http://ec.europa.eu/clima/policies/transport/aviation/index_en.htm accessed 1 April 2016.

European Commission, 'Roadmap: Protection against subsidisation and unfair pricing practices causing injury to Community air carriers in the supply of air services from countries not members of the European Community' (July 2013) http://ec.europa.eu/smart-regulation/impact/planned_ia/docs/2014_move_009_unfair_pricing_practices_en.pdf accessed 19 May 2016

European Commission, 'Social Dimension' http://ec.europa.eu/transport/modes/air/internal_market/social_dimension_en.htm accessed 8 June 2016.

European Commission, 'State Aid control' http://ec.europa.eu/competition/state_aid/legislation/temporary.html accessed 19 May 2016.

European Commission, 'State Aid procedures' http://ec.europa.eu/competition/state_aid/overview/state_aid_procedures_en.html accessed 8 June 2016.

European Commission, 'The EU Air Safety List' http://ec.europa.eu/transport/modes/air/safety/air-ban/index_en.htm accessed 1 June 2016.

European Commission, 'The EU's 2030 Climate & Energy Framework' http://ec.europa.eu/clima/policies/strategies/2030/index_en.htm accessed 8 June 2016.

European Commission, 'The European Aviation Safety Policy' http://ec.europa.eu/transport/modes/air/safety/index_en.htm accessed 19 May 2016.

European Commission, '2050 Low-Carbon Economy' http://ec.europa.eu/clima/policies/strategies/2050/index_en.htm accessed 5 May 2016.

European Commission, 'XXII Report on Competition Policy' (1993).

European Council, 'Comprehensive EU air transport agreements: Council adopts mandates' (7 June 2016) www.consilium.europa.eu/en/press/press-releases/2016/06/07-comprehensive-eu-air-transport-agreements/ accessed 9 June 2016.

European Council, 'Strengthening air passenger rights in the EU' www.consilium.europa.eu/en/policies/air-passenger-rights/ accessed 5 May 2016.

European Low Fare Airlines Association (ELFAA), 'ELFAA condemns proposed extension of Intra-EU only scope for EU ETS' (5 May 2014) www.elfaa.com/pressreleases.htm accessed 12 May 2015.

European Union, 'Public consultation: Proposal for improved protection against subsidisation and unfair pricing practices causing injury to EU air carriers in the supply of air services from non-EU countries' http://ec.europa.eu/transport/modes/air/consultations/doc/2014-01-20-protection-against-subsidisation/policy-context.pdf accessed 12 May 2015.

Ferran E *et al.*, The Regulatory Aftermath of the Global Financial Crisis (Cambridge University Press 2012).

Fioretti J and Bryan V, 'EU Seeks New Air Traffic Agreements in Gulf Carrier Battle' Reuters (online) (7 Dec 2015) www.reuters.com/article/us-eu-aviationid USKBN0TQ16D20151207 accessed 8 June 2016.

Flottau J and Unnikrishnan M, 'Iberia and BA leave AEA in Clash over Gulf Carriers', *Aviation Week* (15 April 2015) http://aviationweek.com/commercial aviation/iberia-and-ba-leave-aea-clash-over-gulf-carriers accessed 19 May 2016.

Freehills LLP competition briefing (February 2013) www.herbertsmithfreehills.com/-/media/Files/PDFs/2013/The%20new%20UAE%20Federal%20

Competition%20Law%20%20Federal%20Law%20No%204%20of%202012%20 concerning%20regulating%20competition%20%2012%20February%202013.pdf accessed 8 June 2016.

Freshfields Bruckhaus Deringer, 'United Arab Emirates: new competition law' (January 2013) www.freshfields.com/uploadedFiles/SiteWide/Knowledge/UAE_new%20competition%20law.pdf accessed 19 May 2016.

GreenAir Communications, 'Chinese and Indian airlines come into compliance with EU ETS as Swiss case moves to EU's highest court' (19 May 2015) www.greenaironline.com/news.php?viewStory=2084) accessed 6 June 2016.

Hoch M, 'New Estimate Puts Gulf Oil Leak at 205 Million Gallons' (2010) www.pbs.org/newshour/rundown/2010/08/new-estimate-puts-oil-leak-at-49-million-barrels.html accessed 22 February 2013.

Humphreys B, 'The Gulf Carrier Row: Real Risk of Pantomime?' *Aviation Strategy* (May 2015) www.aviationstrategy.aero accessed 6 June 2016.

IATA, 'About Us' www.iata.org/about/Pages/index.aspx accessed 13 May 2016.

IATA, 'Building a Greener Future' (2008) www.iata.org/NR/rdonlyres/22669B08-918C-4AB7-8D8F-8F9743BA8FE6/61062/BuildingaGreenerFutureApril2008.pdf accessed 2 August 2008.

IATA, 'Climate Change' www.iata.org/policy/environment/pages/climate-change.aspx accessed 19 May 2016.

IATA, 'Core Principles for Passenger Rights Regulation' (Press Release No 32, 3 June 2013) www.iata.org/pressroom/pr/Pages/2013-06-03-03.aspx accessed 6 June 2016.

IATA, 'Historic Agreement on Carbon-Neutral Growth' www.iata.org/pressroom/pr/Pages/2013-06-03-05.aspx accessed 6 June 2016.

IATA, 'IATA 20 Year Passenger Forecast' www.iata.org/publications/Pages/20-passenger-forecast.aspx accessed 30 June 2016.

IATA, 'New IATA Passenger Forecast Reveals Fast-Growing Markets of the Future' (16 October 2014) www.iata.org/pressroom/pr/pages/2014-10-16-01.aspx accessed 19 May 2016.

IATA, 'Strong Demand for Air Travel Rises in 2014' (5 February 2015) www.iata.org/pressroom/pr/Pages/2015-02-05-01.aspx accessed 25 February 2015.

IATA, 'The "Zero Carbon Future" Proposal' www.iata.org/pressroom/pr/Pages/2007-06-04-02.aspx accessed 29 February 2016.

ICAO, 'Action on the Environment' (2015) 70(4) *The ICAO Journal* 3 www.icao.int/publications/journalsreports/2015/7004_en.pdf accessed 6 June 2016.

ICAO, 'Administrative Package for Acceptance of the International Air Services Transit Agreement' (Chicago, 1944) www.icao.int/secretariat/legal/Administrative%20Packages/transit_en.pdf accessed 8 June 2016.

ICAO, 'Air Navigation Commission: Special 200th Session Commemorative Review' (Fall 2015) www.icao.int/abouticao/AirNavigationCommission/Documents/ANC-200_final_web.pdf accessed 12 January 2016.

ICAO, 'Annex 9: Compliance Issues' (24 March 2015) www.icao.int/APAC/Meetings/2015%20FAL/4.Day2.1200-1230.Annex9ComplianceIssues.2015March04.pdf accessed 22 September 2015.

ICAO, 'Assembly – 36th Session, Plenary, Provision Agenda for the 39th Session of the ICAO Assembly' www.icao.int/Meetings/a39/Documents/WP/wp_001_en.pdf accessed 6 June 2016.

ICAO, 'Assembly – 36th Session, Executive Committee, Draft Text for the Report on Agenda Item 23' www.icao.int/Meetings/AMC/MA/Assembly%2036th%20Session/wp352_en.pdf accessed 6 June 2016.

ICAO, 'Assembly Resolution A38-18: Consolidated statement of continuing ICAO policies and practices related to environmental protection – Climate change' (2010) www.icao.int/Meetings/a38/Pages/resolutions.aspx accessed 22 March 2015.

ICAO, 'Assembly Resolution A39-22/2' (A39-WP/462, EX/179, 5 October 2016) www.icao.int/Meetings/a39/Documents/WP/wp_462_en.pdf accessed 9 October 2016.

ICAO, 'Assembly Resolutions in Force' (Doc 10022, October 2013) www.icao.int/publications/Documents/10022_en.pdf accessed 6 June 2016.

ICAO, 'Aviation and Climate Change' (Germany, June 2011) www.icao.int/environmental-protection/Documents/Presentations/ICAO%20Secretariat%20-%20Opening.pdf accessed 6 June 2016.

ICAO 'Carbon Emissions Calculator' www.icao.int/environmental-protection/CarbonOffset/Pages/default.aspx accessed 6 June 2016.

ICAO, 'Convention on International Civil Aviation Signed at Chicago on 7 December 1944' www.icao.int/secretariat/legal/List%20of%20Parties/Chicago_EN.pdf accessed 6 June 2016.

ICAO, Doc. 7278-C/841, *Definition of Scheduled International Air Service* (1952) 3.

ICAO, Doc. 9511, *Database of World's Air Services Agreements* www.icao.int/sustainability/pages/Doc9511.aspx accessed 26 May 2016.

ICAO, Doc. 9587, *Policy and Guidance Material on the Economic Regulation of International Air Transport* www.icao.int/sustainability/pages/doc9587.aspx accessed 7 June 2016.

ICAO, Doc. 9790, *Assembly Resolutions in Force* (5 October 2001) www.icao.int/publications/documents/9790_en.pdf accessed 6 June 2016.

ICAO, Doc. 9921, *Annual Report of the Council* (2009) www.icao.int/publications/Documents/9921_en.pdf accessed 6 June 2016.

ICAO, 'Draft Assembly Resolution text on a Global Market-based Measure (GMBM) Scheme' (Working Paper, Montreal, May 2016) www.icao.int/Meetings/HLM-MBM/Documents/HLM-GMBM.WP2-Developments_Final_REV1.pdf accessed 6 June 2016.

ICAO, 'Existing ICAO Policy and Guidance Material on Competition', Information Paper (April 2015) www.icao.int/sustainability/Documents/Competition_Existing%20Guidance.pdf accessed 6 June 2016.

ICAO, 'Freedoms of the Air' www.icao.int/Pages/freedomsAir.aspx accessed 8 June 2016.

ICAO, 'High-Level Meeting on a global Market-Based Measure Scheme' (Montreal, 11 to 13 May 2016) www.icao.int/Meetings/HLM-MBM/Documents/HLM-GMBM.WP2-Developments_Final_REV1.pdf accessed 6 June 2016.

ICAO, 'ICAO Council Adopts Core Principles on Consumer Protection and New Long-Term Vision for Air Transport Liberalization' (Montreal, 9 July 2015) www.icao.int/Newsroom/Pages/ICAO-Council-Adopts-Core-Principles-on-Consumer-Protection-and-New-Long-Term-Vision-for-Air-Transport-Liberalization.aspx accessed 6 June 2016.

ICAO, 'International Air Services Transit Agreement' www.icao.int/secretariat/legal/List%20of%20Parties/Transit_EN.pdf accessed 8 June 2016.

ICAO, 'Liberalization of Air Carrier Ownership and Control' (Worldwide Air Transport Conference, Montreal, March 2013) www.icao.int/Meetings/atconf6/Documents/WorkingPapers/ATConf6-wp012_en.pdf accessed 6 June 2016.

ICAO, 'List of Government-owned and Privatized Airlines' (unofficial preliminary compilation) www.icao.int/sustainability/documents/privatizedairlines.pdf accessed 8 June 2016.

ICAO, 'Manual on the Regulation of International Air Transport' (2004) www.icao.int/Meetings/atconf6/Documents/Doc%209626_en.pdf accessed 6 June 2016.

ICAO, 'Member States' www.icao.int/about-icao/Pages/member-states.aspx accessed 13 May 2016.

ICAO, 'NCLB Campaign' http://icao.int/about-icao/NCLB/Pages/default.aspx accessed 19 May 2016.

ICAO, 'New ICAO Aircraft CO_2 Standard One Step Closer to Final Adoption' (Press release, 8 February 2016) www.icao.int/Newsroom/Pages/New-ICAO-Aircraft-CO2-Standard-One-Step-Closer-To-Final-Adoption.aspx accessed 6 June 2016.

ICAO, 'No Country Left Behind' www.icao.int/about-icao/nclb/Pages/default.aspx accessed 6 June 2016.

ICAO, 'Proceedings of the International Civil Aviation Conference (Chicago, 1 November – 7 December 1944) www.icao.int/ChicagoConference/Pages/proceed.aspx accessed 2 March 2016.

ICAO, 'Report of the Economic Commission on Agenda Item 40' (Working Paper, A38-WP/409, 2013) 40–6.

ICAO, 'Resolutions Adopted at the 36th Assembly' (A36-22, October 2007) www.icao.int/icao/en/env/A36_Res22_Prov.pdf accessed 12 May 2015.

ICAO, 'Review of International Governance (Chicago Convention)' Working Paper CWP/13416 (22 June 2009).

ICAO, 'The Postal History of ICAO' www.icao.int/secretariat/PostalHistory/1910_the_paris_convention.htm accessed 13 May 2016.

ICAO, 'USOAP Continuous Monitoring Approach' www.icao.int/safety/cma forum/Pages/default.aspx accessed 6 June 2016.

ICAO, 'Working Paper: A Proposal for a study of policy and programme with respect to examining the international governance of civil aviation' (A36-WP/284, EX/91, 21/9/07, Revision No. 1, 24/9/07) www.icao.int/Meetings/AMC/MA/Assembly%2036th%20Session/wp284rev_en.pdf accessed 6 June 2016.

ICAO, 'Working Paper on the ETS Scheme' C-WP/13790 (17 October 2011).

ICAO, 'Working Paper: Increasing ICAO Council seats to 39' (A37-WP/333, P/28, 1/10/10) www.icao.int/Meetings/AMC/Assembly37/Working%20Papers%20by%20Number/wp333_en.pdf accessed 6 June 2016.

ICAO, '2016 Global Aviation Dialogues (GLADs)' www.icao.int/meetings/GLADs-2016/Pages/default.aspx accessed 6 June 2016.

IPCC, *Aviation and the Global Atmosphere*, JE Penner, DH Lister, DJ Griggs, DJ Dokken and M McFarland (eds), Prepared in collaboration with the Scientific Assessment Panel to the Montreal Protocol on Substances that Deplete the Ozone Layer (Cambridge University Press 1999) www.ipcc.ch/ipccreports/sres/aviation/ accessed 8 June 2016.

Jansen B, 'Emirates, Etihad rebut US Airlines' Charge' (USA Today 17 March 2015) www.usatoday.com/wlna/todayinthesky/2015/03/17/gulf-carriers-etihad emirates-subsidies-us-chamber-aviation-summit/24844191/ accessed 8 June 2016.

Khan N, 'Historical Overview: The 40-year Rise of UAE Aviation' (Aviation Business, *Arabian Supply Chain*, 7 February 2012) www.arabiansupplychain.com/article-6943-historical-overview-the-40-year-rise-of-uae-aviation/4/ accessed 8 June 2016.

Khedr A, 'A Guide to Qatar's Legal System' GlobaLex (New York University, July 2009) www.nyulawglobal.org/globalex/Qatar.html accessed 8 June 2016.

Legal Information Institute '49 U.S. Code §40103 – Sovereignty And Use Of Airspace' (Legal Information Institute, 1982) www.law.cornell.edu/uscode/text/49/40103 accessed 13 May 2016.

Mendelsohn A, 'Unravelling Open Skies' (McGill University Institute for Air & Space Law, Occasional Paper Series No. 1, December 2015) www.mcgill.ca/iasl/files/iasl/2016-occasional_paper_i_unravelling_open_skiesmendelsohn.pdf accessed 8 June 2016.

Ministry of Commerce of the People's Republic of China, 'Anti-Monopoly Bureau' http://english.mofcom.gov.cn/departments/fldj2/ accessed 8 June 2016.

Moloney N, *EU Securities and Financial Markets Regulation* (3rd edn, Oxford University Press 2014).

Monange J, 'De la valeur des choses dans le temps' (Histoire-Généalogie, 1 February 2001) www.histoire-genealogie.com/spip.php?article398&lang=fr accessed 25 May 2016.

Nieuwenhys E and Brus M, *Multilateral Regulation of Investment* (Wolters Kluwer 2001).

O'Connell F, 'Commentary: US White Paper on Gulf Carriers Distorts my Academic Report', *Air Transport World* (26 April 2015) http://atwonline.com/open skies/commentary-us-white-paper-gulf-carriers-distorts-my-academic-report accessed 19 May 2016.

OECD, 'Competition' www.oecd.org/competition/ accessed 8 June 2016.

OECD, 'Competitive Neutrality: Maintaining a level playing field between public and private business' (30 August 2012) www.oecd.org/competition/competitive neutralitymaintainingalevelplayingfieldbetweenpublicandprivatebusiness.htm accessed 19 May 2016.

OECD, 'Globalisation: What Challenges and Opportunities for Governments? (GD(96)64, Paris 1996) www.oecd.org/officialdocuments/publicdisplay documentpdf/?cote=OCDE/GD(96)64&docLanguage=En accessed 6 June 2016.

Oxford Business Group, 'Rules of the game: Legislation for operating a business' *The Report: Qatar* 2012 (2012) www.oxfordbusinessgroup.com/overview/rules-game-legislation-operating-business accessed 19 May 2016.

Partnership for Open and Fair Skies, 'Restoring Open Skies: The Need to Address Subsidized Competition from State-Owned Airlines in Qatar and the UAE', (28 January 2015) available online: www.openandfairskies.com/wpcontent/themes/custom/media/White.Paper.pdf accessed 4 May 2016.

Paylor A, 'British Airways, Iberia Switch Allegiance to ELFAA' *Air Transport World* (27 April 2015) http://atwonline.com/associations/british-airways-iberiaswitch-allegiance-elfaa accessed 19 May 2016.

Peterson J and Bouchard C, 'Making Multilateralism Effective: Modernising Global Governance' in Caroline Bouchard *et al.* (eds), *Multilateralism in the 21st Century: Europe's Quest for Effectiveness* (Routledge 2013) 15.

Piera Valdes A, 'Reconciling CBDR with non-discrimination: A fundamental requirement for ICAO's global MBM success' GreenAir Online (23 September

2014) www.greenaironline.com/news.php?viewStory=1983 accessed 12 April 2015.

Prassl J, 'Case C-410/11 Pedro Sanchez v. Iberia: Shared Baggage, Single Interpretation', *Eutopia law* (3 December 2012) https://eutopialaw.com/2012/12/03/case-c-41011-pedro-sanchez-v-iberia-shared-baggage-single-interpretation/ accessed 8 June 2016.

Qatar Airways, 'Comments of Qatar Airways Q.C.S.C. Re: Information on Claims Raised about State-Owned Airlines in Qatar and the UAE' www.qatarairways.com/images/Internet/qr_commercial/ecommerce/relaunch-2011/5-column/promotions/americas/us/QatarAirways-openskies-white-paper.pdf accessed 8 June 2016.

Skyteam, 'Skyteam Airline Alliance' www.skyteam.com/en/about/ accessed 19 May 2016.

Standing Committee, 'Anti-monopoly Law of the People's Republic of China' (30 August 2007) www.china.org.cn/government/laws/2009-02/10/content_17254169.htm accessed 19 May 2016.

Star Alliance, 'Member Airlines' www.staralliance.com/en/member-airlines accessed 19 May 2016.

The Economist, 'The World in 2009: China's stimulus package', *The Economist* (online) (12 November 2008) www.economist.com/blogs/theworldin2009/2008/11/chinas_stimulus_package accessed 8 June 2016.

The World Air Sports Federation, 'FAI Portal' www.fai.org/ accessed 13 May 2016.

The World Bank, 'Data, Countries and Economies' http://data.worldbank.org/country accessed 1 June 2015.

The World Bank, 'Open Skies for Africa: Implementing the Yamoussoukro Decision' (2010) https://siteresources.worldbank.org/EXTAIRTRANSPORT/Resources/515180-1262792532589/6683177-1285016043773/OpenSkiesForAfrica.pdf accessed 4 February 2016.

U.S. Department of State, 'Air Transport Agreements Between the U.S. and the European Union' www.state.gov/e/eb/rls/othr/ata/e/eu/ accessed 6 June 2016.

U.S. Department of State, 'Air Transport Agreement between the Government of the United States of America and the Government of Qatar' (3 October 2001) www.state.gov/e/eb/rls/othr/ata/q/qa/114294.htm accessed 8 June 2016.

U.S. Department of State, 'U.S. Department of State, Commerce, and Transportation Seek Stakeholder Input on Gulf Carrier Subsidy Claims' (Washington, 10 April 2015) www.state.gov/r/pa/prs/ps/2015/04/240582.htm accessed 8 June 2016.

U.S. Department of State Bulletin, 'The Declaration by United Nations' (6 November 1943) www.unmultimedia.org/searchers/yearbook/page.jsp?volume=1946-47&bookpage=1 accessed 16 March 2016.

U.S. Federal Aviation Administration Category 1 List, www.faa.gov/about/initiatives/iasa/media/IASAWS.xlsx accessed 6 June 2016.

United Nations, 'Atlantic Charter' (Joint Declaration made by the President of the USA and Prime Minister of UK, 14 August 1941) www.unmultimedia.org/searchers/yearbook/page.jsp?volume=1946-47&bookpage=1 accessed 16 March 2016.

United Nations 'Chapter I: Purposes and Principles' (Charter of the United Nations) www.un.org/en/sections/un-charter/chapter-i/index.html accessed 13 May 2016.

United Nations, 'Overview' www.un.org/en/sections/about-un/overview/index.html accessed 13 May 2016.

United Nations, 'Paris Agreement' http://unfccc.int/files/home/application/pdf/paris_agreement.pdf accessed 25 February 2016.

United Nations, 'The United Nations Convention on the Law of the Sea' www.un.org/depts/los/convention_agreements/convention_historical_perspective.htm accessed 26 February 2016.

United Nations, 'Treaty Series' http://ozone.unep.org/en/handbook-vienna-convention-protection-ozone-layer/ accessed 8 June 2016.

United Nations, 'UN Yearbook' www.unmultimedia.org/searchers/yearbook/page.jsp?volume=1946-47&bookpage=1 accessed 13 May 2016.

United Nations Environment Programme (UNEP), 'Environmental effects of ozone depletion: 1988 Assessment' http://ozone.unep.org/pdfs/Environmental-Effects-Assess98.pdf

United Nations Environment Programme (UNEP), Intergovernmental Panel on Climate Change (IPCC), 'Aviation and the Global Atmosphere' [2009] www.ipcc.ch/ipccreports/sres/aviation/index.php?idp=3 accessed 8 June 2016.

UNFCCC, 'Carbon Offsetting Platform' https://offset.climateneutralnow.org accessed 6 June 2016.

Upham P, Bows A, Anderson K and Broderick J, 'Aviation policy options for not exceeding the EU +2 C Threshold' in D. de Jong, B. Kaashoek, and W.J. Zondag (eds), *Blue Skies or Storm Clouds? Essays on Public Policy and Air Transport* (Scienceguide-Aerlines, NOL, 2008) www.tyndall.ac.uk/publications/book-chapter/2008/aviation-policy-options-not-exceeding-eu-2-%E2%97%A6c-threshold accessed 29 February 2016.

Walker K, 'Etihad Report Alleges 3 Major US Carriers have Received $71.5 Billion in Benefits' Air Transport World (14 May 2015) http://atwonline.com/openskies/etihad-report-alleges-3-major-us-carriers-have-received-715-billion-benefits accessed 8 June 2016.

Wit R, 'Giving Wings to Emissions Trading – Inclusion of Aviation under the European Emissions Trading System (ETS): Design and Impacts', CE Delft http://ec.europa.eu/clima/policies/transport/aviation/docs/aviation_et_study_en.pdf) accessed 19 May 2016.

World Trade Organization, 'Agreement on subsidies and countervailing measures' www.wto.org/english/docs_e/legal_e/24-scm.pdf accessed 10 February 2016.

Index